ROMANTICISM IN AMERICAN THEOLOGY

Romanticism In American Theology

NEVIN

AND

SCHAFF

AT MERCERSBURG

By James Hastings Nichols

Wipf and Stock Publishers
199 W 8th Ave, Suite 3
Eugene, OR 97401

Romanticism in American Theology
Nevin and Schaff at Mercersburg
By Nichols, James Hastings

ISBN 13: 978-1-55635-123-5
ISBN 10: 1-55635-123-2
Publication date 12/1/2006
Previously published by University of Chicago Press, 1961

Foreword

In 1945 the Alumni Association and Board of Trustees of the Austin Presbyterian Theological Seminary established a lectureship, bringing a distinguished scholar each year to address an annual midwinter convocation of ministers and students on some phase of Christian thought.

The Thomas White Currie Bible Class of the Highland Park Presbyterian Church of Dallas, Texas, in 1950, undertook the maintenance of this lectureship in memory of the late Dr. Thomas White Currie, founder of the class and president of the Seminary from 1921 to 1943.

The series of lectures on this foundation for the year 1960 is included in this volume.

DAVID L. STITT
President

Austin Presbyterian Theological Seminary
Austin, Texas

Acknowledgments

This study is an expansion of a series of lectures delivered before the Austin (Texas) Presbyterian Theological Seminary in February, 1960. The Introduction and chapters 4 through 7 grew directly out of these lectures and are here presented in fulfilment of the publication requirements of the lectureship. The Swander Lectureship of the Theological Seminary of the Evangelical and Reformed Church at Lancaster, Pennsylvania, gave occasion for an earlier presentation of parts of the study. The author is most grateful to the John Simon Guggenheim Foundation for a grant in aid of research. The University of Chicago Press contributed the financial support for publication.

Many librarians and archivists provided assistance in the search for materials. Thanks are especially due Herbert Anstaett and Elizabeth Kieffer at the library of the Historical Society of the Evangelical and Reformed Church at Franklin and Marshall College, and the late Paul Stonesifer, formerly librarian of the Theological Seminary of that church at Lancaster. Similar kindnesses were extended at other libraries, among them the Western Theological Seminary, Mount Airy Lutheran Seminary, Gettysburg Theological Seminary, New Brunswick Theological Seminary, Eden Theological Seminary, the Presbyterian Historical Society, Notre Dame University, Georgetown University, Union Theological Seminary, Union College, Princeton Theological Seminary, McCormick Theological Seminary, and the Divinity School at the University of Chicago.

Among numerous persons to whom the author is indebted for illuminating conversations on the subject, the late Dr. George W. Richards, Dr. Stonesifer, Dr. Kenneth Plummer, and Dr. Robert Clemmer, at least, must be mentioned. Many students of the Divinity School and the related theological schools at the University of Chicago have also assisted in the clarification of views here set forth. To all these scholarly fellow workers the author owes a debt greater than can be acknowledged.

The Sartain engravings—from an Eichholtz painting, in Nevin's case—were made available for reproduction through the courtesy of Dean David Dunn and Professor George Bricker of the Lancaster Theological Seminary.

Contents

Introduction

Mercersburg is a Pennsylvania village in the foothills of the Appalachians, close to the Maryland border. In the mid-nineteenth century it was the site of the college and seminary of the German Reformed Church. Some of the old buildings are still in use, but the "Mercersburg movement" or "Mercersburg theology" no longer evokes warm partisanship or even widespread recognition.

About 1850, however, the village of Mercersburg provided a distinctive and illuminating vantage point from which to survey the American religious scene. The village was even more remote than it is today. The stagecoach to Greencastle and Hagerstown or Chambersburg provided the chief links to the outer world. The college and seminary were designed to supply the needs of a denomination largely concentrated in the "Pennsylvania Dutch" country between the Delaware, the Potomac, and the Blue Ridge. But the men who gave the institutions their distinction had a horizon far wider than that of their denomination. There were two of them, John Williamson Nevin (1803–86) the theologian, and Philip Schaff[1] (1819–93) the historian. Both came into the German Reformed Church from elsewhere, bringing with them broad perspectives, interdenominational friendships, and a passion for ecumenical unity. They had controversy enough within the German Reformed Church, but this was not the arena of their most significant debates. None of their opponents within the denomination rivaled them in ability or scholarship. The most important discussions of the Mercersburg men were carried on through the mails, with the chief religious weeklies and quarterlies of the nation, and sometimes of Europe also. None of the debates within the German Reformed Church compare in importance with those, for example, with Charles Hodge of Princeton, editor of the strongest theological journal in the English-speaking world; with

[1] Philip Schaf changed the spelling of his name to Schaff in 1847.

Horace Bushnell, the father of romantic liberalism in Congregationalism; with Orestes Brownson, the convert and intellectual champion of Rome in America; or with Isaac Dorner of the Berlin theological faculty.

The Mercersburg men addressed themselves to American Protestantism generally and opposed some of its most characteristic tendencies. The predominant type of religion in the country they habitually described as "Puritan," although what they intended might be better identified as "Evangelicalism" than as classical Puritanism. Philip Schaf set down his first reactions when he arrived in Pennsylvania in 1844, fresh from the University of Berlin and the state churches of Europe.

> Puritan Protestantism forms properly the main trunk of our North American church. Viewed as a whole, she owes her general characteristic features, her distinctive image, neither to the German or Continental Reformed, nor to the German Lutheran, nor to the English Episcopal communion [but to the Puritans of New England]. To this New England influence must be added indeed the no less important weight of Presbyterianism, as derived subsequently from Scotland and Ireland. But this may be regarded as in all essential respects the same life. The reigning theology of the country . . . is the theology of the Westminster Confession.[2]

Congregationalism in New England and Presbyterianism in the middle states and the South had constituted the two largest churches at the beginning of American national life and were still the most influential theologically. Smaller bodies, such as the German Reformed or the Lutherans were deeply influenced by the dominant "Puritan" denominations. And it was against "Puritanism"—or evangelicalism—at large that the Mercersburg guns were leveled.

In American religious history it is customary to think of the middle generation of the nineteenth century first of all in terms of the amazing home missions expansion of the churches and of the increasingly ominous slavery controversy. It was a time of

[2] P. Schaf, *The Principle of Protestantism as Related to the Present State of the Church,* trans. with an introduction by J. W. Nevin (Chambersburg, 1845), p. 114.

revivalism, of the flourishing of the great evangelistic and philanthropic voluntary societies, of numerous experimental cults and model communities. With the first mass immigration of Germans and Irish the foundations were also being laid for Roman Catholic and Lutheran challenges to the virtual monopoly of "Puritan" religious influence on the culture. But Nevin and Schaff had a different concern. They were the chief spokesmen in America for that traditionalist, "churchly," sacramental movement which swept across much of Christendom in the second generation of the nineteenth century. What Moehler meant to Roman Catholicism, Khomiakov to Russian Orthodoxy, Löhe and Kliefoth to Lutheranism, or Newman, Pusey, and Wilberforce to the Church of England—that was akin to what Nevin and Schaff meant to the dominant Reformed and Puritan tradition in America. There were Episcopalians and Lutherans in the United States who belonged to this same romantic current, but none compare with Nevin and Schaff in intellectual power or in scholarship.

The Mercersburg men did not win a wide following in the mid-nineteenth century. Indeed part of their interest lies in the demonstration of just how opposed or indifferent the main body of Americans were to their concerns. In capacity, however, they ranked easily among the first half-dozen American theologians of their generation, along with Charles Hodge, Henry B. Smith, E. A. Park, Horace Bushnell. From the viewpoint of the mid-twentieth century Nevin and Schaff may even seem to be the most relevant of the group.

In part this more enduring relevance is due to the fact that Schaff and Nevin were among the earliest Americans to use the new philosophical and theological idiom of nineteenth-century Germany. The prevailing philosophy in American colleges in the 1830's and 1840's was the empiricism of John Locke, usually in the form of Scottish "common sense." The theology taught at Andover, Princeton, and Union was a related form of rationalistic supernaturalism. Hodge and Park, for example, wrote and taught in this pre-Kantian idiom. The Mercersburg institutions were among the first in America to champion the new German idealism, and to appropriate what Schleiermacher had given to theology. Nevin and Schaff made a major contribution to breaking down American intellectual provincialism, and to opening communications with the live currents of European theology. In the process they reopened many questions which most Americans supposed permanently settled, and they took seriously the thinking of traditions like European Lutheranism and Roman Catholicism, which most American theologians did not even bother to read.

Similarly Nevin and Schaff played a major role in the awakening of the American religious mind to historical consciousness. The American evangelical of the mid-nineteenth century was characteristically uninterested in, and uninformed about, the history of Christianity. Conceiving himself to be directly related to the Bible, he tended to be very cavalier about the experience and tradition of the Christian centuries, even of the century of the Reformation. Nevin and Schaff greatly stimulated serious study of church history, especially of the early church, and of the Reformation. Schaff's seven-volume church history, which was begun in his Mercersburg period, remains to this day the most extended such achievement in the English language.

The new sense of the corporate character of the faith and of its depth in history was related to a responsibility for the whole of the Christian community of a sort scarcely sensed by the typical evangelical. Nevin and Schaff considered the church itself to be the most momentous religious question of their day. Their wrestling with this problem constitutes probably the most significant treatment given it by any American theologians of the nineteenth century. It also establishes them as major prophets of the twentieth-century ecumenical movement.

1/ Nevin's Puritan Career

John Williamson Nevin, theologian of the Mercersburg movement, grew up in "Puritanism." He was himself a Puritan for forty years and it required a major personal reorientation for him to strike out on the new path in which he was to make his mark in history. He once referred to this background in a rare moment of personal confession. "The hardest Puritan we have to do with always is the one we carry, by birth and education, in our own bosom." [1] He was raised in the solidly Scots-Irish Presbyterianism of the Cumberland Valley, converted at Union College by one of the most noted Congregational revivalists of the day, and prepared for the ministry at Princeton Seminary; he taught there and at Allegheny Seminary for a decade before transferring to the German Reformed Church. Even in that church he understood and taught its theology in "Puritan" terms for his first three or four years. We may then approach the "Puritanism" against which Mercersburg campaigned through Nevin's own biography.

Nevin grew up on his father's farm at the base of the Kittatinny range, or "North Mountain," near the present village of Upper Strasburg in the Cumberland Valley. The ridge runs northeast and southwest and at that time was well supplied with deer and wild turkey, with trout in the streams. Dawn rose over the parallel "South Mountain" about fifteen miles away inclosing the long valley. The farm was about equally distant from the Presbyterian churches at Middle Spring and at Rocky Spring. Nevin's grandparents all lie in the walled graveyard of the Middle Spring Church, about three miles out of Shippensburg. The parish school

[1] "Puritanism and the Creed," *Mercersburg Review* (hereafter cited as *MR*), 1849, p. 602.

which young Nevin and his siblings attended was in Shippensburg, where there was also a family of cousins, the children of Major David Nevin, a merchant of the town.

When young Nevin ranged a little farther on his horse, he might ride northeast up the ridge about fifteen or eighteen miles from home to Big Spring, where there was an eighteenth-century mill (which is still standing). Here Nevin was to serve as supply preacher for a time in 1829.[2] And about twenty miles farther toward the Susquehanna lay Carlisle, the seat of Cumberland County, its chief military base, and the location of Dickinson College, where John Nevin, the father, had graduated in 1795.

Down the ridge in the opposite direction, to the southwest, Nevin might ride fifteen or eighteen miles to a village whose name would always be associated with his own, Mercersburg. In his youth there was no school or college here, but the pastor of the Presbyterian Church, "Upper West Conococheague," Rev. David Elliott, was later to join Nevin himself and Rev. Francis Herron, another native of the valley, at the Western Theological Seminary in Allegheny.

The graveyards of these churches contain memorials of the bitter losses of the French and Indian Wars, when this American Ulster was the western march of Penn's colony. Often the settlers had then had to retreat to the fortifications at Carlisle and Shippensburg. After this danger was past, John W. Nevin was still to drill with the Shippensburg military company as a lad of twenty.

Middle Spring Church gathered its congregation every Lord's Day from a radius of about ten miles for the two services. The building was of stone, with a gallery on three sides and a goblet-formed pulpit with sounding board high on the fourth wall. Inclosed by the high sides of the pew, the children could see nothing to distract them from the sober preaching of Rev. John Moodey, though once they were startled by the black face of a visiting Negro clergyman. The psalms, in Rous's version, were

[2] Succeeding Rev. Joshua Williams (1801–29).

led by the clerk from his desk under the pulpit in old "fugue tunes." The people seldom met save on the Lord's Day and at the noon intermission there was family visiting, talk of crops and politics, reading of letters, and some discreet courting until it was time for the afternoon service. When Mr. Moodey was absent, the congregation went to hear Rev. Francis Herron at the Rocky Spring Church.

It was so far as possible the reproduction of the church life of eighteenth-century Ulster or Scotland. The system was sober and formal, with emphases on the churchly means of grace, the sacraments, the preached word, pure doctrine, and daily family prayers, morning and evening. But it was also "evangelical"; the three associated charges of Big Spring, Rocky Spring, and Middle Spring had all been "new side" in the mid-eighteenth-century schism and shared the legacy of "new side" fervor. The parish school was seen as an essential element in the life of the congregation. The schoolmaster examined the scholars weekly in the catechism, as did heads of families every Lord's Day evening. The pastor supervised the whole, making doctrinal teaching the core of his visitation. Sometimes for a year he would visit families one by one for catechizing and, in the next year, gather them by neighborhoods, adults and children, to a common meeting, where assigned portions of the *Larger Catechism* would be reviewed.

The session aided the pastor in family visitation and watched over the good order and morals of the parish. Matters of business ethics, sex and family relations, feuds and fights, drunkenness, swearing, Sabbath-breaking, all these were reviewed by the session and disposed of according to their best wisdom and charity. In 1746, for example, the Middle Spring session rebuked J. P. for taking venison from an Indian and giving him meal and butter for it on the Sabbath Day.[3] There were various grades of reprimand up to excommunication. Restoration to full church privileges was

[3] Alfred Nevin, *Churches of the Valley: or, An Historical Sketch of the Old Presbyterian Congregations of Cumberland and Franklin Counties, in Pennsylvania* (Philadelphia, 1852), pp. 27–28.

effected after a public confession had been made before the congregation.[4]

Members in good standing received from the session the "communion tokens" by which they were admitted to the Sacrament of the Lord's Table. Most congregations apparently celebrated two communion seasons in a year, as in the old country, but some recorded four. In any case, the opportunities were more frequent for members, since congregations usually welcomed communicants of neighboring parishes. The "seasons" were four-day devotional retreats. Friday was a day of fast and preparation; Saturday heard sermons; on the Lord's Day the communion itself was served at the long tables; and Monday was a day of thanksgiving.

In Nevin's youth the valley was a Presbyterian stronghold. The presbytery of Carlisle was second in the church in the number of ministers and third in communicants. For a time Dickinson College had promised to rival Nassau Hall at Princeton, and there were several academies in the Valley, as at Shippensburg and Chambersburg. When the General Assembly decided in 1811 to found a seminary to train ministers, the chief alternative proposal to Princeton was Chambersburg.

But in 1817, when it came time for young Nevin to attend college, Dickinson had lost ground. Captain John Williamson, for whom the boy was named, undertook to finance his nephew's higher education, and evidently it was decided to send him to one of the best colleges in the country. Harvard, Yale, Princeton, and Union then headed the list, and on the advice of another uncle, Dr. Hugh Williamson, the choice fell on Union. Nevin, at fourteen, made the long journey to New York and up the Hudson and Mohawk to Schenectady.

In 1817 Union was just moving into this top rank, a position it would continue to hold until the Civil War. A striking new

[4] Guy S. Klett, *Presbyterians in Colonial Pennsylvania* (Philadelphia: University of Pennsylvania Press; London: H. Milford, Oxford University Press, 1937), chap. vii.

campus had been constructed on the proceeds of state-authorized lotteries, and this had been occupied three years before Nevin arrived. The buildings were laid out in a unified complex in Greek revival style on "College Hill" overlooking Schenectady from the east. The school was rapidly developing in both numbers and reputation. It passed Yale in the former respect, at least, during Nevin's years of residence.

Union College had originally been initiated by the Dutch Reformed of the Mohawk Valley but was finally chartered (1795) as an interdenominational institution. It was located on the "Plan of Union" field, where Presbyterians and Congregationalists co-operated, and indeed that Plan itself had been drawn up by Jonathan Edwards, Jr., when he was president of the college. There was then no suspicion of serious theological division between Congregationalists and Presbyterians. In polity the "Presbygationalism" of Connecticut was more Presbyterian than Independent and indeed the churches of the Connecticut standing order often called themselves Presbyterian. These two denominations and the Dutch Reformed could and did co-operate freely in many ways on their common Calvinist platform. Old-school hostility to the Plan of Union was still a matter of the future.

The dominant personality at Union College was its president, Dr. Eliphalet Nott. In him Nevin first met the orthodox "Presbyterianism" of Connecticut. Nott had been educated at Brown and apparently represented more of Dwight's type of old Calvinism than the Edwardeans. Like Lyman Beecher, Nott made his first reputation with a sermon against dueling—on the occasion of the killing of Alexander Hamilton by Aaron Burr. He was also, like Nevin's father, an early opponent of slavery. From as early as 1811 his baccalaureate addresses were outspoken on the issue. He admired Wilberforce, Clarkson, and the other English abolitionists. Again like John Nevin, the father, who used to hold temperance meetings at the Upper Strasburg farms, Nott was an early temperance champion. A little later, in 1826, there was in the college a temperance society of 130–40 members, and probably in John W. Nevin's day Nott was already a declared temperance man.

One can understand the practical considerations which would push any head of a men's college in this direction. It may have been some of these reforming traits which commended Nott and Union to John Nevin *père* and to Dr. Hugh Williamson.

An early nineteenth-century American college was in its life and organization more like a present-day boarding school on the secondary level than a twentieth-century college. The boys were younger, the average age span being about fifteen to nineteen, and their conduct was closely controlled. Like many a present-day headmaster in an academy of about three hundred boys, Nott dominated the college. He lived in the dormitory and handled the discipline cases personally. This contrasted with the usual collegiate system, whereby the faculty sat as a judicial body and handed down decisions and penalties. Nott was more personal in his administration and was thought by many to be too lenient. Usually one of his faculty assisted him in this matter and maintained order somewhat more rigorously than Nott himself. His readiness to give a second chance to boys who had got into trouble elsewhere earned for Union in some quarters, the nickname "Botany Bay."

Nott was assisted by a faculty of half a dozen men. Nearly all were clergymen, and in accordance with the conception of "Union," they represented the Presbyterian, Dutch Reformed, Congregational, Episcopalian, and Baptist denominations. Of these the two junior members of Nevin's day, Francis Wayland and Alonzo Potter, were to be the most distinguished. Wayland, the Baptist, began as a tutor of languages with Nevin's class, but in the course of the next three years he taught nearly everything in the curriculum as he filled vacancies. He was to end as president of Brown University. Potter, born a Quaker, became Episcopalian. He married Nott's daughter and functioned for a time as vice-president of the college. He left to become an Episcopal bishop in Pennsylvania, where in later years he maintained occasional contacts with Nevin.

To judge from Wayland's account, the curriculum was chiefly

a matter of "recitations" in the languages and mathematics. Relations with the faculty were impersonal and official, and few of the boys were awakened to independent intellectual life before graduation. "Mental discipline or growth . . . was out of the question," [5] wrote Wayland, save for the "conversational lectures" of Dr. Nott to the seniors, where the students first learned how to form their own judgments on men and events. "Attendance upon Dr. Nott's course of instruction formed an era in the life of every one of his pupils." [6] President Nott was an inventor and an active operator in the state legislature; through his influence Union pioneered in both the natural and the social sciences. Nott also usually conducted the required morning and evening prayers.

In the student body from 1817 to 1821 were several men whose later careers were to be notable. Two of the seniors in Nevin's first year, George Doane and Alonzo Potter, were to become Episcopal bishops. In the junior class was Robert J. Breckinridge, the future president of Jefferson College, superintendent of public instruction in Kentucky, professor of theology at Danville, and manager of the Presbyterian ejection of 1837. There also was Job Halsey, who was to turn up at Allegheny as a pastor in Nevin's time. In the class ahead of Nevin were William H. Seward, future governor of New York and secretary of state in Lincoln's cabinet; William Kent, later judge and professor of law at Harvard; and Laurens P. Hickok, to be professor of theology at Auburn and president of Union. Nevin, who was handicapped by shyness, used to marvel at Seward's flow of words in the debates of the student literary societies. Two other fellow students were to become closely related to Nevin: John Proudfit of Nevin's own class and Tayler Lewis of the class ahead. Both men were prepared for Union by Proudfit's father, a minister at Salem, New York. Both were to become college professors of ancient

[5] Francis Wayland and H. L. Wayland, *A Memoir of the Life and Labors of Francis Wayland . . . late president of Brown University, including selections from his personal reminiscences and correspondence* (New York, 1868), I, 33.

[6] *Ibid.*, pp. 35–36.

languages—Proudfit at New York University and Rutgers, and Lewis at New York University and Union. Lewis was to become perhaps Nevin's most notable sympathizer outside his own church, and Proudfit probably his bitterest enemy. An underclassman, Leonard Woods, Jr., son of the Andover professor, was later to sympathize with the Mercersburg theology from within Congregationalism. One can understand the claim that Union College produced more distinguished alumni in the nineteenth century than any other small college in America.

Apart from the curriculum, the most important influence on Nevin at college was the religious revival of his junior year (1819–1820), during which he was converted. Nevin was thus introduced to the piety of the "Second Great Awakening" by one of its most attractive examples, Asahel Nettleton. Nettleton had come to Saratoga Springs in the summer of 1819 to rest from his labors in Connecticut, but he was soon preaching around the area and kindled awakenings in numerous towns. Professor McAuley of the college worked with him, taking some college students along, and in the spring Nettleton came to Schenectady and Union College.

The aspect of the college was suddenly and radically altered. Prayer meetings sprang up in the dormitories. In Wayland's rooms, for instance, a prayer meeting was held every evening, and for a time almost every student in his division attended, each in turn conducting the meeting.[7] The seriousness of the students was increased by the death of one of them, when Professor McAuley gathered them around the body of their departed friend in his study and prayed with them.

This was a restrained type of revivalism, set in the context of high Calvinist teaching on divine sovereignty, the depravity of the natural heart, the electing love of God, and the final perseverance of the saints as the only ground of the sinner's hope. Nettleton was a more "consistent Calvinist" than President Dwight of Yale or President Nott of Union, teaching as he did the "sinfulness even of the religious devotions of the unre-

[7] *Ibid.*, pp. 106 ff.

newed." [8] The focus of his evangelism was not "conversion" but the glory and service of God. For him and for most of those affected by him, the crisis could be described in Edwards' language: "There is wrought in them a holy repose of soul in God through Christ, and a sweet disposition to fear and love him, and to hope for blessings from him in this way, and yet they have *no imagination that they are now converted; it does not so much as come into their minds*." [9] Dr. John Rice of the Presbyterian seminary in Richmond wrote to Dr. Archibald Alexander at Princeton, "I have not heard him utter as yet a single sentiment opposed to what you and I call orthodoxy." [10] This piety must have been essentially the same as that of the prayer meetings spreading in the Cumberland Valley churches at this time.

In the conduct of his work Nettleton was scrupulous to keep within the context of the settled ministry, usually living with the pastor of the congregation with which he labored. He produced emotional reactions, but he did not seek them; and he discouraged confusion and disorder. He feared and opposed the sort of practice which in the hands of James Davenport had given the Great Awakening a bad name, which Finney was soon to bring back off the frontier.[11]

> Dr. Nettleton never adopted the anxious seat, nor any of its kindred measures. He never requested persons to rise in the Assembly to be prayed for, or to signify that they had given their hearts to God, or that they had made up their minds to attend to the subject of religion. He never encouraged females to pray and exhort in promiscuous assemblies. He never held his meetings to a late hour in the night, nor did he encourage loud praying or exhorting. . . . He did not allow himself to denounce ministers and professors of religion as cold and dead, and as the enemies of revivals.[12]

Nettleton similarly opposed the New Haven theology of Beecher and Taylor and attached himself eventually to the rival

[8] Bennet Tyler, *Memoir of the Life and Character of Rev. Asahel Nettleton, D.D.* (Hartford, 1844), pp. 42, 174.

[9] *Ibid.*, p. 240.

[10] *Ibid.*, p. 186.

[11] *Ibid.*, p. 219; cf. p. 246.

[12] *Ibid.*

institution at Hartford, which was to strike hands with the Princeton faculty and the old-school Presbyterians in the war against "Taylorism." In all this he was to find a true disciple in his convert Nevin, who wrote *The Anxious Bench* nearly twenty years later in defense of "genuine revivals," and to stem the spread of Finneyite "new measures" into the German churches.

But that is ahead of the story. Next came a revealing crisis in Nevin's physical and psychological development. He returned to the Cumberland Valley at eighteen, having taken his degree with honors and won Phi Beta Kappa. But his health had broken down. He was afflicted with acute dyspepsia, which defied various diets and cures and left him very depressed psychologically. For weeks and months he could scarcely bring himself even to read. Gradually he recovered strength to work around the farm, and eventually to resume some intellectual interests. He worked on the French he had begun at Union. In the summer he botanized around the countryside; in the winter he attended weekly the debating society in Shippensburg and wrote for local periodicals. He tried his hand at metrical psalmody and other religious poetry, showing an interest in religious music perhaps strengthened in the Union College choir—an interest that was to remain with him. He also drilled with a military company at Shippensburg, of which he was the orderly sergeant.

Toward the end of the second year of his convalescence young Nevin was at last brought to consider further study. This meant study for the ministry, which was the only profession that interested him; but he felt very unsure of his own piety. His conversion had left him highly introspective, and he felt himself unequal to the atmosphere of holiness surrounding the theological students from Princeton who occasionally appeared at Shippensburg or Middle Spring. At length he was persuaded to make trial of his vocation at the seminary, leaving the question of the ministry open. He considered himself the victim, in any case, of an incurable chronic disease and did not expect to live long. And so he matriculated at Princeton Theological Seminary in the fall of 1823, at the age of twenty.

Nevin had the good fortune to reach Princeton Seminary, just as he had Union College, when the institution was achieving a new level of efficiency. The whole pattern of a theological seminary, as distinguished from a theological faculty in a university, was still plastic. The school had been organized just a decade earlier, when Dr. Archibald Alexander and Dr. Samuel Miller had been called from leading pulpits in Philadelphia and New York to become the teachers of theology and Bible, and of church history and government. They had served their apprenticeships as teachers and, now in their fifties, were still in their full vigor. A young instructor, Charles Hodge, had been promoted to a third professorship the year before Nevin arrived. Adequate housing had been enjoyed for five years, with dormitory, refectory, chapel, and library. Princeton now rivaled Andover; they were the two strongest theological institutions on the continent.

The student body at Princeton was between one and two hundred; Nevin's own class numbered sixty-seven. Eight of the class were fellow alumni of Union College, the most important feeder to the seminary after Princeton College. The bulk of the students, like Nevin, were converts from the revivals, and the religious character of the school reflected the Second Awakening. Dr. Alexander, who had been described as "the prince of Methodist preachers," participated in revivals around the Princeton region. He had still deeper influence through his personal interviews with the students, and his Sunday afternoon informal "conferences" on experimental religion were often very moving. Nevin was driven by them repeatedly to a private self-searching quite beyond his earlier crisis at Schenectady, with agony and weeping, yet without achieving the assurance he had been led to expect of the new birth.

It was observed that Dr. Alexander had two preaching styles: his free, informal awakening delivery; and a closely argued, manuscript-bound lecturing style. These reflected the contrast between the curriculum and the religious temper of Princeton. The school had been organized in a mood of theological panic, as illustrated by the extravagant oath of loyalty to the confession drafted for the faculty by Ashbel Green. For his text in systematic theology Alexander went back to the scholastic divines of the seventeenth century and chose Francis Turretin's Latin *Institutes*. Thus, when Nevin arrived, "Princeton theology" was already identified with Turretin and his peculiar views on inspiration. In his course on "polemic theology" Alexander reviewed again all the main points of scholastic orthodoxy, this time in contrast to such errors as deism, Arianism, Socinianism, Arminanism, papism, Universalism. The year before Nevin arrived, Dr. Alexander had preached in Princeton College, on request, a series of sermons on Christian evidences. This became his first published work; his most learned book, a volume on the canon, appeared at the end of Nevin's course.

Princeton owed its reputation as a beleaguered citadel of orthodoxy perhaps even more to Dr. Miller than to Dr. Alexander. Miller's reputation as a historian rested on his two-volume *Brief Retrospect of the Eighteenth Century*. But he was better known for his acute and courtly polemics, his controversies with the Episcopalians, with the Baptists, with the Unitarians. He had challenged Moses Stuart of Andover on the eternal sonship the year before Nevin arrived in Princeton. Similar themes from the controversy with the "New England theology"—imputation, moral and natural inability, the extent of the atonement—preoccupied the weekly meetings of the student theological society in the 1820's. Charles Hodge was soon to inherit Miller's role of defending a revived scholasticism, especially from New England deviations.

John Nevin, meanwhile, was devoting himself especially to Hebrew. He had at first found the subject difficult and unattractive, but by an effort of will he had mastered it and became the best Hebrew scholar in the seminary. When Charles Hodge went abroad in 1826 to study for two years, he approached Nevin with an invitation to teach his biblical courses in his absence. Nevin was in his last term and, still having doubts of his vocation to the ministry, was looking for a teaching post. Hodge's offer seemed to him providential, and so he remained for two more years at Princeton, teaching Bible and Oriental languages.

A literary product of these years was published as *A Summary of Biblical Antiquities; compiled for the use of Sunday-school teachers and for the benefit of families.* At the request of the American Sunday School Union, Nevin adapted this work and the Union published it. As suited their purposes, it made no claims to originality but sought to arrange its materials conveniently and to present them in popular fashion for the use of lay Sunday-school teachers. Nevin enlivened his exposition with modern comparisons and homiletical asides, and the work had considerable success. For example, there is his comment on our Lord's refusal of the drugged wine at his execution: "What a lesson for those who deliberately sacrifice reason and sense for the brutal pleasure of intemperance!" [13] He noted also the freedom of biblical times from tobacco-spitting and fantastic changes in fashion. He contrasted the prescriptions of the Jewish temple concerning reverent carriage with the frequent abuses in modern public prayer: "What roving of the eye . . . what unseemliness of posture and manner, such as sitting without necessity, leaning this way and that, lolling." [14]

The first volume embraced "notices of natural history, with domestic and political antiquities." One of the most remarkable curiosities of the East noted was the poisonous wind called the "samoom." This deadly current was fortunately always quite restricted in extent, generally measuring less than a hundred feet in breadth, and passing any given point in eight or ten minutes. At the same time it always kept about two feet above the ground, with its ceiling generally not more than twelve feet high. Persons who saw it coming, consequently, often managed to avoid its deadly touch by throwing themselves instantly flat on the ground, with their faces downward. Those who were surprised by it, on

[13] Nevin, John W., *A Summary of Biblical Antiquities; compiled for the use of Sunday-school teachers, and for the benefit of families* (Philadelphia, [1829–30]), I, 96.

[14] *Ibid.*, II, 158–59.

the other hand, and breathed the fatal suffocating vapor into their lungs, fell dead instantly. If a limb were shaken, to arouse them, it would fall off, and very soon the whole body turned black.[15]

Most of the data reported, of course, were less sensational than the simoom in their properties. Nevin's second volume was devoted specifically to biblical religion and theology. Here he showed himself to be standing essentially on Hodge's theological grounds. He taught literal inspiration of the sacred text, while remarking that the Holy Spirit accommodated His language to the usage of the day and the individuals involved. He drew a sharp line between the "professing church" and the "true spiritual church," [16] and found the pattern of church organization and worship (except for the Lord's Supper) in the synagogue.

Hodge returned from Germany in 1828 to resume his post. But before Nevin left Princeton he had been approached by Dr. Herron (now of Pittsburgh, formerly of Rocky Spring Church) in the interests of the new seminary to be opened west of the mountains. Dr. Herron also secured for the seminary Rev. Luther Halsey, professor of chemistry and natural science from the apparently dying college at Princeton. The college had dropped to seventy-one students and there was fear that it might close altogether. These developments at Princeton gave the board of Western Seminary two faculty members thoroughly acquainted with all that the church had been able to accomplish in its strongest educational institutions in the East.

Apparently Nevin's scruples about entering the ministry had been in part overcome in his two years of teaching. Although he had examined himself repeatedly for the evidences of grace by the measures of Edwards and Doddridge and could not find full assurance, he was licensed to preach by the Presbytery of Carlisle on October 2, 1828. Since Western Seminary was not yet ready for his services, he lived at home, preaching frequently, in what he later described as "a more or less John the Baptist style." At

[15] *Ibid.*, I, 27–28.
[16] *Ibid.*, II, 8–9.

his father's urging, he trained himself from the beginning to do without a manuscript and was well received.

Nevin had become an ardent and intolerant "temperance" advocate. To him the rapid growth of the organized temperance movement promised "a mighty reformation." (When the American Temperance Society was organized in 1826, there were already some five thousand local societies.) Nevin wrote and preached for the cause, lashing distillers and liquor merchants fiercely. At least one large congregation which had considered him for the pastorate dropped his name for this reason. In his type of "Puritanism" this ascetic discipline was a matter of strict principle.

While living in the Cumberland Valley this year, Nevin became acquainted with Dickinson College affairs. Probably the most distinguished member of the faculty there was Henry Vethake, formerly of Rutgers and Princeton. He taught mathematics and one of the first courses in political economy in the United States. Dr. Nott also had had interests in this direction, which he had communicated to Francis Wayland and Alonzo Potter. Now Nevin too became interested in economics, especially as a demonstration of the working of Providence. He submitted an article on the subject to Ashbel Green's *Christian Advocate.* Although this article was rejected, the theme, which was to occupy a whole generation of American theologian-economists, continued to exercise Nevin's mind.[17]

In December of 1829 John Nevin crossed the Alleghenies to Pittsburgh to join Luther Halsey at the rising Princeton of the West. He found no buildings, no endowment, no library. The school was an appendage of Herron's First Presbyterian Church, in whose session room its handful of students met for classes. Instruction had begun with the local ministers two years before; thus Nevin and Halsey had three classes between them. Nevin

[17] Cf. W. Smith, *Professors and Public Ethics: Studies of Northern Moral Philosophers before the Civil War* (Ithaca: Cornell University Press, 1956).

took the freshmen in biblical studies and Halsey the two upper classes in theology and in church history and government. Nevin lived with the pastor Francis Herron, who treated him as a son.

Pittsburgh then numbered better than ten thousand inhabitants and was profiting largely from its mining and commercial resources. It was predominantly Irish and Presbyterian in religious complexion, a frontier extension of the Cumberland Valley society from which Nevin came. Of the dozen or so churches in town, a third—including the strongest—were Presbyterian. Francis Herron and Elisha Swift, pastors of the First and Second churches, respectively, were also president and secretary of the seminary board. Their churches had been the centers of the revival which two years before had finally made evangelical religion dominant in the city. Up to that time Pittsburgh had resisted such fervor, but when Nevin arrived its church life was characterized by prayer meetings, flourishing Sabbath schools, and a vigorous missionary spirit.

Across the river in the borough of Allegheny a building began slowly to rise in the summer of 1830. Much of the labor on the building was done by students, for the "manual labor plan" of education was then in vogue. Nevin was a convert of T. D. Weld's propaganda on behalf of the "Society for Promoting Manual Labor in Literary Institutions." [18] As Nevin saw it, quite apart from financial considerations, this plan was the only hope of forestalling a progressive physical deterioration of the intellectuals. The building was usable though unfinished in 1831, and that summer the score of students moved into their dormitory. During the year 1830, also, some two thousand books arrived for a library, the proceeds of a begging expedition in Great Britain by one of the directors. But the directors found no success in raising funds anywhere outside the Synod of Pittsburgh. They had to borrow to pay for their building costs, and they were plagued with legal difficulties over the title to their site in Allegheny. In 1834 Nevin reported in the newspapers that the

[18] *The Friend* (Journal of the Young Men's Society of Pittsburgh and Vicinity, Pittsburgh), April 13, 1833.

John Williamson Nevin

(Engraving by John Sartain from a painting by the well-known portraitist Jacob Eichholtz, completed in 1841, in four copies.)

Philip Schaff

(Engraving, about 1850, by John Sartain. Original unknown.)

seminary would probably be forced to close that year. The building was still unfinished and there seemed little prospect of paying faculty salaries.[19] It had been impossible, of course, to fill up the faculty and Halsey in particular was almost breaking under the strain of overwork.

Of Nevin's extracurricular activities in his first three or four years at Pittsburgh we have at least four sermons, although for some reason his ordination was delayed till 1835. Two of the sermons, specifically doctrinal and designed for a collection of Presbyterian tracts, were "The Trinitarian and Unitarian Doctrines concerning Jesus Christ" and "Election not contrary to a Free Gospel." [20] "The Scourge of God" was preached by request at a fast-day set at the time of the cholera epidemic of 1832. Other occasional pieces appeared in the synod newspaper, the Pittsburgh *Christian Herald.*

Nevin was active also in a "Young Men's Society of Pittsburgh and Vicinity," an organization of evangelical but undenominational Christian character, for mutual "intellectual and moral improvement," in short, an early Y.M.C.A. He was persuaded to edit for the society a weekly newspaper, *The Friend*, which he conducted with vigor for two years. In this paper he was debarred from specifically denominational themes but wrote about the biblical bases of evangelical religion and its many evangelistic and reform agencies and concerns. The Synod of Pittsburgh regularly queried its members at this period about Sabbath-keeping, "temperance" (meaning abstinence), colonization, missions. All these interests received extensive treatment in *The Friend*, especially the reports of the various missionary societies, Bible societies, tract societies, Sabbath-school unions, and temperance societies.

Nevin was a representative evangelical—"Puritan," he would have said—in his attitude toward such evangelistic and reform activities. He had a high doctrine of the invisible church, but supposed it to be made visible only in the conversion and

[19] *Ibid.*, May 15, 1834; *Pittsburgh Christian Herald and Western Missionary Recorder* (hereafter cited as *Christian Herald*), September 6, 1834.
[20] *Presbyterian Preacher*, 1833.

obedience of individuals separately. The one indispensable means of grace was the Bible, which must be made available for every man's private study. It was the common ground of all evangelical denominations and provided the way of salvation apart from any denomination.

Nevin vigorously supported the proposal that the Bible Society supply every family on earth with a Bible in two decades.[21] He commended a similar technique used by the missionary societies of Jefferson and Washington colleges and the Western Theological Seminary, to place a missionary paper in every home west of the mountains. All the students of the seminary were employed as teachers in the numerous Sabbath schools of the Pittsburgh area or as tract colporteurs. First Church alone in 1833 used 121 teachers in its dozen schools for some twelve hundred students. The synod was especially missionary-minded, and Nevin once boasted that Western Seminary sent a higher proportion of its graduates into the foreign field than any other seminary. He was a warm supporter of the monthly concert of prayer for the conversion of the world, and became a life member of both the Western Foreign Missionary Society[22] and the American Board of Commissioners for Foreign Missions.

Nevin was also characteristically evangelical in his tendency to moralism and legalism. He was conspicuous even in the Pittsburgh Synod for his devotion to the causes of total abstinence and Sabbath-keeping, and his opposition to frivolous and dangerous amusements, fancy fairs, theaters, and horse-racing. His attitude to the slavery question we must reserve for special attention.

In his sermon "The Scourge of God," Nevin interpreted the cholera epidemic as an evidence of God's controversy with his people. He singled out particularly the sins of manufacturing and vending ardent spirits, citing evidence at the same time that the incidence of cholera was higher among drinkers. No other single theme claimed so much space in *The Friend* as that of temperance —with statistics, reports of temperance organizations, and touch-

[21] *The Friend,* June 12, 1834.
[22] *Ibid.,* May 30, 1834.

ing or horrifying anecdotes about the effects of alcohol. In 1834 Nevin began publishing a fortnightly *Temperance Register*, merely from these materials culled from *The Friend*.

The chief difficulty with regard to the Sabbath, to turn to that cause, was travel on the developing steamboat and stagecoach lines and on the canals. Nevin was made chairman of a presbytery committee on this topic in 1836, and his report called for uncompromising rigor. If a Presbyterian businessman were ruined financially by Sabbath-keeping, he should count it a religious contribution, like giving to missions or to a Bible society. Discipline should be enforced on stockholders as well as users of transportation companies. Better a small church and a pure one! But generally the alternatives would not be thus drawn; prosperity was usually correlated with Sabbath-keeping. The presbytery was so pleased with this report that it ordered ten thousand copies printed and sent it up to the General Assembly as an overture.

Nevin had used the editorial columns of *The Friend* also to censor community morals in other areas. In 1833 he ran a feud with a group of Pittsburgh churchwomen who wished to hold a "fancy fair" for the benefit of an orphan asylum. Nevin attacked fairs as "morally wrong" and "anti-evangelical," ministering—under the pretext of benevolence—to vanity and folly. He illustrated what was really for sale by an anecdote about a visiting tar who paid his fee, stared steadily at the lady in the booth and walked off with no "fancy," saying, "I've had my money's worth." [23] Could one imagine, asked Nevin, the Savior at a fancy fair? But several other local editors opposed Nevin, and the ladies not only had their fair but scheduled another for the winter—while Nevin was east of the mountains for his own wedding. On his return he was only so much mellowed as to apologize grudgingly for having compared the ladies' fair to a bullfight.[24]

The following winter Nevin was a leader in a comparable agitation against a new theater in Pittsburgh. After extended

[23] *Ibid.*, June 6, 1833.
[24] *Ibid.*, June 12, 1834.

debate the Young Men's Society resolved unanimously that the theater was a bad moral influence in the community, although on strictly constitutional grounds they rejected a resolution that members of the society could not hold stock in the company. The consensus was that the theater was vulgar, exhibited vice in specious and familiar form, and was not really capable of reformation. As Timothy Dwight had said, he knew of no play worthy of St. Paul. A writer in the *Herald* intimated that theaters were dying out across the country. But for his part in all this Nevin was threatened with a cow-hiding by supporters of the art of vaudeville.

The most controversial of the social issues in which Nevin became deeply involved was slavery. As we shall see, he became progressively more radical in this respect. In general, however, he subscribed to the notion that the given socioeconomic order was providentially ordered. This direction of thought had been nurtured in him by Nott, Wayland, and Vethake. He read several of Chalmers' writings on these themes with warm approval. Economics, he argued, was the most important science after religion. Every minister should know something of it. Against those with reservations about Malthus and Ricardo, Nevin contended that the speculations of political economics were "lofty and noble" and that its principles conformed to the biblical outlook and the "idea of a perfect moral constitution of life." Pulpit and press, he claimed, often expressed false views in these matters.[25] Legal poor relief, for example, promoted pauperism, as Chalmers had shown, and was outside the proper function of government.[26] Nevin supported the idea of insurance, however, and the Presbyterian Ministers' Fund. Later, in his Mercersburg period, Nevin was to contend that society as well as the individual stood in need of supernatural redemption. The utilitarian social theory would then seem to him simply "infidelity applied to the state."

In addition to its various evangelistic and social concerns, the

[25] *Ibid.*, May 16, 1833.
[26] *Ibid.*, July 4, 1833.

Synod of Pittsburgh regularly estimated its own religious vitality by the criterion of revivals. But at the same time the synod was very critical of the "new measures" reported to be current in new-school New York State. The Pittsburgh *Herald* reprinted Professor Miller's warnings against "anxious seats" in his *Letters to Presbyterians* and expressed distress repeatedly at reports of "new measures" elsewhere in the church. The synod in general probably concurred with the views on the subject collected by the old-school pastor William Sprague for his *Lectures on Revivals.*

In 1834–35 Pittsburgh Presbyterianism witnessed its first demonstration of "new measures" revivalism. James Gallaher, a popular revivalist of the West, opened an evangelistic campaign in December. He did things unheard of in the city. He would come down out of the pulpit during services and parade up the aisles, speaking to specific groups or individuals. He installed a "mourners' bench." He sent singing groups into the streets and hotels. The ministers as a group stood aside and gave him a free hand. Nevin got just near enough to Gallaher's antics, he said, to persuade himself that it was "quackery," "spiritual juggleries"; and he held it his duty to refuse his approbation. It was an experience he "could never afterwards forget," and it strengthened his hostility to "new measures." One suspects that he could have written the first edition of *The Anxious Bench* in 1835.

It is in the context of such irregularities, no doubt, that we are to understand Nevin's introduction for a new edition in 1832 of *Christ's Warning to the Churches, to beware of False Prophets who come as Wolves in Sheep's Clothing, and the marks by which they are known.* The author, Rev. Joseph Lathrop, had been a pastor in West Springfield, Massachusetts, in the last generation of the eighteenth century. He wrote to warn the congregations of the state church against irregular lay preachers and itinerant revivalists. He followed President Ezra Stiles of Yale in contending that in the Congregational church there was an unbroken succession of presbyterially ordained clergy since the apostles. There was divine authority, he argued, not for any particular polity but for an uninterrupted ministerial order in the church. New ministers, consequently, were to be received only if "approved and recommended by Elders of churches." [27] Nevin evidently sympathized with this Congregational argument.

As has already been intimated, Nevin's views on Negro slavery brought him more notoriety than his opposition to revivalistic new measures. From childhood he had been taught to view slavery as a social evil, and up to 1834 he had looked with favor on the scheme of colonizing Liberia with freed slaves from America, the proposal favored by the Kentuckians Robert J. Breckinridge and James Birney. In 1833 Nevin, like many other Americans, followed with great interest the newspaper accounts of the debates on emancipation in the British Parliament and of the bitter resistance of the West Indian planters. Abolitionism was greatly stimulated in America by the West Indian example, and an American Antislavery Society was organized in Philadelphia at the end of the year. Nevin printed its "Declaration" in *The Friend* and organized a debate in its columns between advocates of "immediate" abolition and of colonization, which ran through the spring of 1834.

Such a debate caused offense. Pittsburgh was ruled by a proslavery spirit; "religion, politics, and good manners joined" in silencing protest against slavery. Some of Nevin's readers considered it radical to permit an abolitionist to criticize colonization publicly. But Nevin argued editorially that honest and informed men might differ on the matter. As a case in point he reprinted an article from the *Presbyterian* comparing the two proposals to the great disadvantage of abolitionism.

Nevin never had any sympathies for Garrison, whom he condemned as being irreligious and unpatriotic; but, like Judge Birney, he was won over by T. D. Weld's interpretation of the issue in terms of evangelical moralism. One can follow Weld's activities at Lane Seminary in Nevin's newspaper, and these developments seem to have been the most influential on Nevin, as on Birney. When the Lane students formed their antislavery

[27] App. p. 1.

society, Nevin estimated their bylaws as "wisely and temperately drawn up."

The pressure of English opinion for emancipation was also felt through the letters Nevin reprinted from Dr. Samuel Cox. By midsummer Nevin defined the real issue with regard to the Liberia colony project as being "whether the tendencies and bearings of the system are in their own nature friendly or otherwise to a proper sense of duty, and a proper course of action in the nation, with regard to slavery at home."[28] It seemed to him that the Lane professors Beecher and Stowe had really conceded the abolitionist principle as right.[29] Judge Birney meanwhile had resigned as agent of the colonization society and manumitted his own slaves, convinced at last that slavery was not merely a social problem, but a *sin.* Birney's "Open Letter" caused great distress among his former colonizationist colleagues by its argument that the scheme was a safety valve for the slavery system. Nevin supported Birney, arguing that this man could scarcely be accused of incendiarism.[30] To those who protested that he caricatured the colonization project, Nevin replied that Birney was describing how it actually functioned in the South, not the principles by which it was recommended in the North.

In October, 1834, came the effort of the Lane trustees and faculty to enforce censorship in the seminary and to dissolve the seminary antislavery society. Nevin called this attempt to deny freedom of speech and thought "farcical" and a "moral abomination." "Before God," he declared, "we believe that a fearful weight of guilt is lying upon the land for its apathy on this subject." In abolitionism he now saw "a vast principle" struggling to express itself. He did not believe the abolitionists as a whole were rash and extravagant; rather they showed extraordinary sobriety and discretion and meekness. In his Christmas issue he supported congressional legislation for abolition in the District of Columbia, where no states' rights were involved but where "our national

[28] *The Friend,* July 3, 1834.
[29] *Ibid.,* August 21, 1834.
[30] *Ibid.,* September 4, 1834.

honor is tarnished with the stain of slavery." Slavery was not merely an abomination, iniquity, and evil, but *sin*.

A month later Nevin reported that the Lane students were leaving the seminary rather than submit to the action of the administration. Nevin declared flatly that the trustees and faculty were in the wrong. Since he was not permitted by the Young Men's Society to publish the students' declaration, he announced he would not continue long as editor.[31] Evidently Nevin had not carried the society as a whole with him in his spiritual pilgrimage from colonization to abolition, and his editorials had evoked a storm of protest. There was talk of a move to wreck the office of *The Friend*. A prominent physician said publicly on the street that Nevin was "the most dangerous man in Pittsburgh." Early in March the society resolved that slavery was not to be further discussed in *The Friend*, and they set up an editorial committee to regulate the editor. Nevin took this as an invitation to resign as editor, and he did so.

In his farewell editorial Nevin declared he had never "published as much against colonization as we have in its favor." But now he took the occasion to leave his personal testimony on the subject more explicit than ever.

> Slavery is a sin as it exists in this country, and as such ought at once to be abolished. There is no excuse for its being continued a single day. The whole nation is involved in the guilt of it, so long as public sentiment acquiesces in it as a necessary evil. . . . We glory then in being an abolitionist. . . . It is the cause of God and will prevail. It *has prevailed* within this last year, more we believe, than ever a moral cause did before in this country within the same time.

Colonization, he now agreed with Judge Birney, diverted attention from duty and helped to sustain wicked prejudice against Negroes in general.

Two months later the General Assembly met in Pittsburgh, the first such meeting west of the mountains, and, as it happened, the first in four years with an old-school majority. At least as striking as the old-school gains were the developments on the

[31] *Ibid.*, January 29, 1835.

slavery issue, and these evidently interested Nevin more. T. D. Weld lobbied behind the scenes through this assembly with extraordinary success, reaping the fruits of the year's change of heart, which was so widely felt. Whereas the preceding assembly had included only two "immediate" abolitionists, Weld summed up his conquests in 1835 at forty-eight.

Weld had also tried to organize one or two public meetings during the assembly. At one of these, held in a Methodist church and chaired by the new-school stalwarts Dirck Lansing and N. S. Beman, Judge Birney and John Nevin were scheduled to speak. On the very day of the meeting, June 2, Nevin wrote Weld that he must withdraw. He had been formally advised by a committee of commissioners from the assembly that his participation would seriously injure the seminary. This representation he felt he must respect. On the other hand, he declared, he had the right to resign from the seminary and would

> consider it my duty to do so, as soon as it can be done consistently with what is due . . . to those for whom I act. . . . I look upon the cause of immediate emancipation as so important, that I cannot for any consideration at present consent to be either neutral or silent with regard to it. . . . If I remain in connection with the seminary, it will be as the known and decided advocate of anti-slavery principles.[32]

At this very assembly the Directors of the Western Seminary were requesting an appointment of a professor in Oriental languages and biblical literature, almost certainly with Nevin in mind; but the appointment was arrested, probably by Nevin himself in the light of the situation just described.[33] Shortly thereafter, however, Nevin declined his election as an agent of the American Anti-Slavery Society, perhaps feeling that the prospects at the seminary were better. In any case he continued his in-

[32] G. H. Barnes, and D. L. Dumond (eds.), *Letters of T. D. Weld, A. G. Weld, and S. Grimké, 1822–44* (New York: D. Appleton-Century Co., 1934), I, 222–23.

[33] A. D. Campbell, "The Founding and Early History of the Western Theological Seminary," *Western Theological Seminary Bulletin,* October, 1927, p. 84.

struction—at a nominally increased salary though without formal appointment as professor—for five years more of year-to-year uncertainty.

For the third professorship, that in church history and government, the Assembly of 1835 appointed Dr. David Elliott, formerly of the Presbyterian Church at Mercersburg. Dr. Elliott remained undecided about the appointment for months. In April, 1836, Nevin wrote him,[34] declaring that he considered it of the utmost consequence to the seminary that Elliott become its senior professor, and that he would personally take great satisfaction from association with him. But he did not want to press Elliott, since he had been inclined to think he should leave himself. "I do not wish to leave the seminary," he wrote, "if it can be made to go forward. It *has* seemed to me, however, that it was not likely to be established at present." Consequently, he had intimated in the *Herald* that he was likely to leave himself, to let it be understood "that I did not ask for *toleration*, if any were disposed to refuse it either to my anti-slavery principles or to my views as lately given in the *Herald*," on the advisability of amicably dividing the church.

The concluding reference to an amicable division of the church referred to Nevin's proposal for resolving the bitter "old-school–new-school" hostility which was poisoning relations in the Presbyterian Church. In contrast to his increasing militancy on the moral issue of slavery, Nevin had consistently urged moderation in the doctrinal debates. In this, to be sure, he was following the lead of the Princeton faculty. Like them, he had disapproved of the use of the "Act and Testimony" of the old-school militants as an extraconstitutional test likely to disrupt the church.

The Synod of Pittsburgh, Nevin argued in 1834, was unanimous in its rejection of the doctrinal errors specified in the "Act and Testimony."[35] In fact he personally knew no single case of a Presbyterian holding those errors, although he was prepared to credit the reports that such views were entertained in new-school regions. But the draft, he maintained, had been hastily made and

[34] Unpublished letter, Library of Western Theological Seminary.
[35] *Christian Herald*, October 11, 1834.

was open to valid objections on some minor points. Why should not the Synod draw up its own statement, pruning off these excrescences, and thus achieve unanimity?

Such action would of course have defeated the whole design of imposing the "Act and Testimony" as a test, and those in the synod who desired such imposition resented Nevin's proposal. After debate the synod voted to concur in testifying and protesting against the errors specified, particularly those denying our relation to Adam's sin, and those bearing on native depravity, imputation, human inability, regeneration, and the atonement. The synod declared itself painfully alive to the conviction that these abuses might convert the theological seminaries "into nurseries to foster the noxious errors which are already so widely prevalent." Though probably aimed first of all at Lane Seminary, this observation may have been intended also as a warning in other directions. The synod proceeded to elect two delegates to the convention of "Act and Testimony" signers to be held on the eve of the 1835 General Assembly.

The effort to put brakes to the belligerency of the "Act and Testimony" faction failed, and Nevin then turned to the proposal offered by Archibald Alexander, that the church be divided into several virtually independent synods, meeting infrequently for a merely consultative General Assembly. He presented his case in two series of articles, "Our Synod and Our Paper,"[36] and "Separate Organization."[37] He considered both New Haven divinity and Finneyite new measures to be real dangers, which should be purged from the church. But these were not serious problems in Western Pennsylvania, and he did not want his synod to get involved in the bitter factionalism of the Philadelphia Synod, with its unfortunate consequences for religion. Partisan controversy engendered sinful attitudes and activities, and even the orthodox of Philadelphia were not beyond criticism for refusing to face the slavery issue, if for no other reason. In any case the church could not hold together much longer. Abolitionism would

[36] *Ibid.*, January 15, 22; February 5, 12; March 18, 1836.
[37] *Ibid.*, April 22, 29; May 6; September 16, 1836.

force its way into the General Assembly in a year or two and would divide the church. This, combined with the doctrinal issue, would produce at least three fragments. It was best amicably to divide the Assembly.

Nevin aroused strenuous disagreement and vigorous replies by these articles, but the contributions to the debate of his colleague Halsey were even more sensational. Halsey, who was a widely read historian, damaged the old-school case at a vital point by his historical analysis of the Adopting Act, the basis of the authority of the confessions in the American church. The editor of the *Herald*, T. D. Baird, and Professor Miller of Princeton entered the lists against him. The articles must have been very offensive in the Pittsburgh area, and Halsey's position at the seminary became untenable. He transferred to the new-school seminary at Auburn and to the Presbytery at Cayuga in 1836, just in time to be read out of the church with that new-school presbytery in 1837.

The fateful General Assembly of 1837 met in May in Philadelphia and elected Nevin's new colleague David Elliott as moderator. Nevin wrote Elliott during the assembly, much refreshed to hear that the old school held a majority. "If the Old School do their duty" he advised, "they will make themselves secure of all the power they now possess, and of a great deal more for the next Assembly." Final action of some sort must be taken to resolve the intolerable tensions of party within the church. Nevin hoped the Plan of Union would be abolished and some division of the church effected.[38]

But when news came of the revolutionary action actually taken by the Assembly Nevin was stunned with the shock. Though he did his best to reconcile himself to it, he was borne irresistibly to the conclusion that the measures taken were unconstitutional. However unwise, the Plan of Union had been part of the constitution, and its abrogation could not constitutionally be made to apply retroactively on the ecclesiastical connections of the four

[38] Unpublished letter of May 24, 1837, Library of Western Theological Seminary.

synods so as to expel them. It was not irrelevant that three of the four synods had been organized on the Association Plan of 1808 rather than on the Plan of Union anyway. The judgment of wise jurists who were shocked at the procedure—Wood, Hopkins, and Chancellor Kent—carried Nevin with them. Nevin recognized the extreme pressure on the old school and their sense of desperation. He felt that if they had frankly taken revolutionary ground their case might have been arguable, but what they could not do was to give the color of constitutionality to the measures they had taken. Consequently, when the Ohio Presbytery voted at its June meeting its considered affirmation of the constitutionality and expediency of these measures, Nevin was one of five ministers who voted "no." This was a small minority, but with the "*non liquets*," it included the pastors of the three largest churches in Pittsburgh, the president of Jefferson College, the editor of the *Presbyterian Preacher*, and the Western Seminary professor. One might argue that these were the wisest heads in the presbytery.

Nevin was challenged to explain his vote, and to clear the seminary and himself from suspicion of secret sympathies with the errors of the new school. He finally did so under protest.

> I belong theoretically and experimentally to the Old School in theology, as I have belonged to it theoretically at least from my childhood. I am not conscious of having changed materially in my views as touching the points which divide the two schools, unless it be in coming to see more clearly and fully the emptiness of our modern divinity. . . . [He deplored the spread of] new schoolism even in our orthodox region.[39]

The Presbytery of Ohio tried to conciliate its minority the next year, after the two rival general assemblies had been set up. An "adhering act" was passed unanimously, declaring which general assembly was acknowledged, but stating that brethren might question the constitutionality of proceedings without its being considered an impeachment of their orthodoxy or of their attachment to the church. But Nevin came to scruple even this action. In January, 1839, he recorded for the minority (David

[39] *Christian Herald*, October 12, 19, 1837.

Riddle, Matthew Brown, William McIlvain, Nevin) the meaning of the subscription. For them it signified only their choice of allegiance. They disclaimed the assertion of the old-school assembly that it was "the only true and lawful succession the Presbyterian Church in this country."

In an address entitled "Party Spirit" at Washington College the following fall (September 24, 1839) Nevin set forth the dangers of theological polemics. With obvious if unexpressed reference to the journalists who had whipped up Presbyterian factionalism, he declared that the religious press had too much influence in America. The worst fanaticism was often that enlisted in the service of the truth.

The following month Nevin submitted his resignation, as he had been threatening to do for four or five years. The seminary was thousands of dollars in debt and losing ground continuously. As Nevin wrote,

> All its operations drag, and are maintained from year to year with continual discouragement to the Professors. [Without a different footing financially] it must in the end fail. Of what use then, to cling cold and wet to its leaky bottom, only to assist in keeping it above water a few years longer? . . . For some time past the institution has been a full year behind with me, in the payment of my salary; and latterly the measure of this failure has been steadily on the increase.[40]

The synod voted a crash campaign to raise five thousand dollars to pay the professors' salaries by the end of the year, but like all its predecessors, it failed, and Nevin's resignation stood.

It has been suggested[41] that in addition to the financial difficulties of the seminary Nevin's resignation is to be attributed to the fact that he had "joined the New-School minority in the Presbytery, which destroyed confidence in him to a considerable degree." But Nevin never joined the new-school minority or sympathized with its views. He was, to be sure, linked by ties of

[40] *Presbyterian Christian Advocate and Herald of the West* (from October 1838 replacing the *Pittsburgh Christian Herald and Western Missionary Recorder*), October 30, 1839.

[41] J. I. Good, *History of the Reformed Church in the United States in the Nineteenth Century* (New York, 1911), p. 111 n.

marriage to Dr. David Riddle,[42] the leader of the small new-school presbytery in the Pittsburgh area. But Nevin's position remained consistently that which the Princeton faculty had originally maintained, old-school in theology and constitutional in procedure.[43] This position was no doubt very annoying to the old-school doctrinaires, such as Breckinridge and T. D. Baird, but there is no evidence that confidence in Nevin had been destroyed. On the contrary, Jefferson College awarded him a D.D. that year, and in the very month in which he submitted his resignation his presbytery elected him moderator. One might hazard the guess that if Nevin had changed his affiliations within Presbyterianism, he would have moved, not to the new school, but in the direction of the old-school abolitionists of Ohio, the later "Free Presbyterians."

Instead, however, Nevin accepted an unexpected call to serve as theologian to the German Reformed Church. When first approached he had refused to let his name be presented. But the Germans, at a loss otherwise for a professor, voted to call him anyway. "If we can satisfy him," said S. R. Fisher, who had well taken his measure, "that it is his *duty* to take charge of the Professorship at Mercersburg, the whole Presbyterian Church combined cannot prevent him from doing so." [44] Nevin did become persuaded that this strange turn of events was a special leading of Providence, and agreed to go back over the Alleghenies to his home county to teach at the struggling German Reformed seminary.

Nevin had consulted President Alexander of Princeton and other leading Presbyterians.[45] They encouraged him to view the move as simply a transfer from one to another branch of the Reformed Church. The synod he was entering, as Nevin put it,

[42] Riddle had married a daughter of Dr. Matthew Brown, president of Jefferson College, and Nevin's sister Elizabeth had married the son.

[43] "The authority of Princeton alone was of more weight with me than all the character of the new school put together." *Christian Herald*, October 12, 1837.

[44] J. H. Dubbs, *History of Franklin and Marshall College* (Lancaster, 1903), p. 192.

[45] *Ibid.*

consisted simply of "German Presbyterians," just as the one he was leaving might be called the "Scotch Reformed." The platform on which he would teach at Mercersburg was that on which he had stood at Princeton and at Allegheny, old-school Calvinistic orthodoxy.

In most practical aspects of church life, as well as in ecclesiastical and doctrinal matters, Nevin continued at Mercersburg in the directions laid down in his "Scotch Reformed" days. He remained a conservative Irish evangelical, molded by Princeton scholasticism, strong for private-judgment biblicism and a vigorous promoter of various evangelistic and moralist causes. He got into another dispute about church fairs in Mercersburg and actually reprinted for the new crisis his Pittsburgh editorial on the subject. He remained an intransigent "temperance" man even among the Germans. Sabbath-keeping, however, no longer seems to have claimed a high priority on his list. And there is a rather startling silence on slavery. Mercersburg is very close to Mason and Dixon's line, and to the Potomac, and escaping slaves frequently passed through the region. But there was little or no public controversy in the German Reformed Church over abolition and the most dangerous abolitionist of Pittsburgh seems to have been content with the situation. It was as if he now accepted the old-school gag on the subject which he had resisted in 1836. Apart from this issue Nevin remained a representative "Puritan." The two poles of religion, as he saw it, were conversion, and consequent moralistic and evangelical zeal as evidence of sanctification. Perhaps Nevin was especially militant on the latter score because he nursed some personal anxieties with regard to the former.

2/ A Preparatory Decade

The springs of such radical reorientations as John Nevin experienced at the beginning of his forty-second year are usually difficult or impossible to identify accurately. The period of incubation is often protracted and the evidence of development scanty. Nevin's extended account of his intellectual and spiritual pilgrimage, "My Own Life,"[1] is very useful, but it was composed in old age and under the pressures of recently acquired interests. The fragmentary contemporary evidence from the period of his thirties often corrects the picture significantly. That evidence, unfortunately, is very scattered, consisting chiefly of scores of fugitive articles in newspapers and periodicals, some written in Pittsburgh and some in Mercersburg. Yet some important factors in the process can be identified.

Only when he became editor of *The Friend* in 1833 did Nevin begin to leave sufficient records of his views for any confident assessment. At that time one significant influence on which the autobiography throws no light was clearly at work—the influence of Coleridge. The title of Nevin's paper, *The Friend*, is itself Coleridgian, selections from Coleridge were frequently reprinted in early issues,[2] and the availability of Coleridge for Christian theology was discussed. Nevin was not, at this period, particularly interested in speculative thought. It was probably in the sphere of biblical interpretation that he found Coleridge helpful in the first instance. But now, at the beginning of his thirties, he seemed attracted to an intuitionist, idealist type of thought quite distinct from the Scottish "common sense" of Princeton.

Biblical interpretation at Princeton in Nevin's day followed the

[1] *Weekly Messenger* (hereafter cited as *WM*) March 2–June 22, 1870.
[2] *The Friend*, April 10; June 13, 20; July 4, 18, 1833; January 16, 1834.

principles of Moses Stuart of Andover, the leading American biblical scholar of the 1820's. Stuart brought to America the methods of that German school known as "rational supernaturalism." The *Biblical Theology* of Storr and Flatt, for example, was translated in 1826 under Andover auspices by the American Lutheran theologian S. S. Schmucker. The method was grammatical and historical, assuming that the revealed text would yield its substance directly, as with a work in geology, to the discursive intellect.

When he began instruction at Pittsburgh, Nevin accepted these presuppositions and used as a text in hermeneutics another manual from the same school by Ernesti. Soon, however, he came to question this conception of interpretation. Coleridge, he noted, contended for another organ of interpretation than ordinary common sense. In *The Friend* Nevin reviewed Herder's *Spirit of Hebrew Poetry* and DeWette's *Psalms*.[3] He was scandalized by DeWette's boldness regarding the authorship of the psalms, but agreed with him that religious literature must be apprehended by the "heart" rather than merely by the intellect and that the historical and grammatical method was inadequate. In a series of six articles entitled "Is the Bible of God?"[4] Nevin maintained that one should not expect to assay the evidences of Christianity objectively and rationally, but should seek to know the truth experimentally in the interior life of the spirit. Increasingly he found himself arguing with Ernesti's text as he used it with his students. And as he meditated the hermeneutics implied in his favorite devotional manual, *The Imitation of Christ*, all merely outward modes of mastering the sense of the Bible seemed poor indeed. At times he thought that half his books were better at the bottom of the Allegheny River.[5]

Nevin found help in the Puritan mystics and Platonists of the seventeenth century. Scougall and Shaw used notions of "partici-

[3] *Ibid.*, August 28, September 11, October 2, 1834; January 5, 1835.
[4] *Ibid.*, January 23 to March 27, 1834.
[5] *WM,* June 1, 1870.

pation," "implantation." The works of John Howe, which were reissued at the time, impressed Nevin with their "deep Platonizing thoughts." Archbishop Leighton was one of his chief heroes, in part no doubt because of his freedom from party spirit, but also for the theological orientation he shared with Scougall. Nevin cited Plato's *Republic* and *Phaedo* on the communion possible with the forms of the good and beautiful.[6] The Bible, he had come to understand, presented "Ideas" which kindled corresponding ideas slumbering in the soul. In the same way the natural creation was pervaded by the presence of deity and adumbrated invisible spiritual realities, "the idea of which must be stirred up in the soul itself before either they or their shadows can be apprehended as they are." [7] A Sabbath afternoon lecture series on "The Analogy of the Bible and Nature" (the text of which is apparently lost) probably moved in the same sphere of ideas.[8]

Ten or a dozen of Nevin's own poems, printed in *The Friend*, show that he was preoccupied with mortality and the transitoriness of earthly things, contrasting them sharply with an invisible and eternal realm. This was his well-nigh exclusive theme under titles such as "The Fashion of the World Passeth Away," "Eternity," "Trust not to Earth," "What is Thy Life?" "The Saint's Rest," "Death," "Time."

The positive side of these contrasts was made more explicit in a series on "Worldly-mindedness." [9] Here the world of sense was contrasted to the world of spirit in a Platonic sense. The "present outward world, which should be considered the region of shadows and dreams" is unreal, phenomenal, a symbol or shadow of the invisible stabilities. And faith is a kind of intuition, the "organ of spiritual vision," as sense is that of the material world. Faith is that vision or sensibility by which in the words of the Bible we

[6] "Party Spirit," *WM*, August 26, September 2, 1840; also published separately (Chambersburg, 1840), p. 27.

[7] *The Friend*, January 15, 1835.

[8] *Centennial Volume of the First Presbyterian Church of Pittsburgh, Pa.* (Pittsburgh, 1884), pp. 58, 195.

[9] *WM*, June, July, August, 1840.

hear the living God or in nature constantly sense God's providential rule always encircling us in the events of our practical existence.

Religion and philosophy alike, said Nevin, teach that we do not find our real life in the world that passes. To obey God is to surrender to his direction, not as a mere separate and arbitrary authority, but freely, so as to find in it the proper form of our soul's existence. Salvation is a new life, growing in the soul from the new birth, forming the soul progressively to a recognized citizenship in heaven. The Kingdom of God is thus an inward frame or habit in which God's subjects are bound together in a "complete organic existence." Here, in this "new creation" is our only hope, for the Kingdom of God is really the "ground stream of the world's history." We should look for no earthly paradise like that of St. Simon or Owen, or Pittsburgh's Etzlar. The religious man, to be sure, must live in both spheres, but he should deal with property, honor, politics, art, and science with a measure of independence. Our chief good is elsewhere: the life of God within.

Nevin was fond of the biological analogy for religion. He printed a series of articles entitled "Religion a Life." [10] This phrase was intended on the one hand, in Schleiermacher's vein, to point to the experience which lay behind the doctrine, to argue that religion was "a matter of sentiment more than a mere intellection." But "life" also conveyed the idea of gradual change, growth, development. The new life was inner fellowship with God, initiated by the new birth and maturing in the resurrection of the body.[11]

The theme of growth in holiness had been a favorite with Nevin from the beginning of his publishing.[12] In 1834 he commended a new edition of Scougall's *Life of God in the Soul of Man.* He was inclined to think that modern evangelicalism generally fell short of the classical Reformed and Puritan theologians

[10] *The Friend,* December 25, 1834; January 15, 22, 29; February 5, 1835.
[11] *Seal of the Spirit,* (Pittsburgh, 1838).
[12] Cf. "Trinitarian and Unitarian Doctrines concerning Jesus Christ," *Presbyterian Preacher,* 1833.

on this subject. Multitudes, he observed, had some idea of conversion and regeneration, but not of growth in holiness, of the forming of the "new creation." [13] In fact Nevin's grievance against new-school theology apparently came chiefly at this point, rather than, as with most old-school polemicists, at its supposed Arminian tendency. Nevin charged new-school thought with obscuring the living work of the Holy Ghost and causing "the idea of a divine life in the soul to be regarded too generally as a mystic fancy." [14] He stated a view of justification which was scarcely that of the "Act and Testimony" faction. Christ must be formed *in* us, he contended, before his salvation can reach us.[15] He urged his students to aspire to such inner fellowship with God.

Numerous and subtle counterfeits for this life with God were prevalent, some of which Nevin illustrated in a series of imaginary portraits after the manner of William Law.[16] True faith was not, said Nevin, a matter of intellectual opinion, whether taken on authority or based on some consideration of evidence. One might be completely orthodox intellectually and still outside religion altogether. True faith must be more than correct opinions; it must somehow *touch* its object, *see* divine things as they are. Similarly faith is other than a determination of the will to believe, which is quickly associated with the notion of a meritorious work.

Nevin was also concerned to distinguish faith from mere feeling and imagination. He expressed doubts, in this connection, of the piety of Herder and Goethe, Coleridge and Wordsworth. "Was it all poetry, and nothing beyond?" He warned against the pantheistic cult of nature. Even with true piety, to be sure, it was very difficult to estimate the proper place of the aesthetic and emotional. Nevin appreciated the difference between the "solemn Gothic style" and "a Swiss barn." The use of organs and choirs might be religiously helpful but too often betrayed a mere seek-

[13] Review of Goode's *Better Covenant*, in *Christian Herald*, March 30, 1837.

[14] *Ibid.*, October 12, 1837.

[15] *The Friend*, January 21, 1838.

[16] "Faith," *WM*, February 12, 19, 23; March 4, 11, 18, 1840. Reprinted from the *Presbyterian Advocate*.

ing for effect. In such theatricality Roman Catholic worship was often equaled by "new measures" among Protestants. "Crucifixes and pictures, anxious seats and outward public decision acts come to have very much the same character," an unnatural stimulation degenerating into mummery. No wonder camp meeting converts so generally fell away from grace. Infrequent communion seasons, similarly, tended to nurture a "fictitious piety."

Lastly, when the divine was perceived only as arbitrary power, superstition sought release from guilt by rites and ceremonies which did not involve the heart and will. Pagans and Roman Catholics made much of sacrifices, pilgrimages, fasting in this *opus operatum* sense. Sacraments and ecclesiastical polity by divine right on the ground of an outward apostolic succession might thus be treated as magic. Or a regular Sabbatarian Presbyterian might so understand his religious duties as indulgence taxes. In all this there was no concept of a spiritual, divine habit working freely in the mind.

As he looked back on this period of transition in his old age, Nevin singled out the church historian Neander as the most important personal influence. "How much I owe to him," he wrote, "in the way of excitement, impulse, suggestion, knowledge, both literary and religious, reaching onward into all my later life, is more than I can pretend to explain, for it is in truth more than I have power to understand." [17] It was primarily to read Neander that Nevin learned German, and the first German book he read was Neander's *Tertullian*. Then he read the volumes of the *General Church History* as they appeared.

In part Neander seems to have been the writer in whom Nevin discovered the new perspectives usually associated with Schleiermacher. To Neander religion was a "life," a communion with invisible realities, experience rather than doctrine or theory. Here too was the sympathy for Platonism and idealism generally. The specific contribution which Nevin later singled out, however, was the gift of historical consciousness. To him Neander's history meant "an actual awakening of the soul" whereby he was stirred

[17] *WM*, June 15, 1870.

from his "dogmatic slumber." Not that the full impact was felt at once; rather the new historical understanding grew slowly until it came to condition all his views of life. No element of a true liberal culture was more important, he later felt, than the power of seeing and feeling the historical element in all human existence.

There were at least two aspects of this historical perspective. One was a capacity to appreciate and justify diverse conceptions. As Professor Miller had taught history at Princeton, using Mosheim for facts and Milner for piety, everything was reviewed polemically from Princeton's orthodox point of view. It was, as Nevin said, neither edifying nor truly scientific. History seemed a valley of dry bones, dead facts. The early fathers were an enigma. The history of the church was read in the light of Mede's and Newton's views of the biblical apocalypses. Primitive Presbyterianism had been corrupted in the "great apostasy," first to common prelacy, and then into the full-blown hierarchy of the fourth century. The medieval church was the "synagogue of Satan," for within the "Devil's Millennium" before the Reformation the biblical "Man of Sin" reigned in the papal system. Only a few hidden witnesses to the truth, like the Waldenses, survived in remote regions. Even Lutheranism and the Continental Reformed movement were still over the Princeton horizon. The true church was practically confined to the English-speaking world.

The other aspect of the historical perspective was a sense of unifying direction. History at Princeton was incoherent, a mere arbitrary conglomeration. "Its necessary *a priori* principles and postulates, as connected with the general scheme of the world" had not yet been divined. The concept of an inner purposive dynamic to the process, an entelechy, was to come only with Neander. Previously Nevin would have felt it "well-nigh profane" to suppose that there might be a development of such doctrines as the Trinity or the Atonement. Now, however, even the heresies made some sense in relation to the conception of the developing consciousness of Christian doctrine. They had a role to play, and even in their one-sidedness and error they claimed a new reverence and regard. Neander first reconciled Nevin to the fathers, "not in my Puritanic Presbyterian tongue" but in theirs. Through all the diversities he now traced an objective movement to a divinely ordained purpose. Thus the idea of Providence was recast as the conception of historical development.

By this perspective Neander had opened to Nevin the world of the early church. Many persons, said Nevin, supposed that the doctrine of the first two or three centuries was rigidly orthodox. But in fact the early Christians did not have a mature doctrinal system and often fell into speculative error. It was the Christian *life*, or the insight of the heart, which gave them stability through the intellectual problems, thus illustrating that faith was more fundamental than doctrine and confessions. It was the living sense of the Presence that was basic, prior to conduct and virtue as well as to teaching. Behind forms of worship, also, and such exercises of sentiment as revivalistic conversion stood the facts of the spiritual world.

In 1837, however, when Nevin inherited the church history department of Western Seminary from Luther Halsey, he was not yet in sufficient command of Neander's perspective to teach accordingly. He continued using Mosheim as his text, and despite his new idea of development in history, he still conceived of the papal period as the "great apostasy." In 1840 he commended Joseph Berg's *Lectures on Romanism* to his new German brethren as "large enough to drag some of the most hideous features of the Romish system into the broad light of day."[18] There was, he admitted, some danger of antipapal fanaticism in America, but even greater was the danger of carelessness before the papal threat to civil and religious liberty. "It is the mystery of iniquity, always ready to evolve itself anew from the depths of Satan in the soul of man." If true to itself popery must work for the subversion of American freedoms as well as to undermine the truth as it is in Christ. Similarly in the series "The Heidelberg Catechism"[19] Nevin referred repeatedly to the "Man of Sin," and used such

[18] *Ibid.*, November 25, 1840.
[19] *Ibid.*, 1840–42.

terms as the "popish idol" and the "Moloch of popery." He was not to relax his anti-Romanism until after Schaf had arrived at Mercersburg with a new conception of church history.

When Neander awakened in Nevin some sense of the historical depth of Christianity, this did not yet involve its corporate social character. Nevin remained an individualistic evangelical. He distrusted tradition as a guide to religious truth and urged every individual to search the Scriptures by himself in preference to all secondhand testimony. Neander's pietistic view of Christian history was little suited to develop in Nevin a sense of the meaning of the visible church. Such a conception Nevin first discovered in the Oxford Tracts, which he looked into at Pittsburgh. The idea had thus come over his horizon, but he viewed it with pity and contempt as "Newmania."

When Nevin moved to Mercersburg he was not aware of shifting ground theologically. He was still to work in an orthodox Calvinist church, governed in presbyterian manner. He would now be responsible, not to the Westminister Confession, but to the Heidelberg Catechism, which, he said, could be regarded as the doctrinal groundwork on which the Westminister Confession was erected. The German heritage should be respected in eastern Pennsylvania; and Presbyterianism should have been organized there only as English-language congregations connected with the German Reformed Synod, for otherwise it was out of place.

In that synod in 1840 there was no recognized theological center. The tone was set in Presbyterianism by Princeton and among the Dutch Reformed by New Brunswick, but there was nothing comparable in the German Reformed church. Professor Mayer and his weak seminary had little more influence than any of the three or four leading pastor teachers who had trained a number of ministers. Mayer had never received a college education. His theological text was the work of Mursinna of Halle, and his personal inclinations were apparently rationalist. The older orthodoxy was better maintained by Samuel Helfenstein, Sr., who produced a systematics with his sons, akin to the teaching of Alexander and Hodge of Princeton, and Livingstone of New

Brunswick. The range of theological opinion in Nevin's new synod seems thus to have been much the same as in the Presbyterian church.

If there was no significant difference doctrinally or ecclesiastically between Scotch and German Reformed, what did Nevin consider the German heritage that was to be preserved? To him, it was a matter of culture, literature, language. At Allegheny he had learned to read German and had publicly glorified the language at the expense of the French he had earlier studied. He had developed a real enthusiasm for German historical, theological, and philosophical writers; and this interest was one of the considerations which had led the Mercersburg board to approach him. It may not have been, as Schaf thought,[20] Nevin's primary reason for going to Mercersburg, but it was certainly a factor. In his inaugural Nevin urged the Germans of eastern Pennsylvania not to denationalize themselves. The German mind, with its reflective bent was, he felt, especially adapted to religion, as well as to music and poetry and to the deeper and more spiritual emotions. In 1842 he proclaimed in "The German Language" the distinctive virtues of that tongue. He even once tried to preach in it, at Tulpehocken. No one smiled in church.[21]

It seemed to Nevin that Providence was at work in his call. He had a boyhood familiarity with the Pennsylvania Germans and knew the people well. In more recent years he had developed a marked interest in German theological scholarship. He was returning to his native Cumberland Valley with a determination to help his German neighbors appropriate their own heritage, of the most recent generations as well as of the Reformation.

No doubt Nevin looked forward to the German-trained colleague he would meet at Mercersburg, who might tell him personally much of the new currents in Germany. For two or three years previously Friedrich Augustus Rauch, president of the college, had been commending Hegelian idealism in the seminary,

[20] J. I. Good, *History of the Reformed Church in the United States in the Nineteenth Century* (New York, 1911), p. 111 n.

[21] T. Appel, *Life and Work of John Williamson Nevin* (Philadelphia, 1889), p. 130.

to the enthusiasm of the students and the distress of the aging Dr. Mayer, who taught the old common-sense empiricism. Rauch's chief assignment was with the undergraduates of Marshall College. For them he had written a textbook in psychology (published just about the time Nevin arrived) which was adopted at Dartmouth and the University of Vermont as well as at Marshall. Rauch's *Psychology* was the first presentation in America in English of Hegel's philosophy of mind.

Nevin probably had little opportunity to match idealisms with Rauch personally. The younger man was away much of Nevin's first term and confined by illness during the winter. Nevin later reported that they had never discussed religion intimately, and his impressions of Rauch's German career were certainly erroneous (although Rauch may have conveyed the misconceptions intentionally). Yet, when Rauch died suddenly in the spring of 1841, at thirty-five, he left Nevin as his literary executor. Thus Rauch's chief role in intellectual history was to introduce Nevin in this way to Hegel's anthropology, ethics, and aesthetics.

In his last year Rauch had revised his *Psychology* for a second edition, which was published in the spring of 1841 after his death, with a foreword by Nevin. Rauch had also carried his moral philosophy so far that he had hoped to publish that as well in the summer of 1841. Although Nevin apparently was unable to edit this manuscript for Rauch, he probably taught from Rauch's Hegelian outlines when he inherited the president's course in ethics for the seniors in 1841. What could have been more congenial to a Platonist with a developing historical consciousness!

Rauch's mark on Nevin's religious thought seems traceable first in a discussion of the Eucharist. Not that Rauch was interested in the sacraments, but his psychology seems to have provided Nevin with an apparatus for Nevin's distinctive interests. Nevin had apparently taken a high Calvinist view of the Lord's Supper at Pittsburgh,[22] and he maintained this at Mercersburg, in a church where the prevailing view was rather a Zwinglian memorialism.

[22] Cf. his commendation of a local printing of Willison's *Sacramental Catechism* in 1830.

Nevin's description of Zwingli's Eucharistic doctrine as "low" and "rationalistic"[23] evoked murmurs in the church. For Nevin, however, the Lord's Supper epitomized the core of the gospel, the life of God in the soul of man; and early in 1842 he discussed the Lord's Supper in terms that seemed to reflect study of Rauch's *Psychology*.[24]

In fifteen or twenty pages of that work Rauch had defined a group of related conceptions—life, personality, the relation of soul and body—in a fashion markedly different from Locke's empiricism. These conceptions all bore on theological issues, especially on the Eucharistic presence, the Incarnation generally, the mystical union of Christ and the believer, the resurrection of the body. Rauch made none of these implications himself; he never displayed any of the churchly tendencies of the Mercersburg theology. As Nevin discussed Calvin's doctrine, however, he seemed to be adapting Rauch's definitions. Calvin's doctrine, he said, taught an incorporation with Christ's real person, with the life of his glorified body. It meant a "transfusion of soul and body" in contrast to a merely moral union.

Another element in Nevin's developing views was his study of the Heidelberg Catechism. He worked his way through the catechism in a series of sermons in the college chapel. Evidently he found support here for his views of the Eucharist, for he observed that the catechism was especially happy in its treatment of the sacraments, of Christology, and of justification.[25] This last intriguing point was not explained, but Nevin may have found in the catechism confirmation of his conception that justification is brought home only in the context of the mystical union.

Nevin was to have difficulty later in holding the idea of predestination together with that of sacramental grace, but at this stage it did not seem to embarrass him. He was evidently still a "metaphysical Calvinist" who conceived all events and all redemption as decreed from eternity. He noted that originally both

[23] *WM.*, January 27, February 3, 1841.
[24] *Ibid.*, April 27, 1842.
[25] *Ibid.*, May 18, 1842.

Luther and Melanchthon had been predestinarians, but that after the 1550's the Lutheran and Reformed churches had generally made this issue a point of distinction. Even among the Reformed the sublapsarian view was probably the more common version. The Heidelberg Catechism was wisely silent on this difficult subject, but the idea of unconditional election was nevertheless involved in the system and thus implicit in the catechism.

In the midst of these theological and philosophical preoccupations Nevin was nevertheless displaying extraordinary energy in practical matters. He entered the German Reformed Church like a cavalry charge. "The Church," he said in his inaugural, "is struggling to rise, with a resolution and energy which bid fair to increase every year. What a change has taken place in this respect within the last ten years!"[26] He had in mind, no doubt, the reconciliation of the Free Synod, the erection of the substantial seminary building at Mercersburg, and the vigorous promotion of denominational activities and consciousness by Benjamin Schneck through the *Weekly Messenger*. All that was now needed to furnish the church adequately, said Nevin, might be accomplished in a single year without undue sacrifice. He made himself at once the chief promoter of a year's campaign for the institutions of the church through the columns of the *Messenger*.

He began with a communication headed "Marshall College," in which he reviewed the situation in the tone of a chairman of the board, or at least a president, discussing priorities and ways and means. It had been decided to build a structure for the preparatory school before that for the college, but Nevin wanted to know why both should not be done in the next year. He proposed four different and specific methods of raising the funds, offering a thousand-dollar loan himself. Within a fortnight of his inauguration he launched the educational institutions of the church in an aggressive campaign. His scheme of a loan proved successful and plans for the college building were drawn up. S. R. Fisher urged that all press on with the campaign "to show ourselves properly mindful of the special interposition of Divine Providence

[26] *Ibid.*, May 27, 1840.

in favoring us with one possessed of the enlightened views, enlarged liberality, and commanding influence" of its originator.[27] President Rauch, who had no head for administration, had been discouraged almost to despair in the preceding months, but the injection into the situation of the resourceful and hard-driving Scot changed everything overnight. Rauch, convalescing in Saratoga, wrote him, "I never lose sight of the connection in which I have come to stand with yourself as that in which alone all my enterprises seem to prosper . . . and here let me be permitted in truth and sincerity to acknowledge how greatly my conversations with yourself have instructed and encouraged me."[28]

In the last five months of 1840 Nevin wrote ten or a dozen times in the *Messenger* in favor of the proposed centenary celebration of the organization of the German Reformed Church, a scheme which came out of the Maryland classis and was perhaps his suggestion in the first place. In addition to celebrating past mercies and repenting shortcomings, he urged, such a centenary might furnish the occasion "from which to take . . . a fresh start as a Church." Never before perhaps had a church been in a position to burst the limits of its past existence and emerge before the world in a new character entirely "by a mere act, so to speak, of its own will." Within the church there was little understanding of her capacities, while other denominations were generally ignorant of the theology and character of the German Reformed. As Nevin saw it, all that was lacking in the church was confidence and resolution, and these were the gifts which he would most conspicuously bring her.

Nevin took another bold initiative by proposing a $100,000 campaign for the Mercersburg institutions. These were dimensions hitherto unheard of in the German Reformed Church, but Nevin argued that the wealth was there among the German farmers. He could name ten men in Franklin County alone who would be ready to give $1,000 apiece. And he broke down the $100,000 into a budget of specific needs. He also wrote a series of

[27] *Ibid.*, June 24, 1840.
[28] *Ibid.*, May 5, 1841.

articles detailing a plan of scholarship endowments (by which it was hoped to raise the bulk of the money in the campaign), proceeding to assign quotas to the various districts of the church. One can understand why, when the president of the Marshall College board resigned in September 1840, John Nevin was elected his successor.

Between terms in October, Nevin toured the German country east of the Susquehanna. He venerated the traditionalism of eastern Pennsylvania, its determination to "hold fast to the faith and fashion of their fathers." As an old-school Presbyterian he found this spirit congenial. He conceived that the grand object of a centenary would be to resuscitate in the church its proper life "under its own original and distinctive type" and "her own proper standards." The church was accused of being a cold, lifeless body. Some regarded it as a fair field for proselyting, others for "new measures," but why not revive the original spirit of the Reformation? Nevin prodded the *Messenger* into the field of church history and the history of Reformed theology. Both the continental origins and the American beginnings of the German Reformed church were illuminated, and the Heidelberg Catechism was raised higher in the knowledge and estimation of the church than it had been for generations. By far the most extensive contributions of this sort were supplied by Nevin himself, in the twenty-nine articles on the history and prospects of the German Reformed Church in his series "The Heidelberg Catechism."

At President Rauch's unexpected death, in the spring of 1841, the way of the trustees was clear. Nevin's leadership of the centenary program had proved him a man of the most marked administrative capacity and energy, the natural head of the college. He accepted the election as acting president, with the understanding that he would be released as soon as possible for his primary obligations in the seminary where he was now left the sole professor. Thus, within less than a year Nevin had become president of the college as well as the board and the sole theological professor of the denomination. "He was then a little over thirty-seven years old, but everything about him, with the exception of his dark, black hair, indicated a person of a much greater age. His face was marked with the deep lines of thought, and his gait was that of a person who had been accustomed to carry heavy burdens."[29] His height, his bearing, and his unusually high forehead made an impressive figure, which was increased by a deep, remarkable voice. The Germans took stock of their new theologian and president and concluded, "Gel, ein recht dreistöckiger Mann!"

He declined the president's salary, so that the trustees were able to use the funds for a professor of natural science. In this way they were better off than before, both in teaching staff and in terms of administration. Although they had lost the peculiar appeal of a German-trained professor, they hoped to bring over from Germany a replacement for Rauch.

As Nevin surveyed the condition of the German Reformed parishes, he found certain peculiar problems. For a century the German congregations had been desperately short of ministers and they had become accustomed to a minimum program. The available ministers were spread over so many charges that the average congregation did not expect more than one sermon a month and had no experience of an effective pastoral ministry. Baptisms, confirmations, and an annual communion were often mere formalities, abstracted as they were from a continuous and significant congregational life. Members were generally admitted without inquiry into qualifications, and discipline was rarely exercised for any purpose. The people had not really adjusted themselves to the system of voluntary financial support, and they were hypersensitive to anything resembling the hated church taxation of the old country. Sometimes violent prejudice had been stirred up among them against solicitations for missionary or Bible societies, or for theological seminaries, as devices for cheating them out of their money and working toward clericalism and a church establishment.

The lack of faithful pastoral ministry, Nevin observed, had also

[29] T. Appel, *Recollections of College Life* (Reading, Pa., 1886), p. 297.

left the field open for fanaticism and enthusiasm. The German churches exhibited a tendency to run into "wild and irregular forms of religious feeling." Whole sections of the Lutheran Church were quite given over to the wildfire of Finneyite revivalism. The Reformed Church had not surrendered so completely, but two "ranting sects" had split off, the followers of Otterbein, and more recently, those of John Winebrenner. Both the United Brethren and the Church of God, as they were called, were notorious, reported Nevin, for fanatical, unscriptural disorder in worship, patronage of an ignorant ministry, and a Pelagian tendency in doctrine.[30]

All this was an old story to old-school Presbyterians, who had maintained a steady barrage against "new measures" revivalism ever since the Lebanon Conference. The Princeton faculty had all issued repeated warnings on this subject for years. Now again, in 1842, the *Princeton Review* took the occasion of a review of Woodbridge's lectures on revivals to warn against "anxious seats" and prayers for individuals by name. Nevin, as we have seen, had repudiated Gallaher's revivals in Pittsburgh. For him, as for his Princeton teachers, the greatest danger was theological—the implication in the whole technique that sinners had the inherent powers of decision and self-conversion or that revivalists could manipulate the Holy Spirit. Such denials of God's free sovereignty in man's redemption were the very hinge of new-school heresy. For Nevin the old issue was now reopened in his new synod: was the area between the Delaware and the Potomac to be given up to Arminianism? [31]

When Nevin's articles in the *Messenger* were called to Winebrenner's attention, he wrote the author, charging misrepresentation and requesting retraction. Nevin replied that he would retract if shown incorrect. What he had called fanaticism, he said, included loud groaning, crying and shouting, clapping of hands, jumping, falling down, permitting women to pray in mixed assemblies, admitting unlearned ministers and frequent attacks on

[30] *Ibid.*, August 10, 1842.
[31] *Ibid.*, August 24, 1842.

educated ones, and the assumption that all who came to the anxious seat and declared they had found peace there in the midst of the animal excitement were truly converted.[32] His charge of a Pelagian tendency was based on the "Church of God" teaching of the sinner's inherent moral ability to repent and believe. The Church of God was also very largely given over to the Millerite excitement over the imminent second Advent.

Winebrenner did not deny that these were prevailing features of his camp meetings; he merely insisted they were scriptural rather than fanatical. "Who made you a judge of these things?" he demanded.[33] If Nevin had itinerated as an evangelist half as long as he had, he would better understand the character of the German Reformed Church. It was "a fallen and corrupt church," a "synagogue of Satan," marked by a "diabolical . . . spirit of pride, bigotry, and persecution" from which it was sinful *not* to secede.[34] All converted ministers had a duty to break with the German Reformed Church immediately, on the injunction "Be ye not unequally yoked together with unbelievers." [35]

Nevin saw no point in continuing the debate and declined Winebrenner's challenges. He wrote instead:

> You must not think that I cherish towards you any personal ill will. I think honestly, you erred in breaking away from the German Reformed Church when you did. Your acknowledged system of religion, practically considered, is to my mind, whether in your hands or in the hands of others (for under different names it abounds in the country), radically defective and full of danger. In the fire and whirlwind system of converting sinners, I have less confidence the longer I live; I believe four are deceived by it for every one that is saved, if it be overruled to the salvation of any. Such are my views. I do not utter them in the way of railing—and it is not necessary at all that in holding them I should hate those who like yourself think differently.[36]

[32] August 11, 1842, as cited in *Gospel Publisher* (Harrisburg), October 18, 1843.
[33] December 30, 1842, in *GP*, November 15, 1843.
[34] September 30, 1842, in *GP*, November 1, 1843.
[35] July 6, 1843, in *GP*, December 6, 1843.
[36] June 29, 1843, in *GP*, November 29, 1843.

Nevin was equally outspoken against rationalistic formalism. As he wrote Winebrenner, a German paper in the West had given him two columns of abuse for saying that the German immigrants needed spiritual religion. After personal investigation, in fact, he defended the revival in Reading in the winter of 1842–43. So far as he could learn, all things had proceeded decently and in good order, "not by the blind mummery of new measures"; and the charges of fanaticism and Methodistic extravagances were not justified. He sharply rebuked those who attacked prayer meetings, family worship, or heart religion as Strablerism or new measures. Such things were as different as light and smoke, he declared. The great interests of evangelical piety imbedded in the catechism, the old hymns, and the Bible had nothing to do with "anxious benches, shouting, clapping, and the whole babelism of false excitement." [37]

Ambiguity about the meaning of "new measures" is amusingly illustrated by a letter to the *Messenger* of February 9, 1848, entitled "A Plain Man's Thoughts," which sounds suspiciously like the style of William Nevin:

> Our minister is always talking about new measures, or *schwaermerei*, as it is called in German, and telling us to take care it doesn't get in among us. By what he says, one would think the Church was full of it; and he sometimes hints too that you, Mr. Editor, and Dr. Nevin and Schaff and the young men they're teaching in the Seminary are all of you strabblers, or not much better at any rate. Now . . . I never saw any jumping or shouting or using the anxious bench, as strabblers do. . . .
>
> Now what I think about the matter is just this: our minister knows well enough that you and the Professors don't go in for shouting nor for the anxious bench: but he calls you strabblers because you're in favor of Sunday schools and scripture instruction, prayer meetings, and giving Bibles to poor people that can't buy them, and sending missionaries after our children out to Ohio and Michigan, and to the Heathen, and because you sometimes hint that as God tells us to keep *all* his Sabbaths holy, so we ought to have preaching on *every* Sunday, instead of once a month. . . . Let him come right plain out, and say so, and not keep hinting against them, and calling them new measures, when everybody knows they ain't new measures.

[37] *WM*, June 14, 1843.

And the worst is I'm afraid he's taking the very plan to make strabblers.

The issue over new measures came up also in Mercersburg village. The German Reformed congregation in the Old Stone Church was looking for a new pastor in 1842. They heard, probably at Nevin's suggestion, a sermon by his Princeton classmate, W. Ramsay, back from missionary work in China. When at the end of the service Ramsay unexpectedly issued an "altar call" and swung into the Finneyite routine, Nevin was taken aback. He made some remarks which were not wholly in the spirit of the occasion and later wrote Ramsay, who had received the call of the church, that he would not support him if he tried to introduce new measures. Ramsay, offended, declined the call and blamed Nevin. Some of the students had been favorably impressed by Ramsay and expressed their disappointment. In the class on pastoral practice, Nevin delivered several lectures on the theme of new measures, which probably became the core of the little tract published in the fall of 1843 as *The Anxious Bench*. Winebrenner had persisted by mail in seeking a debate, and this publication enabled Nevin to deal with the issues without becoming involved with Winebrenner.

The Anxious Bench was given that title as less ambiguous than the term "new measures." True revivals, prayer meetings, protracted meetings, and the work of the evangelistic societies were sometimes labeled "new measures" also; and Nevin wanted to indicate precisely what he meant. He was writing about those new measures to which the "anxious" or "mourners'" bench was the door; "all beyond this is only something worse."

The Congregational and Presbyterian churches, it was noted in *The Anxious Bench*, had largely freed themselves from Finneyite techniques. Several critical comments on the system by Alexander and Miller were cited. Now it was invading the German churches, especially the Lutherans, with the commendation of Dr. Kurtz and his *Lutheran Observer*. As yet there was comparatively little of it in the German Reformed Church, and Nevin hoped to rally the church against it, a hope which was to be largely gratified.

"Anxious bench" excitement, he maintained, was a form of quackery. Its appeal was to emotions of fear and sympathy rather than to genuine religious feeling. It was the refuge of inadequate ministers, lacking the capacity to teach or to enforce the claims of religion soberly, unwilling to restrain themselves to study and the retired cultivation of personal holiness. Where this system was adopted, wrote Nevin, "Conversion is everything, sanctification nothing. Religion is not regarded as the life of God in the soul, that must be cultivated in order that it may grow, but rather as a transient excitement to be renewed." [38]

Nevin repeatedly compared the "anxious bench" system to forms of Roman Catholic "quackery," pilgrimages, *opus operatum* baptism,[39] vows. The decision to "come forward," he contended, was confused with a decision for Christ, and under the circumstances men were distracted from the real issues of repentance and faith. Only a small proportion of camp meeting converts gave later evidence of regeneration; no "conversions" were more precarious. The whole atmosphere militated against genuine prayer or solid instruction: in fact, the devotees of the system tended to drop religious education entirely and to show little concern for growth in grace. The basic theory was false. The Kingdom of God was not advanced by such methods, but rather by a teaching ministry, by preaching with light and unction, by faithful systematic instruction, by pastoral visitation, church discipline, and zeal for holiness—what Nevin called the "system of the catechism."

In all this argument Nevin was setting forth the accepted view of the conservative leaders of the main American Calvinist churches ever since Finney had appeared. He might have written essentially the same tract a decade earlier in reference to Gallaher's Presbyterian revivals in Pittsburgh. The religious press also reacted as one might have expected. *The Anxious Bench* was favorably reviewed in the *Princeton Review* [40] and in Engles' *Pres-*

[38] *The Anxious Bench* (2d ed.; Chambersburg, 1844), p. 27.
[39] *Ibid.*, p. 34.
[40] January, 1844.

byterian[41] (both Presbyterian), and by the *Christian Intelligencer*[42] (Dutch Reformed). Methodist papers, on the other hand, took issue, as might also have been expected, and so did those of the United Brethren. A new-school Presbyterian[43] replied at length, and a Lutheran pastor.[44] The most sustained defense of Finney's techniques came in a series of articles in Dr. Kurtz's *Lutheran Observer*. Dr. Greenwalt's *Lutheran Standard* (Ohio), however, deplored the fact that Lutheranism had not taken the same line as Nevin, but that instead "a large proportion of her ministers and newspaper writers have taken extreme ground in behalf of new measures" and had denounced opponents as unconverted.[45]

The Anxious Bench sold out in a month or two, and in preparing a second edition Nevin added new materials. He had published a series of six articles in the *Messenger*, chiefly in reply to the *Lutheran Observer*. Here he showed his respect for the Lutheran Reformation. It seemed to him that the very existence of the distinctive Lutheran tradition was at stake, even more so than with the Reformed. The *Observer* would transform the church of the Augsburg Confession into mere Methodism. Better Methodism than nothing, to be sure, but these were not the only alternatives. "Let this system prevail . . . and the old regular organizations, if they continue to exist at all, will not be the same churches."[46] There was no viable combination of genuine Lutheranism with the system of the bench. The issue was ultimately theological: Finneyism was informed by the Arminianism of the New Haven theology.[47]

The second edition of *The Anxious Bench*, which finally appeared in March or April, 1844, at the end of the winter term, incorporated most of Nevin's arguments from the *Messenger* series and was nearly three times as large as the first edition. In

[41] October 7, 1843.
[42] October 14, 1843.
[43] J. W. Davis, "A Plea for New Measures."
[44] R. Weiser, "The Mourner's Bench."
[45] October 18, 1843, as cited in *WM*, January 14, 1844.
[46] *Ibid.*, January 31, 1844. Cf. *The Anxious Bench*, pp. vi–vii.
[47] *WM*, January 24, 1844. Cf. *The Anxious Bench*, p. 124 n.

addition, a new seventh chapter had been written, purporting to state the theological ground of the "system of the catechism" as opposed to the "system of the bench." The author himself noted that it "might well form the theme of a separate tract." It did not wholly fit into the structure of the debate. Later in the same year [48] Philip Schaf was to call attention to this chapter as stating a position with which he concurred enthusiastically. In fact, it was the first enunciation of what was to become the Mercersburg doctrine of the church. In the context of a controversy with revivalistic new measures, Nevin had decided to take a significantly new theological tack, the further course of which was to carry Mercersburg into deep waters.

In his attack on new measures Nevin now found the fatal flaw in the individualistic presuppositions of the system. "Sin . . . is not simply the offspring of a particular will . . . in the form of actual transgressions, but a wrong habit of humanity itself, a general and universal force, which includes and rules the entire existence of the individual man, from the very start." [49] Similarly, he claimed, man's restoration begins beyond the individual in the general life of humanity resurrected in Christ. The whole of the human drama is thus organized by the relations of the communities of the first and second Adams.

> The sinner is saved then by an inward living union with Christ, as real as the bond by which he has been joined in the first instance to Adam. This union . . . constitutes a new life, the ground of which is not in the particular subject of it at all, but in Christ, the organic root of the Church. . . . Religion in this form becomes strictly a life, the life of God in the soul.[50]

The church then is no mere "aggregate of parts mechanically brought together," is "in no sense the product of individual Christianity as though a number of persons should first receive the heavenly fire in separate streams" and then come together. Rather, the church is the mother of all her children, imparting

[48] P. Schaf, *Das Prinzip des Protestantismus* (Chambersburg, 1845) p. 154, Anm.
[49] *The Anxious Bench*, p. 124.
[50] *Ibid.*, pp. 125, 128.

her life to them. "Christ lives in the Church, and *through* the Church in its particular members, just as Adam lives in the human race generically considered, and through the race in every individual man." [51] Under the stimulus, apparently, of the biblical commentator Olshausen and the Lutheran theologian Sartorius,[52] Nevin had now developed the formula of the first and second Adams into a key to the understanding of Christ and the church.

A still fuller indication of Nevin's new direction was given a few months later in midsummer. The Dutch and German Reformed Churches, which had been so intimately associated in America from the beginning, were now in the process of drawing together more closely. A joint convention was held at Harrisburg, and there the keynote sermon was preached by Dr. Nevin, as the chief theologian of his denomination.

Although the occasion naturally suggested a discourse on church unity or co-operation, Nevin's treatment of the theme was not a conventional one. He called it "Catholic Unity," [53] for one thing, and he expressed a passionate concern for the unity of the visible church, as the "most important interest in the world." To many of his hearers this may have seemed merely pardonable homiletical overemphasis, but Nevin meant just what he said. This ecumenical thrust was to be a main feature of the Mercersburg movement.

The interpretation of the church in terms of the new humanity of the second Adam was repeated here and further developed. Individual Christianity, said Nevin, is a "moral solecism." All individual existence arises within an organic, generic common life, and in the case of the church, this life grows from the root or germ of Christ. Implanted in an individual as a divine seed, it

[51] *Ibid.*, pp. 129–30.

[52] *Ibid.*, p. 124 n.; cf. p. vii. Sartorius claimed that in his lectures of 1831, he had revived the idea of resting the Atonement on the union of the human and divine in Christ. He and Olshausen used the formula of the two Adams to explain imputation. Nevin drew out the implications also for the church.

[53] Printed as an Appendix to P. Schaf, *The Principle of Protestantism as related to the present state of the Church*, trans. with an Introduction by J. W. Nevin (Chambersburg, 1845), pp. 191–215.

grows to fill the whole man and is completed in the glorified body and glorified soul of the resurrection. The union of the believer with Christ is thus not merely a moral one, but substantial and real, and is epitomized in the sacramental incorporation with the glorified body of the Lord.

A distinction new to the American discussion emerges as Nevin speaks, not between the visible and invisible, but between the actual and ideal church. The ideal is for him a potency struggling to actualize itself—not something unreal or merely mental, but the power which moves events. The Holy Catholic Church is thus already one in potency or ideal and is struggling to realize itself so in history. Church unity is not our achievement; if the church were not already one, we could not make her so. But she *is* one and is becoming so more visibly. Her catholicity and unity are obscured but not destroyed by her apparent division into a number of denominations. "The whole Church then must be regarded as inwardly groaning over her own divisions . . . as though Christ could not rest until such unnatural violence should come to an end."

What then is our duty with regard to church unity? The first duty is repentance. The rampant sectarianism and individualism of modern Protestantism, declared Nevin, is a lamentation. "The present state of the Church involves the sin of schism to a most serious extent." To be sure, denominations are not necessarily schismatic, and church unity does not necessarily require organizational unity, as Episcopalians and papists suppose; but the "spirit of sect and party as such is contrary to Christ." Were this repented of and overcome, Protestant Christianity would appear very different. The first duty then is "the conviction of deep and radical defect."

Nevin had no respect for crusades against sects, as proposed by several contemporaries such as Alexander Campbell. It was not possible to sit free of the denominations in the hope of starting all over. Nor were strategems and devices of an institutional sort useful. The problem lay at a deeper level. It was a matter of the growth of charity in the church, of entering into Jesus' concern for the unity of his followers. It would come as a gradually ripening process, in ways no one could anticipate. But every opportunity "to pull down a single one of all those walls of partition" must be greeted as a great responsibility.

Nevin set this ecumenical vision in the perspective of Protestant history generally. The work of the Reformation, as he saw it, was still incomplete. A kind of gradual paralysis had led the Protestant churches to a one-sided development. In Germany they had produced rationalism; in Great Britain, dissenting radicalism; in America, a licentiousness of private judgment and the multiplication of sects. Now a widespread reaction was being felt, lending a mysterious charm to popery and the Anglo-Catholic movement. The friends of truth might well tremble. For this was "the grand rebounding movement of the Reformation itself, by which more fully than ever before" the truth and stability of Protestant principles were to be tried. The work of the sixteenth century must now be taken up again and brought to a completion.

The popular evangelical protest against popery and Puseyism seemed to Nevin mere negativism. It "sinks the Church to the level of a temperance society, strips the ministry of its divine commission and so of its divine authority, reduces the sacraments to mere signs, turns all that is mystical into the most trivial worldly sense, and so exalts what is individual above what is general and catholic" as to open the door to sectarian license.[54] A more responsible course must be followed, facing seriously questions supposed to have been settled long since and doing full justice to the valid elements in the papal and Anglo-Catholic position.

In this recovery of a sense of the "catholicity" of the church, Nevin was apparently thinking in terms of the churches of the Reformation heritage as a whole. Similarly Moehler and Khomiakov had rediscovered catholicity in *their* communions. The glory of God and the honor of His truth, Nevin preached, required that the Reformed churches "should stand out to the world not as many, but as one, *the Church,* (not churches) of the Reforma-

[54] *Ibid.*, p. 214.

tion, the body of Christ."[55] How he conceived the relation of Lutheranism to the Reformed is not made clear, but he was explicit in the unity of the Dutch and Germans at least, in "the one great communion of the *Reformed*, as gloriously represented in the ever memorable synod of Dort. The faith of Switzerland, the faith of the Palatinate, and the faith of Holland in the sixteenth century were emphatically one faith." In this last connection the joint convention committee on action, under Nevin's chairmanship, recommended a kind of Plan of Union for home missions in the West, a common text in theology for the seminaries of the two churches, and an effort to make the liturgies conform as closely as possible.[56] It is ironical that it was to be precisely the recovered sense of catholicity at Mercersburg which was to frustrate even these modest proposals.

[55] *Ibid.*

[56] *WM*, July 20, 1842.

3/ Evangelical Catholicity in Prussia

Philip Schaf, under appointment to the Mercersburg Theological Seminary, had landed in New York at the end of July, 1844. On August 5 he left the city and traveled by train and stage to Easton, the gate to the "Dutch" country. From that point on, he heard German or Pennsylvania German constantly —with stops at Reading, Womelsdorf, Tulpehocken. At Harrisburg, the triennial convention was in session and Schaf first met Dr. Nevin, who delivered there his sermon "Catholic Unity." Schaf was delighted. He wrote shortly after in his journal, "I think I could not have a better colleague than Dr. Nevin. I feared I might not find any sympathy in him for my views of the church; but I discover that he occupies essentially the same ground that I do and confirms me in my position. He is filled with the ideas of German theology."[1] How had the young instructor from Berlin come to *his* views on the church, so similar to those of Nevin?

Schaf was half a generation younger than Nevin, a Swiss by birth, with a German education. Born in 1819 in the high mountain country of the Grisons, of a poor and humble family, he was raised by a widowed mother. He grew up speaking German and Italian in the streets and quickly showed marked talent in the canton school. The chief preacher of Chur took an interest in the gifted boy and arranged for him to enter the academy at Kornthal, in Württemberg, when he was fifteen. Schaf made the journey on foot, with all his possessions in a knapsack. He was to spend the next five years in the kingdom of Württemberg, to which, he later said, he owed his spiritual life and the best part of his education.

[1] D. S. Schaff, *The Life of Philip Schaff* (New York: Charles Scribner's Sons, 1897), p. 103.

Kornthal, where Schaf spent his first academic year, was a village seven miles out of Stuttgart, next to the royal summer palace. It was a pietist colony not unlike the Moravian settlements where young Schleiermacher received his early training. Here, in his first year and amid the pangs of homesickness, young Schaf experienced a conversion experience of the pietist sort and was confirmed by the Lutheran village pastor. He now determined to prepare for the ministry, relinquishing his previous ambition to be a poet. For the rest of his life he was to be characterized by the fervor of Württemberg pietism and by the heightened eschatological expectation especially characteristic of Kornthal.

The next year Schaf transferred to the Stuttgart gymnasium, where he was given a thorough humanistic preparation for the university. Weekly essays were written alternately in Latin and Greek, and the pretheological students also mastered Hebrew. Much of this period Schaf lived in the home of one of the leading merchants of the city, sharing the room of his son, Wilhelm Julius Mann, who was to be a lifelong friend. In the Mann home, which was a center of pietist activities in Stuttgart, Schaf made many friends and acquaintances who confirmed the direction of his religious development.

At eighteen, in 1837, Schaf matriculated at the University of Tübingen, the capital of "higher criticism." He was venturing into the lion's den, for the strongest intellectual current among the students there was Hegelianism, and the most influential theologian was Ferdinand Christian Baur, then in the prime of life. Baur was a magnetic and compelling teacher, who was the first to apply rigorously to the documents of early Christianity the critical nineteenth-century methods of general historical and literary analysis. He revolutionized the study both of the New Testament and of early church history. He was not satisfied merely to challenge the reliability of the gospel accounts, as Strauss had done two years before in his famous *Life of Jesus*. Baur sought to determine the occasion and tendency of each of the New Testament writings separately and then to reconstruct the actual history of the first two centuries. Baur's genius claimed Schaf's respect and admiration, although his critical conclusions must often have been very distressing to the devout student. From him, Schaf later wrote, he had gained his "first idea of historical development or of a constant and progressive flow of thought in the successive ages of the church." [2] Schaf thus learned in his teens that historical perspective which came to Nevin as a revelation in his thirties.

A conservative opposition in the theological faculty was led by Professor C. F. Schmid, but Schmid could scarcely match Baur in gifts and productivity. Schaf's closest personal relation was with a new professor, Dr. Isaac Dorner, whose first courses on apologetics and dogmatics he attended. Dorner had been trained under Hegel and Schleiermacher and was ideally suited for students who wished to master the new critical and speculative problems without losing their Christian faith.[3] Since the first edition of Dorner's *History of the Development of the Doctrine of the Person of Christ* was published in Schaf's last year at Tübingen, this theme must have been his intellectual preoccupation when Schaf was most intimate with him.

Since the Napoleonic Wars Tübingen had possessed a dual theological faculty—one Protestant, one Roman Catholic. Just two years before Schaf arrived, the most distinguished member of the Roman Catholic faculty, Johann Adam Moehler, had left for Bavaria. But in the preceding decade he had made Tübingen the center of the most powerful theological movement in Roman Catholic Germany and had put his Protestant colleagues on the defensive. Schaf must have felt the reverberations of this debate throughout the theological community at the university.

Moehler might be described as the Schleiermacher of Roman Catholic theology, in the sense that he had reacted against the rationalism and moralism prevailing in South German Catholicism and restated the faith in the terms of romanticism and idealism. But Moehler stressed the corporate aspect of Christianity more than Schleiermacher did. Moehler's teacher Drey was influenced

[2] *Ibid.*, p. 20.
[3] *Ibid.*, p. 23.

by Fichte and Schelling and had enunciated the central conception of *organism*, of a living, dynamic tradition, as the nature of Catholicism. Tradition was not a mere static body of teachings and practices, but the collective consciousness of a social organism capable of change while remaining true to type. Before his appointment to the faculty Moehler had visited Planck and Neander, and the patristic studies of the latter especially had come as something of a revelation to him. In his first major work, *Die Einheit in der Kirche* (1825), he had combined Neander's vivid appreciation of the fathers with the theme of organism, the corporate living unity of the ancient church whose animating social psyche was the Holy Spirit. Moehler had further commended to fellow Roman Catholics this vitalistic approach to Christianity by publishing in 1833 the most substantial Roman Catholic polemic against Protestantism since Bossuet, *Symbolism, or Exposition of the Doctrinal Differences between Catholics and Protestants.* Among the numerous Protestant replies Baur had written one of the most elaborate, although scarcely the most representative or orthodox, and the rebuttals were still being exchanged in Schaf's time of residence at the university. In Schaf's own later thinking the romantic conception of the church as a social organism would be as important as Baur's interpretation of intellectual history as a dialectical exfoliation of ideas.

After two years in the intense intellectual activity of Tübingen Schaf migrated, after the German custom, to another faculty. He went first to Halle, where he had the good fortune to be taken up at once by the leading light of the theological faculty, Professor F. A. G. Tholuck. Tholuck was one of the most conspicuous representatives of the "Awakening" in north Germany, where his autobiography was a more influential document than Schleiermacher's *Speeches on Religion.* Having been appointed to the Halle faculty when it was controlled by the rationalists, he had endured mockery and persecution as a pietist. Now, however, he had become the most popular teacher and preacher, while the classes of Wegscheider, the rationalist, had dropped from four or five hundred students to six or eight.

By cultivating close personal relations with his students Tholuck exercised a strong religious influence on them. He took a particular interest in his American students, who included Charles Hodge of Princeton; Edward Robinson, Henry B. Smith, and George L. Prentiss of Union; and Edwards A. Park of Andover (some of whom were later to be Schaff's associates). For a time Schaf was employed as Tholuck's librarian and secretary, and ate with the family several times a week. In Tholuck's home he first met an American.

Julius Mueller, a colleague who shared Tholuck's religious orientation, was more profound if less brilliant. The first volume of his *Christian Doctrine of Sin* appeared while Schaf was a student at Halle.

Over the Christmas holidays Schaf visited the Prussian capital and its young but brilliant university. Professor E. W. Hengstenberg, to whose *Kirchenzeitung* he had contributed, offered him a tutoring post if he should come to Berlin. When Schaf decided to go to Berlin, Tholuck went with him and introduced him to the Baron von Kottwitz, the patriarch of the "Awakened" in Berlin, whom Tholuck honored as his own spiritual father. Schaf tutored a son of the Baroness von Kroecher, of the Prussian nobility. The baroness was generous, accomplished, and devout, and left Schaf ample time to attend lectures at the university. Of the two years that Schaf remained in this position, the second was spent in travel in southern Europe. In the meantime he had completed his course, passed his examination, and received the licentiate in theology.

At the University of Berlin, as at Tübingen, history was the dominant theological discipline at the end of the 1830's. Hegel and Schleiermacher were both gone, and no speculative thinkers of comparable rank remained, save for Schelling, who came back from retirement in 1841. The most influential theologians of the day were both church historians, Baur at Tübingen and Neander at Berlin. As Tholuck had told his American students, the controlling and central feature of the theological thought of the day was "Entwicklung" (development, evolution). Schaf heard only one of Neander's courses, modern church history, the one period Neander never dealt with in print; but Neander helped him more than anyone else through personal association. Schaf thought of himself thereafter as a student of Neander, first of all. (Fifty years later the Berlin faculty sent him a testimonial, describing his *Church History* as "the most notable monument of universal historical learning produced by the school of Neander.") [4] Schaf's writings also bore the evidence of Baur's influence, but his religious orientation was much closer to that of Neander.

Schaf also heard the historian Leopold von Ranke, the geographer Karl Ritter and the Norwegian philosopher Heinrich Steffens. When Schelling delivered his famous lectures on the philosophy of mythology and revelation in 1841, Schaf was there with all the rest of educated Berlin. He was also a student of Hengstenberg, who taught exegesis at just the opposite pole from Baur, arguing for literal inspiration and traditional interpretations with orthodox zeal. (Neander's position on hermeneutics was somewhere between the two and not very clearly defined.) In the spring of 1841 Schaf's first book, *Die Sünde wider den heiligen Geist* (*Sin Against the Holy Spirit*), was published, and he sustained examination at the hands of Neander, Hengstenberg, Philipp Konrad Marheinecke, and Karl Twesten.

Schaf's year in the Mediterranean immediately thereafter was a marvelous opportunity for an historian. He spent a month or so in Sicily, with its architectural monuments from the Athenian expedition on down to the time of Frederick II. In papal Rome he acted as chaplain of the Prussian Embassy for some weeks. Here he visited the catacombs and churches, the temples and palaces, of the burial ground of the world's history. He met artists, such as Thorwaldsen and Overbeck. He observed the pageantry of Holy Week at St. Peter's in 1842, with its illuminations and foot-washing. He even had an audience with Gregory XVI and constrained himself to kiss his red slipper. On his way north he made a pilgrimage to Assisi and the Waldensian valleys. Back in Switzerland he came to know the theologians of Geneva and

[4] *Ibid.*, p. 467.

Lausanne. From his first travels in Württemberg Schaf had made a practice of calling on distinguished clergymen and scholars wherever he went, and he usually won a cordial welcome with his engaging manners and easy conversation. Consequently he had a remarkable range of acquaintances for a man of his age, having already met most of the leading theologians of Germany. These early contacts and personal traits were qualifying him to be the unique ecumenical ambassador he later became.

On his return from the grand tour in the summer of 1842 Schaf resigned his tutoring post and went back to Berlin to hang out a shingle as a *Privatdocent*, at the age of twenty-three. His first offerings were in theology and New Testament—courses in the Catholic Epistles and on the theology of Schleiermacher. One of his students was Dr. Park of Andover, who asked for private instruction in the latter topic. (It was from Park that Schaf first heard the name of Jonathan Edwards.) Meanwhile, he was at work on his *Habilitations-schrift* on James, the brother of Jesus, which was published in 1842; he also contributed articles to Hengstenberg's *Kirchenzeitung* and Tholuck's *Literarischer Anzeiger*.

Toward the end of Schaf's second term in Berlin as a docent, two tall strangers called on him. They were seeking a professor for a theological school off across the Atlantic in the mountains of Pennsylvania. They had been refused by the famous preacher F. W. Krummacher; but Krummacher, Tholuck, Hengstenberg, and others had highly recommended the young docent from Switzerland. Would he accept a call if it were offered? This was too serious a proposition to be answered without thoughtful consideration. Schaf's friends and advisers, such as Neander and Dorner, counseled acceptance; and Hengstenberg and Minister Eichhorn assured him that there would be a university post for him when he returned to Germany. So Schaf agreed, and in the fall of 1843 he accepted the call. He was ordained in April, 1844, in Krummacher's church at Elberfeld but spent six weeks in England before crossing the Atlantic, thus arriving in New York in midsummer.

Schaf's high-church views cannot be explained by his academic preparation. None of his teachers taught the doctrine of the visible church which was to characterize him in America. Those closest to him, Neander and Tholuck, were pietists tinged with idealism, who somewhat feared the institutionalizing of religion. Schaf evidently developed his churchly views from extracurricular associations, in particular those of the Gerlach circle in Berlin. Of parallel developments elsewhere in Germany he doubtless heard reports, but he acknowledged himself a disciple of Ludwig von Gerlach.[5]

Two months after Schaf's migration to Berlin, Frederick William IV had been crowned at Königsberg. He brought to power with him the group of "Bible hussars" who had been his particular friends for the preceding decade or more when he was crown prince. Members of the landed aristocracy who had been caught up in the religious awakening, they now represented a combination of political and social reaction with theological orthodoxy. There were significant variations among them—the Roman Catholic Radowitz, the philosopher Stahl, the Gerlach brothers (especially the general, Leopold, and the jurist, Ludwig), the theologian Hengstenberg, and the king himself. They were united, however, in their earnest Christianity, their counterrevolutionary passion, their fear of liberalism and nationalism, and their insistence on the need of authority in state, society, and church. The new regime was to set itself against the currents of the day much as the Stuart kings had done in seventeenth-century England.

Schaf came to Berlin as a protégé of Hengstenberg, who was at that time in virtual control of theological appointments. Hengstenberg manipulated these to further his orthodox party. Part of his procedure was to recruit promising students like Schaf and, through tutoring posts and academic appointments, place them in strategic positions. Schaf heard Hengstenberg's course, wrote for his *Kirchenzeitung*, attended his soirees, and faced him on his examination committee.

[5] *Ibid.*, pp. 66–67.

Even more influential on Schaf's thought was President von Gerlach, the most important theorist and publicist of the court circle. For a decade or more, von Gerlach had been associated with Hengstenberg in the conduct of the *Evangelische Kirchenzeitung*, in which much of his important writing is found. At least in his years as a docent, if not already as a graduate student, Schaf attended Gerlach's Saturday evening gatherings and here shaped his high-church views.

It is not clear whether the student from republican Switzerland adopted the theocratic medievalist politics of Gerlach entire. For Gerlach, the existing social hierarchy and political authorities were divinely authorized as such, part of the primordial architecture of creation, unchangeable. All social and political authorities, from the head of the family up to the prince, shared in this divine responsibility—each in his own degree. Private rights, as of the feudal nobility or of various corporations, were part of this divine order, and these were to be defended against royal absolutism as well as against constitutional liberalism. The realization of the Kingdom of God required this particular political order. Schaf was to reflect at least one inference from this position—that political revolution was false *religion*, apostasy from the divine order. His American hearers, heirs of the War of Independence, must have puzzled over his remarks about political revolution as a disease of Protestantism.[6]

Gerlach's distinctive conception of the church had taken form about the revolutionary year 1830. In the twenties he had been an individualist pietist, inclined to private religious assemblies. But about 1830 he displayed a new interest in the doctrine, sacraments, and order of the institutional church. It was first generally apparent in his anonymous and notorious article in the *Evangelische Kirchenzeitung* attacking professors Wegscheider and Gesenius of Halle as false to their doctrinal obligations. Even more striking was his new stress on the visible church as the Body of Christ, outside of which there was no ordinary prospect of salvation. The church as an institution was prior to the Bible as well

[6] P. Schaf, *Principle of Protestantism* (Chambersburg, 1845), p. 98.

as to doctrinal formulations, and within the church the priestly office was authoritative. "First Christ, the apostles, the ministry; only then the faithful and the faith."[7] Maintenance of the constituted ecclesiastical authorities was as important as the defense of doctrine. In this Gerlach was aware that he was correcting the Reformers, who—in his judgment—had gone too far and had lost the sacramental character of the institution.

Gerlach's high-church doctrine was set, of course, in the context of the Prussian United Church as organized by Frederick William III. That church was as if designed for Schaf. Raised in the Reformed Church in Switzerland but converted and confirmed in Lutheran pietism, he felt himself at home in the Union faculty at Berlin. The Union involved a degree of harmony or consensus of the Lutheran and Reformed confessions, at least in so far as the common liturgy was concerned. And the *Evangelische Kirchenzeitung* regularly distinguished between essential and non-essential doctrines in this connection. Gerlach was more interested in insisting on the three ancient creeds, as the basis of unity with Roman Catholicism and the ancient church, than on defining a position among the more elaborate and distinctive Protestant formulae that followed the Augsburg Confession. He used the appeal to consensus in this connection to define the common doctrinal tradition of orthodox Christianity. He sympathized with the "old Lutherans" under persecution, but not to the extent of supporting their wish to separate. He coveted their doctrinal orthodox support within the Union but could not condone their defiance of the authority of the godly prince as *praecipuum membrum ecclesiae*. Within the canon of universal agreement Gerlach conceived the church to be infallible.

Such a view of catholic tradition emphasized the doctrinal continuity through the Reformation. Gerlach described the Reformation as the finest flower of the Middle Ages. It had been a necessary development of the catholic tradition, but it was un-

[7] Cited from Gerlach's Rundschau in the *Neuen Preussischen Zeitung*, May, 1853, by E. Jedele, *Die Kirchenpolitischen Anschauungen des Ernst Ludwig von Gerlach* (Ansbach: C. Brügel & Sohn, 1910), p. 32.

fortunate that schism had resulted. Gerlach's attitude toward contemporary Roman Catholicism was so cordial that his conversion was prophesied. He was of those few who frankly dreamed of eventual reunion with Rome, employing the term "evangelische Katholizität" to describe his position. In the Cologne conflict over mixed marriages he supported the Roman Catholics, even against Hengstenberg and his own brother Leopold. He gloried in the expansion of Roman Catholic power in Prussia and felt far closer to the Jesuits than to the Protestant theological liberals, the "Friends of Light." In line with this policy, Frederick William took several actions in favor of Roman Catholicism in Prussia.

Gerlach admired Roman Catholicism not only for its traditionalism and authoritarianism but also for its power to penetrate and mold culture, in which it seemed to him superior to Protestantism. He refused to accept the Enlightenment's secularization of culture as well as of politics. His theocratic dream encompassed the Christianization of all society and culture, a conception which was largely shaped by his romantic theory of the Middle Ages and had little bearing on the realities of his own day.

In effect Gerlach's church theory was a "branch" theory of catholic Christendom analogous to that of the Oxford movement. His Christian universalism was expressed by his support of the Holy Alliance as the structure of the *corpus Christianum* in the nineteenth century. This league of orthodox Christian peoples under three sovereigns—Austrian Roman Catholic, Russian Orthodox, and Prussian Protestant—was the greatest idea of the century, Gerlach believed, the Christian alternative to revolutionary nationalism and liberalism. Frederick William IV actually tried to shape Prussian policy in the light of this conception, just as he subordinated particular Prussian interests to the dream of a renewed Holy Roman Empire under Austrian leadership.

Schaf derived his "catholic" high-church understanding of the Prussian United Church from Gerlach, though similar views were if anything more frequent among the exclusive Lutherans who opposed the Union, as well as among Roman Catholic followers of Moehler. Wilhelm Loehe, for example, the organizer of confessional Lutherans in Bavaria, had been conspicuous, through the 1830's, for an organic conception of the church. His view, which was similar to Moehler's, apparently developed independently. He came to repudiate the individualism of his former pietism. One is baptized into *koinonia,* he now said; "you cannot be blessed with Christ by yourself." He also stressed the catholicity of the Lutheran tradition. The Lutheran Church did not arise at the Reformation but continued the main stream of the old catholic church in a fullness found nowhere else. "Members of the true church may be found in other churches," he conceded, "but somewhat confused and out of communion with our dear Mother Church." Whatever had been maintained by Christians at all times and places was part of the catholic tradition of Lutheranism. This common heritage was especially obvious in liturgy. Lutheranism was the middle way, the unifying way, between the one-sidedness of Rome and that of the Reformed. Loehe's most famous work, *Drei Bücher von der Kirche* (1843), which appeared a year before Schaf's *Prinzip des Protestantismus,* was in some ways a parallel phenomenon, even though Loehe pleaded eloquently for the unity and catholicity of Lutheranism against the Reformed movement.

From about 1833 Loehe had also contended for a conception of the ministry as deriving its authority, especially in absolution, from Christ by apostolic succession. Ordination thus imparted a special power in which the laity had no share. A chief practical concern was the desire for holiness and sanctification in the church through Eucharistic discipline in private confession. Loehe felt that he needed to exalt the authority of the pastor in this relation.

After Loehe, probably the most important of the German high-church Lutherans was Theodor Kliefoth of Mecklenburg. He had studied at Berlin a decade before Schaf, under Schleiermacher as well as Neander and Hengstenberg. He then became tutor to two of the Mecklenburg princes and, later, their adviser on ecclesiastical affairs. He became increasingly confessionalist and "catholic." For half a century he was to be the dominant figure in the administration of the Mecklenburg-Schwerin church, from which his influence passed to the high-church movement in Swedish Lutheranism. He sought to break up the Prussian United Church in the interests of strict Lutheran confessionalism. Kliefoth also continued Loehe's revival of historical Lutheran liturgics, and his liturgical writings left traces on the Mercersburg movement. To a strict confessionalism Kliefoth joined an un-Lutheran doctrine of the ministry and an un-Lutheran stress on the sacraments even over the Word.

Both Loehe and Kliefoth were out to unchurch the Reformed. Loehe's own decisive religious turn had come through Krafft, a Reformed leader of the Awakening at Erlangen, but the controversy out of which his *Drei Bücher von der Kirche* arose focused on his desire to force the exclusion of the Reformed from the sacraments in Bavarian parishes. In Hesse, similarly, a minor persecution of the Reformed was led by Vilmar, who—though of a Reformed background—adopted Moehler's organic view of the church and the Osiandrian view of the ministry.

A related but distinct view of the church had already emerged in the Lutheran Church of Denmark. Even before Gerlach or Loehe, N. S. F. Grundtvig, the Danish poet and historian, had announced a new conception of the church. First awakened by idealist influences, such as those of Steffens, Fichte, and Schelling, Grundtvig had then passed to a pietist biblicism. The biblical critics, however, made him feel very insecure, and he cast about desperately for an invulnerable point of authority. About 1825 he made his "great discovery" and left biblicism altogether for the sacramental and dogmatic tradition of the church, especially as focused in the baptismal creed.

This discovery did not mean simply the substitution of the creed for scripture. Since the creed included all indispensable dogma, the layman needed no longer worry about what the professors were doing to the Bible. But the baptismal covenant was for Grundtvig also the *living* voice of the Spirit in the church. He believed that God the Spirit is present in the sacraments as nowhere else and Grundtvigianism became the most sacramental type of Lutheranism, developing weekly communion in addition to the great stress on the ever renewed baptismal covenant. From 1837 Grundtvig published the hymns which were to give great vitality to his concern for the fellowship of the Spirit and the priesthood of all believers. At first he was inclined to ascribe a special significance to the ministry in apostolic succession, but he soon abandoned this notion in favor of the indefectibility of the church as a whole. He came out thus with a sort of unclerical or even anticlerical lay catholicism. English observers commented that Grundtvigian Lutheranism seemed to combine the liturgical and sacramental feeling of the Anglican high church with the warmth and spontaneity of a nonconformist prayer meeting. Actually, the nearest English parallel to Grundtvig's orientation was the Coleridgian tradition (especially as seen in Frederick Denison Maurice), which was more familiar to the Mercersburg men than Grundtvig was.

During Shaf's six weeks in England he was exposed to two other schools of thought which belonged to the catholic movements of the generation. In England, when he arrived, the great topic of conversation in church circles was the Tractarian movement. The explosion over Tract 90 had taken place three years before, and Newman's contentions in that tract had been disallowed by the bishops as well as the Oxford authorities and Anglican opinion at large. Schaf called on Newman in his retirement at Littlemore but could not draw much from him. With Pusey, whose name was generally attached to the movement on the Continent, Schaf seems to have been more successful. After calling on him at Oxford (where Pusey was left in command), Schaf recorded in his journal the heads of an extended conversation. He also had several meals at Guy's Hospital in London with the chief proponent of the Coleridgian perspective on the church, Maurice. Schaf found in Maurice "a German temper of mind" and a position distinct from both the evangelicals and the Puseyites.

The Tractarian movement was the English equivalent of the French traditionalism of de Maistre, de Bonald, and Lamennais; and of the Christian patriarchalism of the Gerlach circle in Prussia. All three were conservative reactions to the reforming tendencies of liberalism in church and state. All three hoped to secure the foundations of community life against reform and revolution by asserting the divine right of ecclesiastical government and the necessity of adherence to defined doctrine. In England the liberal movement of constitutional reform had begun with Catholic emancipation and the repeal of the Test and Corporation acts, and proceeded through reform of the parliamentary franchise and municipal government to consideration of the abuses of the church itself, especially in its finance and administration. A long overdue reorganization of dioceses in Ireland had led to Keble's call to arms in 1834, his sermon on "National Apostasy." Then the *Tracts for the Times* laid down the program for the next six or eight years.

A deep and genuine piety is evident in the sermons of the Tractarians, but the tracts themselves placed administrative matters in the foreground. The social affiliations of the Anglo-Catholic leaders were with the English equivalents of the Prussian Junkers, but the movement was largely of and for the clergy, as contrasted with the Gerlach circle. Though they accepted the idea of the church as the Body of Christ, the Tractarians were less interested in the church than in the exclusive prerogatives of the Episcopalian clergy based on their peculiar view of apostolic succession. They had a stronger sacramental interest than most Anglicans, but interpreted the sacraments still in largely individualistic terms. Newman's famous remark about the two luminous realities, God and his own soul, exaggerates only slightly the religious individualism of the Tractarians. They had less sense of the corporate church than Schaf had found in Moehler and Gerlach or might have found in the Lutheran high churchmen, such as Loehe and Grundtvig.

Schaf was delighted with the town of Oxford, which gave him more sense of history, he said, than any other city save Rome.

He found Pusey a rather humorless ascetic scholar, rigidly devoted to his static unhistorical orthodoxy, compiled out of selected fathers and councils. Luther had no right, Pusey told him, to pronounce new doctrines. "We dare not go outside the first six centuries." [8] Schaf unsuccessfully pressed on him a more dynamic concept of the church as the Body of Christ living and developing in history. Similarly he urged in vain on Pusey a view of the indefectibility of the church which left room for error along with the teaching of the truth. The Tractarian image was of a closed and perfect and unchangeable system of doctrine and order supposed to have existed sometime about the fourth and fifth centuries.

Like Schaf, Pusey was distressed at the confusion of sects in America. He would have wished the field cleared of all but Episcopalians and Roman Catholics because they alone possessed the episcopal successions which were the talisman of the true church. When talk touched on the Reformation Pusey seriously inquired, "Why could not the Reformers have applied to England for ordination?" Schaf left him, hoping that God would use the Tractarian movement for the good of the universal church and would bring the leaders to an understanding of the Reformation.

Schaf no doubt felt closer to Maurice than to Pusey. Maurice had at first read the Tracts with sympathy and had been considered close to the movement. Like the Oxford men, he considered the evangelical focus on sin unsound. Theology should rather find its center in God. He agreed with the Tractarians in setting the Atonement in the context of the Incarnation; and he rested the Christian's assurance not in feeling, as did the evangelicals (and the Reformers, according to the Tractarians!), but on God's faithfulness to his promises. On reading Pusey's tract on baptism, however, Maurice realized that he was separated from Pusey by a chasm. Pusey made baptism a magical charm, effecting a change in the child's nature by virtue of the act alone. Maurice's own experiences with baptism had been poignant, and with a different meaning. Out of the germ of a reply to Pusey on baptism grew

[8] Schaff, *Life*, p. 89.

Maurice's first book, *The Kingdom of Christ* (1838), a more substantial and profound study of the nature of the church than anything yet written by the Tractarians. Maurice's great concern was the unity of the church. He held ministry, sacraments, and the Bible essential to the church; but he defined the unity of the church otherwise—as lying rather in personal relations to Christ, its Head. Maurice often compared church unity with the unity of the family, whose personal relations still hold despite differences of doctrine or institutional connections (as he knew so vividly from personal experience). The Kingdom of Christ thus lives under different denominations. Maurice was not eager, like the Tractarians, to set the limits precisely for the sake of exclusion. He believed in the real presence at the Eucharist, in real binding and loosing of men's sins, but he had a more corporate sense of the church than the Tractarians. Maurice did not share Newman's religious individualism; like Loehe, he did not want "a separate life, here or hereafter." It seemed to him that the Tractarians became sectarian in their desire to possess Christ's catholicity. They craved the living God but settled for a fiction of ecclesiastical authority. He defended their right to speak against those who would silence them, but he disliked their opinions.

The split was made broader by a controversy over the Anglo-Prussian bishopric of Jerusalem—a proposal that had come from Frederick William IV. Deeply impressed by the Anglo-Catholics, the king dreamed of an episcopal reorganization of the Prussian United Church, with the succession derived from English and Swedish archbishops. He felt a vocation to work both for a unified German Protestantism and for closer interconfessional relations, especially with the Roman Catholics. Having been convinced by the Anglo-Catholic claim to be a "bridge church," he had sent his ambassador Bunsen to England in 1841 to work for a joint Anglican-Prussian bishop in Jerusalem as a first step in ecclesiastical rapprochement. Prussian as well as English candidates for this appointment were to subscribe to the Thirty-nine Articles and receive Anglican consecration. Even Gerlach, with all his respect for the episcopal system, disliked the king's open preference for it and denied that it was essential to the being of the church.

Nor did the Tractarians reciprocate the interest and admiration of Frederick William. Viewing the Prussian church as a compound of Lutheran and Reformed "heresy," the Tractarian W. Palmer had attacked the whole scheme of the Jerusalem bishopric. In reply Maurice argued that no principle for which the Church of England should stand was sacrificed by the terms of the proposal and that an important ecumenical witness would be made. Maurice, of course, had the great advantage of historical knowledge of the Reformation, without which the Tractarians operated on a basis of prejudice and misinformation. He was also governed throughout his life by a passionate desire for the realization of the unity of Christ's kingdom. He lived in an eschatological urgency, seeing the sects breaking up about him and the one church catholic emerging in a great ecumenical reformation.[9] No one in England so closely matched Schaf's concern in this matter.

In his inaugural lecture in America Schaf gave an estimate of the Anglo-Catholic movement which startled and offended some of his hearers.[10]

> It has brought into clear consciousness on all sides, spiritual tendencies and wants which were not previously understood. Already thus it appears clothed with a world-historical importance. I have myself hardly ever before had such an impression of the objective power of the "idea," as during the course of my late travel, through Germany, Switzerland, Belgium, England and North America; encountering as I did everywhere, in the persons of distinguished ministers and laymen, if not precisely Puseyism itself, at least aspirations and endeavors of a more or less kindred spirit.

Puseyism, he said, was "an entirely legitimate and necessary reaction" against the sectarian, rationalistic, and subjectivist tendencies which had forgotten or at least undervalued the significance of the church "in favor of personal individual piety, the sacra-

[9] Frederick Maurice (ed.), *The Life of Frederick Denison Maurice, chiefly told in his own Letters* (New York: Charles Scribner's Sons, 1884), I, 206.

[10] Schaf, *Principle of Protestantism*, pp. 122–28.

ments in favor of faith, sanctification in favor of justification, and tradition in its right sense in favor of the holy scriptures." Schaf hoped to bring into the German Reformed Church a new concern for the church, sacraments, historical tradition, sanctification of life, and ecumenical unity. He admired the "deep moral earnestness" and "spiritual dignity" of the Oxford men, their filial homage to the church's past and recognition of its authority over the individual, their realization of Christ's "actual living presence" in the sacraments. Their restoration of weekday services, church festivals, frequent communions, and cultivation of church art seemed to him calculated "to hold within the Protestant communion such as feel themselves urged to forsake it through dissatisfaction with the usual nakedness and barrenness of its worship."

The Oxford men had done much to bring home to the Protestant consciousness the great problem of the age, but they were in danger of discrediting the cause by their unskillful efforts at solution. Their doctrine of the church and episcopacy was external and mechanical. The apostolic succession they limited to the order of bishops, in isolation from the laity and lower clergy, as though they were specifically different in their nature. This position involved the denial of "the episcopal and apostolical character of every inwardly and outwardly called minister of Christ." It also hung the apostolical legitimacy of churches on a question of history about which no conclusive result was ever possible. The apostolic succession of ministry and doctrine was indeed essential to the church catholic, but the Tractarians had narrowed this to a "crazy foundation."

Again, the Puseyites surrendered—if they had ever understood—the religious and doctrinal gains of the Reformation.

> The *sola fide* on which the Reformers lived and died, they have never had experience of probably in themselves, and accordingly they let it go for a small price. The sanctity on which they insist appears thus on closer examination to carry rather the character of an outward legalism, an unfree anxious piety, reminding us of monkhood, with undue stress laid on the observance of particular Church forms, fasts and self-imposed discipline.

Oxford had also abandoned the scripture principle "for the Roman dogma of tradition . . . without any critical sifting by means of science or God's word." Schaf noted that the *New York Churchman* even defended in many respects the last papal bull against Bible societies. The points on which the Puseyites differed from Rome were "comparatively subordinate and unimportant." In essence, thus, the program was one of pure archaism. The grand defect was the "utter misapprehension of the divine significance of the Reformation, with its consequent development, that is, of the entire Protestant period of the Church."

The Tractarians lacked, in fact, any sense of historical development, despite their reverence for the past. They fixed upon one phase of the life of the historical church as complete and final and could not conceive of the living process of the church through different historical stages. In contrast, Schaf, like Gerlach, proposed to do historical justice to the whole sweep of Christian history, and thereby to achieve a genuinely "evangelical catholicism." This was the program he brought to Mercersburg.

4/ *The Reformed Doctrine of the Lord's Supper Recovered*

The Mercersburg movement might be called essentially a sacramental, more particularly a Eucharistic, revival. From the beginning the Lord's Supper had been Nevin's central concern, and he was the dominant personality. When the movement was first publicly challenged and issues brought to a head at the heresy trial at the York Synod of 1845, four of the five charges bore on the meaning of the Lord's Supper.[1] Nevin's most extended formal debate—with his former instructor, Charles Hodge—dealt specifically with the definition of the Reformed doctrine of the Lord's Supper. Probably this aspect of the Mercersburg position was the most thoroughly worked out and consistently maintained, and in this lay much of its enduring contribution.

The Mercersburg program, in brief, was the affirmation of the full classical Reformed or Calvinist understanding of the Lord's Supper in a church which had nearly forgotten it. This understanding was sometimes identified in the debate as the doctrine of the "spiritual real presence." Nevin insisted upon the idea of communion and incorporation with the "glorified humanity" of Jesus Christ in the sacrament, a concept which occasioned the greatest scandal. All the other points at issue, he would say, were presupposed or involved in this central conviction.

Nevin also notified his readers plainly that the Mercersburg views of Christ and the church were to be best interpreted from this vantage point. The starting point was not, as at Oxford, the prerogatives of the hierarchy, or even baptismal regeneration.

[1] See Appendix.

As the Eucharist forms the very heart of the whole Christian worship, so it is clear that the entire question of the Church, which all are compelled to acknowledge the great life-problem of the age, centers ultimately in the sacramental question as its inmost heart and core. Our view of the Lord's Supper must ever condition and rule in the end our view of Christ's person and the conception we form of the Church. It must influence at the same time, very materially, our whole system of theology, as well as all our ideas of ecclesiastical history.[2]

For Nevin himself it had taken some years for the Calvinist view of the Lord's Supper to correct his individualist evangelicalism with regard to the church. He had apparently believed in the spiritual real presence at Pittsburgh, and perhaps even at Princeton.[3] In his first year at Mercersburg, Nevin had declared that in addition to commemorating the cross, the Lord's Supper has the effect of "incorporating us with the real person of Christ." In 1842 he had laid down in outline what were to be, four years later, the main contentions of his most famous theological work, *The Mystical Presence*. "In the Lord's Supper," he wrote, "an actual union is realized on the part of the believer with the life of the Savior's glorified body; involving a communion with him in his whole nature, as real as the bond which identifies us, in virtue of our natural birth, with the general nature, soul *and* body, of our first father Adam." [4] Such, Nevin held, had been the teaching of all the major Reformed confessions. In his own day, he claimed, the Reformed churches had generally withdrawn to a Zwinglian view, wherein the sacraments were only commemorative symbols, stimulating at best a merely moral union of the believer with his Lord, rather than effecting an actual incorporation.

The implications for the church of this conception of the two Adams were not drawn, however, until the second edition of *The Anxious Bench*, and his sermon on "Catholic Unity." Yet Nevin at this time would apparently not have traced the continuity

[2] *The Mystical Presence: A vindication of the Reformed or Calvinistic doctrine of the Holy Eucharist* (Philadelphia, 1846), p. 3.

[3] Nevin later expressed surprise to find Hodge repudiating Calvin's teaching on this subject. *Weekly Messenger* (Chambersburg) (hereafter cited as *WM*), July 12, 1848.

[4] *WM*, April 27, 1842.

of the church through medieval Romanism, which was to him still "the great apostasy." Nor would he have appealed to tradition as an authority beside the Bible.

Both "Catholic Unity" and Schaf's *Principle of Protestantism* made polemical references to recent publications of a fluent and facile theological writer, Dr. Joseph Berg, pastor of the Race Street Church in Philadelphia. Berg, who was not the man to decline a debate, is said to have remonstrated privately without getting satisfaction. In any case, he precipitated the first great Mercersburg controversy by an article in his *Protestant Banner* accusing the professors of teaching the heresy of the "spiritual real presence." [5] Nevin in turn defended the idea of sacramental participation in the body as well as the soul of Christ against those who "pour contempt on all this as the obsolete mysticism of the Reformers." [6] The chief periodicals of the Lutheran and the Dutch Reformed Churches lent themselves to the hue and cry against Mercersburg. The whole Philadelphia Classis of the German Reformed Church, which was dominated by Berg and the Helfenstein family, drew up a true bill of five charges to submit to the Synod.[7]

Nevin replied to the charges by admitting that he had so taught but contending that the Reformed confessions and liturgies were explicitly on his side. "The whole Church," he wrote, "in Switzerland, France, Germany, Holland, Scotland and England, united in maintaining a real communication of the whole substantial humanity of Christ to the believer in the sacrament of the Lord's Supper." [8] And he stood ready to document this claim.

Most of Nevin's opponents, on the other hand, were ill-grounded in the confessions and church history generally and were really appealing to the current consensus in the church. Some of them were even disrespectful to the standards of the church. Berg, for instance, had declared that he was not ready

[5] Cf. J. I. Good, *History of the Reformed Church in the United States in the Nineteenth Century* (New York, 1911), pp. 219–25.
[6] *Ibid.*, p. 199. Cf. *WM*, September 10, 1845.
[7] Cf. Appendix.
[8] "Pseudo-Protestantism," *WM*, August 27, 1845.

"altogether to deny that the devil may have had some hand in originating Luther's notion of consubstantiation; it savors so much of transubstantiation, the *chef-d'oeuvre* of the evil one, that it would be hard to disprove the devil's agency in its invention." [9] As for the doctrines of Calvin and the Heidelberg Catechism, they were still more absurd, Berg maintained, than those of Luther.[10] All this made a shaky platform from which to launch a charge of disloyalty to the Heidelberg Catechism against the Mercersburg professors. The anti-Mercersburg writers were largely reduced to the accusations that Nevin's language about the humanity of Christ could only mean a corporeal local presence in the sacramental elements, and that ascribing any objective character to the sacrament implied an *opus operatum* view. The professors had denied these interpretations from the beginning, and the Synod of York had to dismiss the charges as groundless.

This decision of the synod, though nearly unanimous (40–3, 1 *non liquet*) by no means settled the controversy. Although Berg and Nevin came to a qualified personal reconciliation, with harsh expressions both ways forgiven and forgotten,[11] Berg recorded his continuing protest against the York decision. And the exchange of arguments in Lutheran, Dutch, German Reformed, and other periodicals continued unabated. Nevin himself published half a dozen articles on the Lord's Supper from the summer of 1845 into the next spring; and Berg, the Helfensteins, the Lutheran Kurtz, and others kept up a constant barrage. Nevin comprehensively summarized his case in his monograph on the Calvinist doctrine of the Lord's Supper, which was finally published in June, 1846, as *The Mystical Presence: a Vindication of the Reformed or Calvinistic Doctrine of the Holy Eucharist.*

Even the publication of *The Mystical Presence* did not end, or even climax, the controversy. The Philadelphia classis that year renewed its charges, supporting Berg's protest against the synod action; and Berg and Nevin began a formal debate in the *Weekly*

[9] *Lectures on Romanism* (Philadelphia, 1840), p. 233.

[10] Cited by Schaf, *What Is Church History?* (Philadelphia, 1846), p. 71 n., from Berg's *Protestant Banner.*

[11] *WM,* December 24, 1845.

Messenger. For months no significant review of *The Mystical Presence* appeared—surely a commentary on the level of interest and competence in the subject in American Protestantism generally. At length, however, two men of stature declared themselves: Nevin's old college friend, now the brilliant lay theologian of the Dutch Reformed church, Professor Tayler Lewis of Union College; and his former instructor, Charles Hodge. Lewis gave the only sympathetic and judicious American opinion,[12] but Hodge severely attacked the book in a long article in the *Princeton Review* (April, 1848).

Across the water, meanwhile, German opinion declared itself definitely on the Mercersburg side, to the surprise and dismay of men like Berg and Kurtz and Schmucker. From Zwingli's old chair at Zurich, Professor J. H. A. Ebrard, the historian of sacramental doctrine, voiced his commendation. And Krummacher, the famous preacher and chief advocate in Germany of the American German Reformed, declared the Mercersburg teaching unexceptionable. Germans and Americans were thus brought to a startled awareness of their radically divergent tendencies on the sacraments.

The real climax was reached in Hodge's *Princeton Review* article. "The weight of his single name," Nevin recognized, "is with multitudes sufficient to outweigh any amount of favorable judgment on the other side." [13] Neither Krummacher nor any other German divine exercised equal authority in America. Princeton was certainly one of the best theological faculties in the country, if not *the* best; and Hodge was the "central theological organ" of the old-school Presbyterians, the most influential and theologically powerful body south of New England.

Recognizing that he must either surrender or defend himself, Nevin took up the gauntlet. At once he requested the *Weekly Messenger* to reprint Hodge's attack. Then, abruptly cutting off

[12] T. Lewis, "The Church Question," *WM*, January 21, 28; February 4, 1846, reprinted from the *Biblical Repository*.
[13] *WM*, May 24, 1848.

his debate with Berg, he accompanied Hodge's work with his rebuttal. Throughout the summer of 1848 the columns of the *Weekly Messenger*, and probably most of its readers, groaned under the burden of seemingly endless historical and theological argument. Nevin had tried to secure publication in a more specialized theological journal, but could not find a publisher. This widespread boycott was a major cause for the launching of the *Mercersburg Review* the next year. In the second volume of that *Review* (1850) Nevin reprinted a revised form of the historical part of his reply to Hodge—an article of 128 pages—which constituted one of the first significant American contributions to the history of theology.[14] Hodge did not reply. He was beyond his depth and, whether he fully realized it or not, he had been demolished.

The debate between Hodge and Nevin was largely historical, in answer to the question, "What was the doctrine of the Reformed church on the Lord's Supper?" The contrasts between the two briefs are a startling illustration of the change effected in the early nineteenth century by the rise of historical consciousness. Nevin's argument resembles the work of a modern scholar, but Hodge's is still the production of an orthodox scholastic, with no sense for the meaning or movement of history.

Nevin attempted to show how the Reformed movement gradually took shape out of diverse and sometimes confusing tendencies in Switzerland. The great influence in this clarification was of course the work of Calvin, and the definitive doctrinal formulations were those which showed Calvin's influence, especially the five great national confessions of the French, Scots, Dutch, Palatines, and Swiss (Second Helvetic). These confessions superseded all the earlier statements and remained thereafter the rec-

[14] A contribution extensively quoted without mention of Nevin in A. Barclay, *The Protestant Doctrine of the Lord's Supper* (Glasgow, 1927), pp. 134 (Nevin, 475), 188–98 (487–96), 280–84 (506–10), 107–11 (464–66 and 467 n.), 117 (473); cf. R. Clemmer, "The Present Significance of the Mercersburg Theology," *Bulletin of the Theological Seminary of the Evangelical and Reformed Church in the United States*, 1950, p. 19.

ognized authorities in Reformed theology. Nevin made every effort, consequently, to establish the Eucharistic doctrine of Calvin and of these definitive confessions.

Hodge, in contrast, handled the history arbitrarily and without regard for chronology. He selected one set of formulations which he found congenial, chiefly those derived from Zwingli, and another set with which he could not come to terms, those showing the influence of Calvin. He then arranged a third category of formulations exhibiting both emphases, which he interpreted as Zwinglian. Although he offered a pretentious parade of sources, all the important documentation, with one exception, he had borrowed without acknowledgment from *The Mystical Presence.* In effect what he had done was to comb over *The Mystical Presence* in a fortnight or so, with no significant independent study, and to rearrange its historical evidence completely out of context in accordance with his own ideas of theological propriety. It was not that he was dishonest; he just lacked understanding of what history is. For him the past was an armory of theological tenets, and a man had a right to pick and choose as he would.

Hodge identified himself with the doctrine of the Zurich Consensus of 1549, the only significant document he added to Nevin's list. This document he proceeded to interpret to suit himself, with no regard for what its author, Calvin, said that he meant by it. (In his exposition of the Heidelberg Catechism, Hodge also ignored the extended commentary by *its* author, Ursinus.) Hodge admitted that Calvin had many passages not congenial to his own opinions, but these he disposed of as compromises with the Lutherans or ill-considered slips. The French, Dutch, and Scottish confessions he must concede to Nevin. The Heidelberg Catechism and the Second Helvetic Confession, on the other hand, he placed in his third category, as patient of a wholly "Zwinglian" exegesis. The other, "mystical" strain was not to be found, he pointed out, in the scholastics Pictet and Turretin, on whom his whole theological system was modeled. And he assigned Nevin to a highly original theological position, calling him Sabellian, Eutychean, monothelite, Roman Catholic, mystical, Socinian, rationalist, Schleiermacherian.

Hodge would have done better to concede the historical case from the beginning, like Berg. Berg granted early that, apart from some Zwinglians, the leading Reformers were all tainted with "that bias which has its full development in the monstrous figment of transubstantiation." [15] Berg was happy to say that this bias had been almost obsolete for centuries and, so far as he knew, had never been held in America.[16] But Hodge, whose sacramental theory was very similar to Berg's, made such a play of orthodoxy that he could not afford Berg's cavalier attitude to the standards of the church. He made the mistake of challenging a man whose command of the field was vastly greater than his own.

Nevin successfully refuted Hodge's exposition of the Heidelberg Catechism, the Second Helvetic Confession, the Zurich Consensus. Ebrard had just published his 800-page volume on the sacramental controversies of the sixteenth century, the fullest account that had yet been made. Armed with Ebrard's researches, Nevin could even go far to reclaim Zwingli himself from mere memorialism (although he reserved judgment on this point).[17] Hodge and the "modern Puritans" were left with little to fall back on but Karlstadt. Hodge's famous assertion that no new idea had ever come out of Princeton was thus shown to rest on a rank underestimate of his own originality in face of the Reformed standards. Princeton, as represented by Hodge, was caught as far off base as Hodge had ever caught the new school.

Such, in brief, was the course of Mercersburg's single-handed five-year war with the surrounding unsacramental hosts of American Protestantism. The debate itself had demonstrated Nevin's case: that a general defection from the Reformation position was to be observed in American Protestantism. The largest denominations, the Baptists and Methodists, as he said, were un-

[15] "The Reformation," *Protestant Quarterly Review* (hereafter cited as *PQR*), 1846, p. 164.

[16] "The German Controversy," *PQR*, 1846, p. 304.

[17] "Doctrine of the Reformed Church on the Lord's Supper," *Mercersburg Review* (hereafter cited as *MR*), 1850, pp. 462–63.

sacramental and unchurchly in principle; and those of the Reformed tradition were hardly to be distinguished from them in fundamentals. They too had in effect reduced the whole idea of a sacrament to an ordinance, a mere outward commandment.[18] Nevin canvassed the sacramental views of the New England theologians from Jonathan Edwards, Samuel Hopkins, and Joseph Bellamy to Timothy Dwight, and even down to Albert Barnes, the new-school Presbyterian disciple of Yale's Nathaniel Taylor. He cited Moses Stuart, the chief ornament of the other major Congregational theological faculty, Andover Seminary.[19] On the Presbyterian side Princeton had spoken through Hodge. Ashbel Green, the old-school wheel horse, was also on record; and from Scotland, John Dick, whose textbook Nevin used for lack of a better. The Dutch Reformed Church through its periodicals and professors had almost officially repudiated the Calvinist position that Nevin was urging.[20] And yet the Belgic Confession, as Nevin pointed out, was actually higher than the Anglican in sacramental doctrine. Of all these branches of the Reformed church, the classical teaching of the Reformation, as Nevin said, was "almost lost even to the knowledge of the Church. When it is brought into view, it is not believed, perhaps, that the Reformed church ever held, or taught, in fact, any doctrine of the sort." Although Nevin had found more support in the Episcopal Church than elsewhere, here too, he continued, "few are willing to receive in full such representations of the Eucharistic presence as are made either by Hooker or Calvin."

Most startling of all was the declension in the sacramental faith of the Lutheran church in the United States. The representative spokesmen, President S. S. Schmucker of Gettysburg and editor Kurtz of the *Lutheran Observer*, rejected even the Calvinist doctrine as too high and had abandoned Luther completely. Kurtz, Nevin observed, licked the boots of the *Princeton Review*, while Hodge coolly brushed aside Luther's own position as gross

[18] *Ibid.*, p. 546.
[19] *Ibid.*, p. 540.
[20] *The Mystical Presence*, p. 98 n.

superstition. "Methodism itself," said Nevin, "can hardly be said to make less account of the sacraments, practically or theoretically."[21] Ebrard similarly commented on the difference of reception his book had been accorded from that given Nevin's. Both set forth the classical Reformed doctrine and both had been attacked by the Lutherans. But the German Lutherans opposed Ebrard from the point of view of a local, corporeal presence, whereas the American Lutherans held up against Nevin the view of Luther's opponent Zwingli![22]

A significant outcome of the whole controversy was an increment of self-knowledge for all American Protestantism. Nevin did find scattered individual support among Lutherans, Episcopalians, Presbyterians, Dutch and German Reformed, and even Congregationalists. But on the whole the generalization held good. As has been observed in our own day, American Protestantism, in comparison with that of the Continent, seems constitutionally unsacramental. The very awareness of this contrast was an outcome of the Mercersburg debate. At the beginning Berg could confidently declare that Calvin's and Luther's views were almost obsolete, and that those of Zwingli prevailed "throughout the world."[23] A year or so later, however, Berg found it necessary to relinquish the weight of German Protestant opinion to Nevin and to fall back into what Nevin called "theological nativism." As Nevin drove home his historical case for the early church and the Reformation, the Americans gradually discovered that in fact they seemed to be, as Nevin said, in conflict with "the faith of nearly the whole Christian world from the beginning."[24] In the historical and ecumenical marshaling of the whole church, the Americans were startled to find themselves well off the main highway.

For Nevin personally, meanwhile, the general unsacramental temper of the church was the source of deep pain and near

[21] *Ibid.*, p. 109.

[22] "Doctrine of the Reformed Church on the Lord's Supper," *MR*, 1850, p. 457 n. 1.

[23] "The German Controversy," *PQR*, 1846, p. 305.

[24] *The Mystical Presence*, p. 6.

despair. If the Reformed church necessarily tends to "Zwinglianism," he declared, then "we may well despair of the whole interest." For him this was the article that distinguished the standing from the falling church. "Most assuredly no Church can stand, that is found to be constitutionally unsacramental." [25] Here, we may guess, was a major factor in his later breakdown.

What, precisely, were the differences between the Calvinist teaching as restated by Nevin and the view of men like Berg, Hodge, and Schmucker?

One comprehensive difference, already mentioned, lay between a *sacrament* and an *ordinance,* although the terms were not used consistently by all concerned. The Berg-Hodge view maintained ordinances as scripturally enjoined practices with devotional value, but emphasized the warning that the ordinances of the church cannot of themselves convey religious life. Only the Holy Spirit can achieve this result. The Holy Spirit kindles faith in many different circumstances and situations, among which sacramental ordinances are in no way unique. "The Spirit," as Nevin somewhat wryly illustrated their view, "may work on men's minds, exciting pious thoughts or feelings of devotion, by the presence of a majestic cataract, or a whirlwind, or a smiling beautiful landscape; and why not then with equal ease through the graphic and affecting representation of the blessed eucharist?" [26] Neither Niagara Falls, however, nor the Lord's Supper, was always or necessarily so blessed to the spiritual nurture of the Christian participant; and in either case the effect was to be understood as a normal process of religious psychology.

The Calvinistic theory of a sacrament, by contrast, involved by definition the conjunction of grace with an outward ordinance. A sacrament was an act of God through the institutional practice, resting on God's faithfulness to His promise and received by faith. The last point ruled out any *opus operatum* understanding; but an objective divine potency was intrinsic in

[25] *Ibid.*, p. 74.
[26] "Doctrine of the Reformed Church on the Lord's Supper," *MR*, 1850, p. 449.

the whole action. Its efficacy in any individual case was conditioned on faith, but faith did not cause the presence of the divine power. Psychology could not explain the sacramental action, for it was a mystery, rooted in God's declared intention.

This difference had extensive practical implications. For Nevin, as we have seen, the Lord's Supper was the center of all Christian worship and the epitome of the gospel. He had been brought up on the awesome four-day communion seasons of the Presbyterians—more solemn and moving, probably, because of their relative infrequency. In the German church likewise he had experienced an equally solemn ceremonial meal, with all seated at long tables in the presence of the Holy One. For him the deepest and highest in the religious life transpired at these times. For Hodge, on the other hand, this evidently was not true. As he somewhat ingenuously confessed at the beginning of his review of *The Mystical Presence*, he had let the work lie on his desk for nearly two years because he always found it hard to apply himself to books on such themes. Though very conservative in outward forms, he really had given up the substance and meaning of both sacraments. In this respect, in fact, he stood on the same religious and theological ground as a Baptist.

A second notable contrast between the two teachings lay in what each believed was conveyed in the Lord's Supper. What was signified by the reception of Christ's body and blood? All agreed that—whatever else it was—the Holy Supper referred to the atoning sacrifice, to Jesus' body as broken and his blood as shed for the remission of sins. It was a memorial of the cross and passion in which the benefit of the victory there won was made over to the believing recipient. All the Reformed confessions and theologians had been clear on this.

The Reformed tradition had also taught, Nevin insisted, that the Supper meant actual communion with the present living Christ, so as to participate in his very life. Hodge conceded that this meaning was unmistakable in Calvin and in the confessions of the French, Dutch, and Scottish churches; but he argued—unconvincingly—that it was not also taught in the Heidelberg Catechism and the Second Helvetic Confession. In any case he rejected the truth and validity of the conception. It had dropped out of the teaching of the Reformed church generally, he said, because it was really not compatible with the main thrust of Reformed theology.

Where was the difficulty? The teaching of Nevin, Calvin, and Luther seemed to Berg and Schmucker and Hodge to qualify dangerously the Protestant doctrine of forgiveness, of forensic justification or imputation. Nevin indeed protested against a merely abstract conception of imputation. "The Bible knows nothing of a simply outward imputation, by which something is reckoned to a man that does not belong to him in fact." [27] With sin, it is because every particular sinner shares in Adam's fallen life that guilt and condemnation are imputed to him. Similarly with the second Adam, the legal imputation of Christ's righteousness is grounded on the actual sharing of Christ's life and righteousness by the sinner. In the act of our justification we are inserted into Christ himself and his righteousness is accounted to be ours. The forgiveness of past sin and the power to holiness become ours only in virtue of the indwelling in us of the life of Christ. As Calvin wrote, "I see not how any man can attain a solid confidence that he has redemption and righteousness in the cross of Christ, and life in His death, unless he first has a real communion with Christ himself; for those blessings would never be imparted to us, if Christ did not first make himself ours." [28] Nevin asked:

> Could the sacrifice of Calvary be of any avail to take away sin, if the victim there slain had not been raised again for our justification and were not *now* seated at the right hand of God as our advocate and intercessor? . . . Surely it is the perennial, indissoluble *life* of the once crucified Redeemer, which imparts to his broken body and shed blood all their power to abolish guilt. . . . The priesthood and sacrifice of Christ are *one*, as always remaining. . . . His one offering needs no repetition; but just for the reason, that it never comes to an

[27] *The Mystical Presence*, p. 190.
[28] *Institutes of the Christian Religion*, IV, xvii, xi.

end and passes away. . . . The atonement, in this view, is a quality or property of the glorified life of the Son of Man.[29]

Berg thought that this position made justification consist in the implantation or infusion of Christ, and he compared it to Newman's attempt to combine forensic justification and infused righteousness. Hodge also accused Nevin of holding a Romanist view of justification.

Tayler Lewis defended Nevin at this point. He cited Howe, Owen, and Baxter to show how the Puritans as well as Calvin had grounded imputation on the mystical union with Christ. Other writers, Lewis pointed out (Swedenborg, Coleridge, Morell), had so interpreted the mystical union as to neglect or deny the forensic element. There was a real danger here, Lewis admitted, against which Nevin should perhaps have been more emphatic, but he felt that Nevin had successfully and honestly maintained the grace of God in forgiveness while setting it within the context of our actual relation to Christ.[30]

Hodge had accused Nevin of being a follower of Schleiermacher and consequently inadequate on sin and the need for forgiveness. Yet Nevin had introduced *The Mystical Presence* with an essay of Ullmann's which purported to correct Schleiermacher just at this point.[31] Ullmann sought to assert and hold together as the two highest ideas of Christianity, the doctrines of sin and grace and those of the mystical union of the believer with God. And it is precisely in the Lord's Supper, Nevin felt, that these themes are held together indissolubly.

With Hodge there was no apparent sense of the need of explaining our solidarity either with Adam or with Christ. The connection was wholly arbitrary. As Nevin pointed out, one could, on Hodge's grounds, as readily explain the imputation to us of the sin of the fallen angels as of Adam. In similar fashion,

[29] "Doctrine of the Reformed Church on the Lord's Supper," *MR*, 1850, p. 547. Cf. *The Mystical Presence*, pp. 137, 180.

[30] "The Mercersburg School of Theology and Philosophy," *Literary World* (New York), April 7, 14, 1849.

[31] *The Mystical Presence*, pp. 26–27.

the Incarnation was a purely temporary expedient to make expiation possible. It was as if a divine Christ had been let down in a blanket and then caught up again to heaven, leaving earth as before. The imputation of sin and of righteousness were both perfectly arbitrary acts of God. There was no sense of a real involvement of man either in Adam or in Christ.

Nevin accepted Hodge's assertion that there was a certain incompatibility between Calvin's sacramental doctrine and other aspects of his theology. The tension came, however, not—as Hodge and Berg thought—with forensic justification, but with an abstract understanding of election, the divine decrees. Furthermore, Nevin frankly rejected double predestination. Here he apparently had learned from Schaf, for there seems to be no evidence that he had qualified his predestinarianism until after Schaf's arrival. Schaf, while still in Germany, had explicitly rejected double predestination in his dissertation *The Sin against the Holy Ghost* and suggested the possibility of future probation for those dying in ignorance of the gospel. He declared:

> I cannot see how, in presupposing that the heathen, too, after the present time of probation, had no farther grace, we can avoid admitting of an absolute double predestination. . . . Justly our sympathy for our fellow beings revolts against such an uncouth proposition. Shall all the longing minds of the gentile world, who make numberless Christians blush—an Aeschylus, Pindar, Sophocles, Socrates, Plato, Plutarch, Marcus Aurelius, and men, too, like Saladin, etc., never hear anything of the comfortable words of the gospel? . . . those who could not here receive the news of the redemption through Christ, shall have it offered to them beyond this life.[32]

For this speculation he had been widely attacked in the summer of 1846 and his view rejected by the synod of that year—in the first official censure of Mercersburg ideas. Nevertheless, Nevin adopted both the theory of the intermediate state (after death and before resurrection) and the denial of double predestination—a point that he justified as continuing the Melanchthonian heritage of the German Reformed Church.

[32] Quoted in Berg, "The German Controversy," *PQR*, 1846, pp. 314–15, from Guldin's translation in the *Christian Intelligencer*.

In these matters the Mercersburg men foreshadowed the actions of the American Reformed churches generally in the next fifty years. By the 1890's the Presbyterians and Congregationalists were ready to disavow formally the scholastic theory of the decrees, and in that decade Schaf's battle for "future probation" was fought over again by the missionary candidates of the American Board of Commissioners for Foreign Missions. Although the Calvinist view of the Lord's Supper has not been generally established in these churches, it is certainly far stronger than it was in the 1840's.

It may even be that in the light of modern Calvin scholarship Nevin and Schaf let Hodge off too easily. Nevin argued effectively that Calvin's sacramental views were much more definitely declared in the Reformed confessions than were the divine decrees, and that consequently they should be considered more central when there was conflict as to the definition of the Reformed tradition.

> The sacramental interest and that of the decrees, in his system, are not free from some inward conflict, and . . . the one has a tendency continually to overthrow the other. Hence it is, no doubt, that in those sections of the Reformed church where the doctrine of the decrees has been regarded as the main interest in theology, the original Calvinistic view of the sacraments has fallen more and more into the shade, so as frequently to be of no authority whatever. And yet the doctrine of the decrees as held by Calvin never belonged at all to the constitution of the Reformed Church as such; whereas the sacramental doctrine entered in truth into its distinctive character as a confession.[38]

Perhaps Nevin should have carried the same argument into the exposition of Calvin himself. If he had noted the point at which election was set in Calvin's thought and its function, he might have made a case that for Calvin himself the Eucharistic view was more central. He conceded too easily to Hodge, however, that "with Calvin, God's absolute decree is made to be the *principle* of the Christian salvation" from which all else followed. As a

[38] "Doctrine of the Reformed Church on the Lord's Supper," *MR,* 1850, p. 523. Cf. "Hodge on the Ephesians," *MR,* 1857, pp. 46–82, 192–245.

result, he tended increasingly to relinquish Calvin to Hodge and other scholastics, and to appeal rather to Melanchthon.

A third significant point at issue between Nevin and his opponents generally was the understanding of the meaning of *body* or *flesh*. For Nevin communion with the person of Christ meant particularly communion with his flesh, his humanity. Only by and in his humanity was the divinity of Christ accessible to men. So Calvin had maintained, "I do not teach that Christ dwells in us simply by his Spirit, but that he so raises us to himself as to transfuse into us the vivific vigor of his flesh."[34] But Berg, Hodge, Schmucker, and the other "modern Puritans" admitted a communion with Christ at most in his divine nature, as the eternal Logos, or as Spirit conceived separately from his incarnate humanity. The presence of humanity or body in the Lord's Supper seemed to Berg to imply inescapably corporeality and thus transubstantiation.

In *The Mystical Presence* Nevin had explicitly corrected Calvin's psychology. It seemed to him that Calvin did not sufficiently distinguish the plastic organic law of life from the chemical materials of body. His further investigations, however, under the stimulus of Hodge's challenge, and with the aid of Ebrard's analyses, satisfied him that Calvin had not needed correcting nearly as much as he had thought.[35] In his attempts to restate Calvin in terms of modern psychology he had been even more true to Calvin's intention than he had realized.

Nevin had taken care to point out that the essence of a living body is not the matter of which it is composed. This matter might be wholly changed in a matter of hours and the body still remain itself. The identity of the body lies in its immaterial animating power, the capacity to assimilate and organize mere matter into its own distinctive structure and functioning. In ref-

[34] "Secunda defensio . . . de sacramentis contra Joachimi Westphali calumnias," *Opera* (Amsterdam, 1667), IX, 669; "Opera Calvini," IX, 76, in *Corpus Reformatorum* (Brunsvigae, 1870), XXXVII. Cited in *The Mystical Presence*, p. 124. Cf. "Catholic Unity," in Schaf, *Principle of Protestantism*, p. 198 n.

[35] *WM*, July 26, 1848.

erence to the sacrament, thus, a tactual incorporation with the mere chemical matter of Christ's body would be Capernaitic eating—and valueless. What the believer seeks is incorporation with the animating power of his life, what Calvin called the "vivific virtues" of his flesh. This vivific virtue is not received in the mouth as if it had dimensions, but enters into the central stream of our life, the core of personality, by faith. It is not attached to the elements as a thing, but is conveyed through the sacramental action as a meaningful whole.

This formulation of the nature of the life communicated in the sacrament baffled most of Nevin's opponents. The synod of the Dutch Reformed Church, for example, which met at Albany in June, 1846, was deeply troubled by the reports their fraternal delegates brought back of the actions of the German Reformed synod the fall preceding in the Mercersburg controversy. They heard Dr. Wolff, as delegate from the German church, in explanation of the Mercersburg use of the term *body:*

> The scene when the parting address was made was quite a graphic one. The members, scattered through the Synod chamber, left their seats, and crowded toward the speaker, and appeared by drinking in every word, to catch the true features of what was generally deemed something new; and after he closed, there was mutually a general expression of surprise and dissatisfaction, avowals of entire inability to apprehend the philosophy advanced. . . . our flesh is not our body . . . that *it* is nothing but a compound of salts and gases and minerals and earth and alkalis and that which holds them in combination, which embodies them, is body.[36]

The only sense which the Dutch synod could make of all this was what Berg and Proudfit and Hodge read into Mercersburg thought, and the synod acted accordingly.

Nevin ran up against popular materialistic conceptions also on the question of whether heaven is a place. Calvin, faithful to the language of the Bible, placed the risen body of Christ at God's right hand in heaven. In order to effect communion with the believer "notwithstanding such vast separation in space," Calvin

[36] *Christian Intelligencer,* July 16, 1846.

then had to take recourse to a miraculous action of the Holy Spirit in raising the believing communicant to the presence of the Savior on high. This device, said Nevin, was violent and unsatisfactory. If Calvin had substituted for the localized humanity of Christ, "the idea of the organic law of Christ's human life," a local and material contact would no longer have been necessary to establish continuity of existence.[37] Calvin's theory would thus be freed of that awkward aspect which had been so derided by the Lutherans.

Henry Harbaugh, a young pastor, requested a review from Nevin of his popular work on the sainted dead, in which he argued that heaven was a definite fixed locality. Nevin demurred on this point.

> Heaven of course involves the conception of *place* [he conceded to Harbaugh], but we have no right to think of it as holding only under such local relations and limitations, in this form, as are found to characterize our present mortal life. . . . Place itself becomes what it is, by the way in which it is occupied and apprehended; a new sense imparted to us (like sight for instance to the consciousness of a world born blind) might of itself be sufficient to change our existence, immeasurably more than a translation without it to the most remote part of the universe.[38]

In similar fashion, Nevin interpreted what Calvin had meant in speaking of the ascent of the soul to Christ's glorified body in heaven.

> The soul must be directed subjectively, in the sacrament, to heaven, or the higher sphere in which Christ dwells, and not to the sphere of matter and sense, for the accomplishment of the grace it seeks; while on the other side, the power of Christ objectively meets this upward look of faith, by actually breaking through the limitations of space, and from the bosom of his own higher order of life itself, causing the vigor of his glorified humanity to reach over into the persons of his people in an immediate and direct way. Neither ascent nor descent here are to be taken in any outward or local sense; they serve merely

[37] *The Mystical Presence*, pp. 156–57.
[38] *MR*, 1849, p. 398.

to express metaphorically the relation of the two orders or spheres of existence, which are brought into opposition and contrast.[39]

In this way Calvin's conception was brought closer to what Luther was struggling for in his theory of ubiquity.

Another dimension to these questions of body and place in relation to life and consciousness was the subject of the relation of body and soul. Nevin declared:

> We have no right to think of the body as the prison of the soul in the way of Plato; nor as its garment merely; nor as its shell or hull. . . . the Bible knows nothing of that abstract separation of soul and body which has come to be so widely admitted into the religious views of the modern world.[40]

Princeton and New Brunswick and popular American Protestantism, however, were accustomed to think in Platonic rather than biblical categories on this matter. That was why they were interested only in communing with the spirit of Christ.

Nevin found himself again defending Calvin against the Calvinists in insisting on the real unity of soul and body. In their ground, he taught, soul and body are but one life, "holding forever in the presence and power of the self-same organic law." [41] "Life" in this connection is "the central consciousness of the subject . . . that to which we refer both body and soul, when we say *my* body and *my* soul. . . . For what is personality if it be not the absolute centralization of its subject at last in the power of a single consciousness that pervades and rules at every point the entire compass of his life as a whole?"

In reference to the Incarnation, this conception meant "such a union of the two natures in Christ as makes them to be one life, one personal consciousness." [42] So it had been with Calvin; but Hodge and Berg, and with them a very large section of American Protestantism, seemed to hold a dualistic Nestorian view of the

[39] "The Doctrine of the Reformed Church on the Lord's Supper," *MR.*, 1850, p. 504.

[40] *The Mystical Presence*, p. 171.

[41] *Ibid.*

[42] *WM*, July 26, 1848.

relation of Christ's divinity and humanity. They seemed to imply, in fact, two centers of consciousness in Jesus Christ, one human and one divine. For Nevin, as for Calvin, it was the whole Christ, the incarnate God, divine and human, at once and indissolubly, with whom we seek incorporation.

In all this discussion it is difficult to sift out the specifically religious from the philosophical or psychological. Nevin was employing psychological theories learned from Rauch in relation to the Eucharistic presence, the nature of the risen Christ, and the conception of the final resurrection state. On all these topics Hodge, Berg, and most Americans were accustomed to a different vocabulary and set of categories. Most of them, however, were so naïve as to be unaware that they had made philosophical commitments of this sort; they were only talking common sense. It was Nevin, in their minds, who was mixing up theology with philosophy, and bad philosophy at that. The discussion never got to the point, consequently, of an open-minded endeavor to see whether there were equivalent philosophical formulations in which the same religious apprehensions might be couched.

One last distinctive conception urged by Nevin was his analysis of the generic and the individual aspects of personality.[43] The idea did not play a major role in the debate, but it illuminates the context of his Christological thought. Nevin put it in terms of the parallel of the first and second Adam. Adam was both an individual man and man generically, involving in himself and his reproductive potentialities the whole of humanity. As generic man, Adam still lives in us all, soul and body (since soul and body are manifestations of the one underlying life); yet as an individual man, he does not live in his posterity.

Similarly, Jesus Christ is a distinct individual, man and God; at the same time he is the head and sum of a new race, a new creation, still living in his people as truly as he continues his personal existence. "His person is always the actual bearer of our

[43] *WM*, January 14, 1846, and *The Mystical Presence*, pp. 160–61. Nevin probably derived the idea from Dorner.

persons," yet is not fused with them. The new creation is to be conceived as "an all-present, everywhere active personal life."

Although Hodge accused him of it, Nevin does not seem to have meant that Jesus Christ had no human personality, that he was God incarnate in impersonal humanity.[44] He acknowledged that the relation between Christ and his people cannot be conceived in full analogy to that of Adam and his descendants. But the analogy held sufficiently "to show that there may be a real communication of Christ's life to his people, without the idea of anything like a local mixture with his person. . . . He lives in himself, and yet lives in them really and truly at the same time." [45]

Nevin himself summed up the several contrasts between the classical Reformed doctrine and that of the "modern Puritans."

> It makes a great difference surely, whether the union of the believer with Christ be regarded as the power of one and the same life, or as holding only in a correspondence of thought and feeling; whether the Lord's Supper be a sign and seal only of God's grace in general, or the pledge also of a special invisible grace present in the transaction itself; and whether we are united by means of it to the person of Christ, or only to his merits; and whether finally we communicate in the ordinance with the whole Christ, in a real way, or only with his divinity.[46]

How is Nevin's achievement in the theology of the sacraments to be evaluated? He had certainly made a major contribution to the history of theology in America, and he had increased the authority of the Heidelberg Catechism and of Calvin, in his denomination and beyond.

On the whole he had interpreted Calvin accurately and perceptively, much more so than the Princeton Presbyterians. His polemic position was such, however, that he developed only one side of the Reformed doctrine. His whole attention was directed to the spiritualist and Baptistic left wing, against whom he cer-

[44] *WM*, July 19, 1848. See also Schaf, *What Is Church History?* (Philadelphia, 1846), pp. 33-35.
[45] *The Mystical Presence*, p. 161.
[46] *Ibid.*, p. 126.

tainly declared authentic Reformed concerns. On the other side, however, he was, to say the least, unguarded.

Nevin is very brief, for example, regarding the heresy of the propitiatory mass. He states the point but does not seem to feel the full weight of it. Recognition of a divine presence in the sacrament seemed to him essentially the same in both interpretations. In the same way, he assumed a continuity between the sacrificing Roman mass priest and the Reformation minister of the Word and Sacraments. An indication of Nevin's insensitivity to issues on this side was his habitual use of the term *altar*, showing his unawareness of Reformation views about the difference between the Sacrament of the Holy Table and a propitiatory sacrifice at an *altar*. (The American German Reformed may merely have picked up this language from the Lutherans, with whom they were often closely associated.)

One last indication of the same sort was that his attempt to restore the authority and value of the Eucharist was carried out partly at the expense of the preached word. No doubt other factors were involved. The fully audible and intelligible liturgy of the Eucharist in the nineteenth century could stand of itself without preaching better than the dumb show and Latin mumbling of the sixteenth-century mass. Still it is hard to recognize the Calvinist accent in an argument which would deprecate and restrict the preaching of the Word.

With these necessary qualifications, then, one should acknowledge in Mercersburg the measurable accomplishment of the goal Nevin had set: the recovery of a genuine Reformed Catholicism, particularly regarding the Holy Eucharist.

5 / Schaf's Theory of the Historical Development of the Church

The year 1845 saw the publication of two works which, for the first time in the English-speaking world, tried to restate the Protestant–Roman Catholic debate in terms of historical development. Neither was well received by the church in whose interest it was presented. In England John Henry Newman sought to persuade Anglicans of the Roman Catholic case in his *Essay on Development*. In the United States Philip Schaf offered in his *Principle of Protestantism* an alternative type of anti–Roman Catholic argument to that which was current there. Each seemed to many or most of the theologians of his own church to have made dangerous or fatal concessions. Roman Catholics protested that Newman's was really a Protestant book, and Protestants accused Schaf of being a crypto–Roman Catholic. There were few in either England or America who had enough grasp of Christian history to appreciate the considerations which had led to this new type of apologetics.

The prevailing habit of thought in both American Protestantism and in Roman Catholicism generally, outside Germany, was unhistorical. Each sought to claim the support of historical evidence for his dogmatic position, but neither would admit the force of inconvenient evidence. Joseph Berg illustrates the popular American Protestant approach. As retiring president of the German Reformed Synod, Berg preached the sermon at the opening of the synod in October 1844 on the historical background of the Reformation. He argued that the doctrines and practices of the Reformation derived unchanged from the apostolic church, having been preserved down the centuries by the medieval Waldenses. The synod then adjourned to Reading to hear Schaf's inaugural lecture as professor of church history. Therein Schaf developed a rival thesis which he had already set forth at Berlin in articles on "Katholizismus und Protestantismus," [1] that the Reformation was the direct offspring, not of the Waldenses, but of the papal church of the Middle Ages. In its later printed form, if not also in the address as delivered, Schaf brushed aside Berg's contention as preposterous. Both men promptly expanded their addresses to small books, which were published in the following spring. Berg's bore the title, *The Old Paths, or a Sketch of the Order and Discipline of the Reformed Church before the Reformation, as maintained by the Waldenses prior to that Epoch, and by the Church of the Palatinate in the 16th Century*. Schaf's, which was published about the same time, was called *Das Prinzip des Protestantismus*. Nevin had been laboring over the translation, and by June, 1845, the English version was also before the church, with Nevin's introduction and appended sermon.

Berg's position was that of a stable orthodoxy. "Christianity is a system of divinely revealed truth, which is perfect, and consequently admits of no improvement." [2] It had been proclaimed as complete and so maintained, at least by a faithful minority in the Waldensian valleys. With an eye on Schaf, he attacked the conception that Protestantism "is merely a Reformed Romanism." "If we admit," he argued, "that the Church of Rome has ever been the Church of Christ, you concede the entire ground." [3] For if she once was, she must be still. If her doctrines and practices were ever those of the true church, such are they still. The papal church has either always or never been owned by the Lord. It has always been either the apostasy or the church. Contrariwise, if they are now true, the doctrine and practices of the Re-

[1] *Literarische Zeitung* (Berlin), October 31 and December 16, 1843.
[2] *The Old Paths* (Philadelphia, 1846), p. 14. Cf. J. Helfenstein, *Weekly Messenger*, September 9, 1846.
[3] Berg, *op. cit.*, p. viii.

formed Church must always have been maintained. Christ promised to be forever with his church.

Schaf knew that the historical evidence could not support any such contention. The Reformation was no such revolutionary break with medieval Catholicism, "holding connection at best, perhaps, with some fractionary sect of the Middle Ages, and only through this and the help of certain desperate historical leaps beside, reaching back to the age of the apostles."[4] This kind of argument could only survive in an atmosphere of historical ignorance, which was, to be sure, the general American condition. When the pressure of historical evidence increased, Protestants of Berg's type generally retired from the historical field altogether. The Presbyterian (new school) editor of the New York *Evangelist,* Dr. G. B. Cheever, contended that true Protestants recognized no historical connection of any sort with the apostolic church. Berg's view had been "entirely given up," wrote a successor, J. I. Good, in 1911. "The true view of historic succession is through the invisible church."[5] Historians, of course, can neither prove nor disprove an invisible succession.

One may observe the same argument from stability and the same ultimate dismissal of historical evidence on the Roman Catholic side. Orestes Brownson, the theological spokesman for the Roman Church in America, deplored Newman's book. The Roman *magisterium* had never "developed"; it sprang into history full-grown and armed like Minerva. Was or was not the Roman hierarchy, he demanded of Newman, able to teach truly and infallibly "the whole Catholic faith, and the precise Catholic faith, on any and every point" in the time of Clement, Polycarp, Justin, and Irenaeus? If what she then taught was sufficient for salvation, why is it not now? The alleged variations in doctrine which Newman allowed—regarding purgatory, episcopacy, and infant baptism, for instance—could be conceded by no Catholic.

[4] *The Principle of Protestantism as Related to the Present State of the Church* (Chambersburg, 1845), thesis 31.

[5] J. I. Good, *History of the Reformed Church in the United States in the Nineteenth Century* (New York, 1911), pp. 318–19.

The Protestant Schaf had a right to such views; in him the theory of development was "bold, manly and consistent."[6] But for a Catholic to take historical evidence seriously against church teaching was to appeal to private judgment. Consequently, as the evidence mounted, Roman Catholics of Brownson's ultramontane stamp would retreat into frank obscurantism. The Vatican Council was to dispose of the evidence against the dogma of infallibility on Manning's principle, "Dogma must conquer history."

Romanists and Puseyites alike treated the Reformation and Protestantism generally the way the pseudo-Protestants did the Middle Ages. They could see nothing here but a great "apostasy"; they must *a priori* deny that God had here also been faithful to his promises and had owned his church. As Schaf wrote of the Puseyite program of archaism, "they wish to shut out of view the progress of the last three centuries entirely; to treat the whole as a negation, if possible; and by one vast leap to carry the Church back to the point where it stood before the separation of the Oriental and Western communions."[7]

Such was the prevailing mentality, at least outside Germany, in 1845. Schaf and Newman were seeking honestly to wrestle with historical evidence, which the dominant theologians of their respective churches were accustomed either to twist out of shape or to deny altogether. Were Newman, Schaf, and history to be respected, whole libraries of apologetic must be junked and a laborious process of rethinking undertaken. Schaf indeed referred, with more accuracy than tact, to the "poor, stale reproductions of the worn out theology of New England, still appearing among us."[8] One can understand why he was not welcomed.

Newman similarly described the prevailing great ignorance with respect to church history in England.

[6] Orestes Brownson, "Newman's Development of Christian Doctrine," *Brownson's Quarterly Review*, 1846, pp. 361, 351 n.
[7] *Op. cit.*, pp. 124–25.
[8] *What Is Church History? A vindication of the idea of historical development* (Philadelphia, 1846), p. 19.

> Our popular religion scarcely recognizes the fact of the twelve long ages which lie between the councils of Nicaea and Trent, except as affording one or two passages to illustrate its wild interpretations of certain prophecies of St. Paul and St. John. It is melancholy to say it, but the chief, perhaps the only English writer, who has any claim to be considered an ecclesiastical historian, is the infidel Gibbon.[9]

After quoting this passage, Schaf observed, "The same may be affirmed, of course, with equal or with still greater right of our America." [10] In both countries, history was written and viewed as "a mere conglomeration of notices thrown together," with no grasp of meaningful continuity or development. At least with regard to Christianity, one could hardly say that historical consciousness had yet emerged in the English-speaking countries.

Newman's and Schaf's essays on development did not constitute a formal debate; they were written independently, each without knowledge of the other. To a degree the authors seemed to talk past each other. Each wrote apologetically, to account for what seemed to him the greatest historical embarrassment of his church. Newman labored to show that the contrast between the apostolic church and the full-blown papal system was more apparent than real. Schaf argued that Protestantism had not begun in the sixteenth century, as the unwary might suppose, but was the proper continuation of the main stream of Christianity up to that time. "Where was your church before Luther?" was the challenge he was answering. "Where do you find popery in the New Testament and the early fathers?" was Newman's problem. Newman canvassed primarily the history of the ancient church, Schaf the church of the late Middle Ages and those following.

The 1845 fall term began at Mercersburg amid all the excitement attending the trial of the professors for the heresy of the *Principle of Protestantism.* Schaf opened his course on church history with a lecture on historical method. As with his inaugural lecture of the preceding year, he then expanded the address for

[9] *Essay on the Development of Christian Doctrine* (American ed.; New York, 1846), p. 14.

[10] *What is Church History?* p. 4.

publication. It was translated by Nevin [11] and published in June, 1846, under the title *What Is Church History? A Vindication of the Idea of Historical Development.* In this work Schaf was able to clarify further the point of view he had set forth in *Katholizismus und Protestantismus* and in the *Principle of Protestantism.* He also took the opportunity to express briefly his opinion of Newman's *Essay*. A comparison of their views may help to clarify Schaf's conception of development.

Schaf agreed, of course, with Newman's presupposition, that there had been a development of views and practices between the first-century church and the medieval papacy. Newman's attempt to minimize the extent of these changes, however, went beyond what Schaf would allow in many particulars. As Schaf described Newman's procedure, "the slightest and most indistinct hints of Christian antiquity are taken as sufficient proofs by themselves for the existence at the time of doctrines and practices that belong to a much later period." [12] (Five or six years later, as we shall see, Schaf's colleague Nevin was to come to Newman's assistance in this argument.)

A second distinction between his own and Newman's theory of development was pointed out by Schaf. For Newman the growth of doctrine, order, and practice was cumulative and irreversible. Heretical forms might appear and disappear in time, but no valid development, once achieved, could thereafter be rejected. The whole of tradition that was true to type, partook as it were of the character of divine revelation. For Schaf, on the other hand, the forms in which the church apprehended the Christ of the Bible were always in principle subject to correction. A given historical development, like episcopacy, or the medieval papacy, or Protestant denominationalism, might have justification and necessity relative to its historical situation, without being universally and permanently necessary. Even the dogmas of the ecumenical creeds were in principle subject to correction by

[11] D. S. Schaff, *Life of Philip Schaff* (New York: Charles Scribner's Sons, 1897) p. 140.

[12] *What Is Church History?* pp. 46–47 n.

Scripture.[13] The essential and changeless continuity of the church could not be identified definitively in terms either of explicit doctrine or church order; it was to be found in the bond to the Christ known through the Bible. Thus Schaf's view might comprehend a legitimate Reformation; Newman's could not. And yet, while Newman made far less room for legitimate Christian development, he had already, in Schaf's judgment as in Brownson's, conceded more to the facts than Rome could or would allow. The full recognition of historical development in Christianity was possible only from the viewpoint of reformed or evangelical catholicism.

Schaf wrote the first history of church history in English,[14] which, indeed, was published before his former professor, F. C. Baur, published his pioneering *Epochen der Kirchlichen Geschichtsschreibung* in Germany. In his sketch (*What Is Church History?*) Schaf grouped the chief writers of church history since the Reformation according to their basic conceptions of the nature of history and the church. He displayed a high degree of self-consciousness concerning the relation of his view to those of his predecessors.

The first group of historians discussed by Schaf were the representatives of orthodoxy, whether Protestant or Roman Catholic, for example, Baronius and the Magdeburg "centuriators," Bossuet, Du Plessis, Daillé, Usher, Bull. Whether Roman Catholic, Lutheran, Reformed, or Anglican, they agreed on the assumption of doctrinal immobility. For them whatever system was espoused was defended as apostolic and unchanging; variation in doctrine was by definition heretical. The only changes admitted were such outward matters as missionary expansion or influence on society. We have already seen how such representatives of this view of history as Berg and Brownson contrasted with Schaf. Most Americans who read any church history were raised on Mosheim, a late and rather latitudinarian representative of this

[13] *Principle of Protestantism,* p. 51.

[14] *What Is Church History?* Much of the material is reproduced and expanded in the introduction to Schaff's *History of the Apostolic Church* (New York: Charles Scribner, 1859).

school. Mosheim still conceived of Christian doctrine as a fixed and unalterable system, although he was disposed to view heresies mildly, as errors of thought or imagination, or forms of enthusiasm. Long since superseded in Germany, Mosheim still monopolized the textbook market in America.[15]

Although pietism, in the main, held the orthodox faith and, like orthodoxy, rejected any idea of development in doctrine, it nevertheless formed a transition to rationalism. The great figure here was Gottfried Arnold, especially with his *Unparteiische Kirchen und Ketzerhistorie* (1699). By substituting devotional intensity and ethics as criteria in place of doctrine and church order, Arnold quite reversed the orthodox evaluation of the state churches and the sects. He found the true church generally a faithful remnant among the latter. Justice was thus done at last to many hitherto despised movements, but at the price of a pervasive suspicion and disillusionment with the main church bodies. Not all pietists approved. P. J. Spener, for example, would not read the book. J. S. Semler, on the other hand, the proper founder of rationalist church history, considered Arnold's work the best available.

Rationalist church historians championed heretics generally in the interest of free thought and Pelagius in particular for his moralism. More radical still was their disintegration of any unity to the story of Christian history. The history of doctrine became "a confused chaos of opinions," mere motion and flow, a "vast tumultuating waste without guiding principle or certain aim." The cause of this activity was understood to be "a purely subjective play of human passions," a "history of human folly." "God was excluded from history altogether" and supposed to be at most "a private indifferent spectator merely of human events, from beyond the clouds." [16] Here, we may assume, Schaf would have located Newman's one English "church historian," the Gibbon of the *Decline and Fall.*

Modern historiography, Schaf continued, is distinguished from

[15] Schaf, *What Is Church History?* pp. 42 ff., 56.
[16] *Ibid.*, pp. 70, 71.

that of rationalism in two chief particulars. On the one hand, it is far more disposed to take the lives of other generations at their own valuation, to respect their individuality, and not to measure them so obviously by the standards of the historian's society. At the same time the new history finds a principle of continuity and unity in the idea of the progress of humanity conceived as an organic development. J. C. Herder was the prophet of both themes back in the days of rationalist predominance, with his *Philosophy of History* (1774) and his *Ideas for the History of Humanity* (1784). Herder gloried in the variety and richness of historical life, defending the Middle Ages, for example, from the fashionable contempt. At the same time he believed he discerned the signs of a divine purpose working itself out through the sequence of generations and cultures toward some hidden future meaning.

The historians of the Romantic Movement exploited this conception of history in many directions, especially in the recovery of sympathy and understanding for the Middle Ages. The notion of development, meanwhile, was clarified especially by the philosophers Schelling and Hegel. Hegel had "contributed more than any other influence, to diffuse a clear conception of the interior organism of history, as a richer evolution continually of the idea of humanity." [17] To be sure, Hegel and his followers had carried the idea of an immanent purpose in history to the point of pantheism and the undermining of personal responsibility, so that they were unsafe guides in church history.

The most important church historian of the day, in Schaf's judgment, was Augustus Neander. Neander was less intellectualistic than Hegel and, like Schleiermacher, sought the experience behind the formulation of dogma as the essence of religion. Like Hegel, he gave great weight to the idea of the developing process in history. His church history, completed by that time down to the age of Boniface VIII, was by far the most important monument of church history of the nineteenth century. Even although Schaf desired to correct Neander in the direction of a more dis-

[17] *Ibid.*, p. 76.

tinct orthodoxy and more definite churchly feeling, he accounted himself a disciple of his Berlin teacher. This was the orientation he had been trained in.

The guiding metaphor in Schaf's historical thought was the idea of biological growth, in which change is regulated by an inner power, preserving unity through diverse stages of maturation. Each new stage both negates and fulfills its predecessor. Pursuing this analogy, "every stage of development has its own corresponding *disease*," [18] the more advanced stages being exposed to more dangerous diseases.

An alternative metaphor to that of the growing biological organism is the movement of a river down its predestined course. The advantage here is the picture of the side currents which may stagnate and dry up unless they return to the main stream. Here Schaf put the Dunkards, for example, or even Eastern Orthodoxy, or those sections of Roman Catholicism out of contact with Protestantism, which is the main river bed in the modern period.[19]

Neither image, the growing plant nor the winding river, was permitted by Schaf to argue that the agency of the historical process is wholly immanent in it. This regularity of successive epochs, each building on its predecessor, follows a pre-existent divine plan. The great ideas which determine the significance of historical epochs are "actual single emanations from the primal Truth," which is God. This providential direction of history finds its focus in the history of the church, the main stream of the world's history, and the vehicle in the first instance of the Spirit of Christ in history. Divine Providence allows nothing in vain and uses to its purposes even the passions and errors of men.[20]

From this providential conception of historical development, with its emphasis on great ideas, it was not far to the Hegelian dialectical scheme. This pattern Schaf also used as a subordinate motif (thesis 17) although not always with rigor. His antitheses

[18] *Ibid.*, p. 98.
[19] *Ibid.*, pp. 106, 107.
[20] *Ibid.*, pp. 64, 82, 27.

were often alternatives of emphasis rather than logical contraries. The synthesis often turned out—as in the iconoclastic controversy, or the Laudian-Puritan struggle—to be rather the path of moderation, or the golden mean. There is an inherent contradiction between development through logical contraries and the continuity of type essential to biological growth. When it came to a choice, Schaf usually held to the analogy of organism.

Schaf felt himself closest to Neander of all his church history teachers, but in the critical analysis of the anatomy of history Neander was of little help. For the great organizing generalizations and the grounds of periodization Schaf had to look elsewhere. He seems to have utilized two radically divergent theories of development without ever bringing them into full harmony with each other. At times the *Principle of Protestantism* seems to be presenting the high-church Lutheran conception of cumulative growth, as set forth, for example, in Kliefoth's *Einleitung in die Dogmengeschichte* (1839). Then at other times Schaf obviously was drawing on the Hegelian schematism of the Tübingen dean of the "higher critics," F. C. Baur.

In the spirit of the high-church historians Schaf represented the Reformation as an organic development of ancient and medieval catholicism. The Reformation was not a movement to overthrow and reconstruct the work of the church "in the case of its great cardinal doctrines as already positively defined by the general councils, but to carry forward and complete that work, by going on to define and settle what had not yet been made the subject of action in the same positive style. . . ." The essential fundamental doctrines of the Reformation fall within the sphere of soteriology, which had not been occupied by any conciliar decisions, as in the case of the Trinity and Incarnation, and "where accordingly it was possible to advance new scriptural statements, without contradicting the true Catholic Church." [21]

From the point of view of the theory of development it is significant that these were "new scriptural statements." The progress or development which is to be observed in church history "is

[21] *Principle of Protestantism*, p. 52.

never in the strict sense creative, but in the way only of reception, organic assimilation and expansion."[22] As a new order of life Christianity was perfect and complete in Christ and the apostles, but the church has gained in the apprehension and appropriation of this life and doctrine and spirit. That life was not fully actualized from the beginning in the general mass of the church, but has been increasingly actualized since (thesis 29).

The principles on which the church had always lived, which were only wholly articulate at the Reformation, were not really two, but one. Justification by grace alone through faith and the final authority of the Bible are joined as content and form, as

> but two sides of one and the same principle . . . *Christ all in all.* . . . Christ, or in an immediate view his Spirit, is ever in the word and with the word; never without or beyond the word, written or preached; yea, he is himself the living personal Word. The word again can be understood only by faith, in union with the spirit of Christ speaking to us through the letter.[23]

As "life" and "spirit," the power of the new creation has made itself felt at the subconscious level even where it has not been doctrinally articulated.

> We may bring forward indeed many passages from the writings of Augustine, Anselm, Bernard of Clairvaux, and other men . . . which seem to teach the cardinal doctrine of justification by grace; and it may be affirmed with truth, that all real Christians, from the beginning, had lived upon this doctrine at bottom, unconsciously to themselves. But still their piety, in its general character, must be admitted to carry with it more or less of a legal complexion. Only in single, exalted moments of their existence at best, were they enabled to lay hold of the freedom, the assurance of salvation, and full triumphant faith to which we have been raised by the Reformation.[24]

In a more general sense, Schaf continued, "*the entire Catholic Church as such, so far as it might be considered the legitimate bearer of the Christian faith and life,* pressed with inward nec-

[22] *Ibid.*, p. 51.
[23] *Ibid.*, pp. 93–94.
[24] *Ibid.*, p. 51.

essary impulse towards Protestantism." This church was predominantly legalist in temper, a church of law and authority, well fitted "to exercise a wardship over the nations, still in their childhood, till such time as they might be ripe for a fuller appropriation of the evangelical principle, and the use of a manly independent freedom." But it is of the nature of the law to create dissatisfaction, and a craving for reconciliation with the lawgiver.

> Thus the Jewish dispensation looked always toward the gospel; and in like manner the discipline of the Roman Church involved an inward struggle, that became satisfied at last only in the evangelical emancipation of Protestantism.[25]

So seen,

> the Reformation is the legitimate offspring, the greatest act of the Catholic Church; and on this account of true catholic nature itself, in its genuine conception: whereas the Church of Rome, instead of following the divine conduct of history, has continued to stick in the old law of commandments, the garb of childhood, like the Jewish hierarchy in the time of Christ, and thus by its fixation as Romanism has parted with the character of catholicity in exchange for that of particularity.[26]

Schaf's theory of development, in contrast to Newman's, could interpret the Reformation as a valid development of catholicism. The Reformers themselves, Schaf pointed out, so conceived it. They never conceded the name "Catholic" to their opponents, nor did their followers until the second half of the seventeenth century. The Reformers were and understood themselves to be Catholics, holding faith and organic continuity with the ancient and medieval Catholic Church. The "papists," or "Romanists," by contrast, had ceased to be catholic, and with the Council of Trent became formally particularistic and heretical. This did not mean that catholicism was extinguished within the modern Roman church. Schaf quoted St. Martin with approval on the point:

[25] *Ibid.*, p. 48. Cf. thesis 33.
[26] *Ibid.*, pp. 49–50.

"Le catholicisme est la force du papisme, mais le papisme est la faiblesse du catholicisme." [27]

As soon as Schaf moved on to the later course of Protestantism, however, he put aside the high-church scheme of progressive expansion of the Christian tradition in favor of a pattern which admitted significant reversals of direction. When Schaf had studied at Tübingen, F. C. Baur was making his great attempt to see Christian history in terms of the Hegelian dialectic. Schaf had evidently learned from Baur, even though he disagreed sharply with Baur's theological and critical radicalism.

In Baur's scheme of church history the Reformation marked the great crisis, whose correct understanding was the key to the meaning of the whole. The whole history of Christianity fell into two great epochs on either side of this watershed, and neither could be understood properly apart from the other. Christianity was the religion of the unity of God and man in the person of Christ. The ancient church was driven to actualize this unity in dogma; the medieval church proceeded to externalize it in hierarchy and institutional fabric. The whole momentum of Christianity through these two phases was toward the objectification of the "Idea" of Christianity, but with the Reformation this lower stage of Christian consciousness was transcended. It was now comprehended that the principle of Christianity could not be adequately objectified in concrete history, but must remain in tension with it. The Reformation and Protestantism thus signified "the principle of subjective freedom, of the liberty of faith and of conscience, of subjective autonomy, in contrast to all the heteronomy of the catholic conception of the church." [28] The individual and the state alike were now emancipated from clerical control. At first the protest was primarily against the usurpations of the papal hierarchy, but then the authority of dogma also was involved in the process of dissolution, and in Baur's own hands the Bible itself.

[27] "Katholizismus und Protestantismus," *Literarische Zeitung*, December 16, 1843.

[28] F. C. Baur, *Epochen der Kirchlichen Geschichtsschreibung*, p. 257.

When Schaf surveyed the state of modern Protestantism he found much justification for Baur's themes of autonomy and subjectivity. We even find him reading the Reformation in these terms, apparently without sensing a significant incompatibility with his conception of its catholic character.

With the reformation of the 16th century, the main stream of the Church took a direction wholly opposite to that which it had before. Thus far, the history of Christianity had been a development of the principle of objectivity, authority, obedience, Jewish Christian legalism. This was carried so far, that the power of the church became at last an unsupportable bondage. Then the spirit of personal freedom, trained by such discipline to ripe self-possession, rose in revolt, and struck into quite another way. With this begins the evolution of the principle of subjectivity, the Gentile Christian element, evangelical liberty and independence. At the first, this movement carries along with it still the force of the old church life, as derived from the Middle Ages; but in proportion as it recedes from where it started, it is found to lose more and more its objective church character. . . . Thus for the papacy of the one bishop of Rome, is substituted the papacy of endless sect-systems and sect heads. No wonder then, that the historical stream should even now be turning from this pseudo-protestant extreme, towards a higher form of true church life in the opposite direction.[29]

In Schaf's description of Protestant development three or four kindred manifestations of this subjectivist current were noted. In Germany and Lutheranism the tendency showed itself on the theoretical side, as theological *rationalism*. In the Reformed tradition of the English-speaking world the center of interest has been practical and organizational. Here subjectivism meant ecclesiastical fragmentation, *sectarianism*. But the two, Schaf points out, are internally related: rationalism is theoretical sectarianism, sectarianism is practical rationalism. Also on the practical side is the third subjectivist tendency, to *political revolution*. *Cultural responsibility*, finally, Protestantism has largely abdicated, consenting to the secularization of modern civilization. Protestant history as a whole, as dominated by these "diseases," is a malfor-

[29] *What Is Church History?* pp. 94–95.

mation. It has been a story of regression into "unchurchly subjectivism."

The first step toward rationalism, in Schaf's view, did not appear for more than a century after the Reformation began. It was then implicit in the pietist reaction against scholastic orthodoxy. Schaf regarded the intellectualization of religion in orthodoxy as a degeneration, but did not follow the logic of his own argument and admit it as in itself a step toward rationalism. It was rather the anti-intellectualism of pietism, he argued, which undermined the authority of the confessions, and thereby the sense of the authority of the historical church, and then the biblical writings themselves. Semler illustrates the transition from pietism to biblical criticism and neology. By the beginning of the nineteenth century rationalism had in Germany "almost universal possession of the pulpit and the professors' chair . . . the general superintendents and counsellors of consistory." [30]

The deistic rationalism of the eighteenth-century tradition, to be sure, was relatively harmless in comparison to the new atheistic and pantheistic movement of left-wing Hegelianism. Strauss dissolved the gospel account into myths thrown up by the pious imagination of the early church, and Feuerbach pushed the tendency to the point of making all religion an illusory projection of man's fears and aspirations. Here, Schaf argued, was the most dangerous intellectual enemy of genuine Protestantism, not, as most of his American readers supposed, the Catholicism of Rome.

> Must not all serious believing Protestants feel themselves more closely related in spirit to a Bellarmine or a Moehler, who agree with them in acknowledging the trinity, the deity of Christ, atonement by his blood, and the divine inspiration and infallibility of the scriptures, than they are to Strauss and Bruno Baur, by whom all these articles are rejected? [31]

In contrast to the strategy of men like Berg and Brownlee, Schaf urged

[30] *Principle of Protestantism,* pp. 99, 100.
[31] *Ibid.,* p. 103.

. . . let us never forget the much that we hold in common with the Roman Church, the bond of union by which she is joined with us in opposition to absolute unbelief. . . . Let us first with united strength expel the devil from our own temple, into which he has stolen under the passport of our excessive toleration, before we proceed to exorcise and cleanse the dome of St. Peter. At least, let this be our main business.[32]

Schaf sensed that most of his American readers would feel little concern about this new and alien infidelity. They would be confirmed by his account in what they had long suspected of German Lutheran philosophy and theology, but they would find it hard to believe that rationalism could rival in America the threat from a militant and expanding Roman Catholicism. In Schaf's judgment, America's relative immunity from philosophical infidelity was due primarily to the low estate of American intellectual life. As the nation matured, and especially as it came out of its cultural isolation, it would be exposed to all these European currents. And there were traces already, not merely in the Unitarian heresies, but among "many respectable divines" who thought themselves orthodox, of German rationalism. Schaf had evidently been shocked also at the rationalist elements he had found in the liturgies and hymnals of the German American churches. "A cold abstract intellection to which all that is mystical or supernatural in Christianity is found displeasing" [33] was in fact far from insignificant in the orthodox American churches.

If rationalism has been the characteristic vice or disease of Lutheranism, the second disease, sectarianism, is rather typical of the Reformed tradition in England and America. As with theological subjectivism, Schaf found the beginning, not in the Reformation century, but in the seventeenth century. Pietism had been the first important manifestation of the disease that resulted in rationalism. Puritanism seemed to Schaf an early manifestation of sectarianism. Luther, Calvin, and Elizabeth of England had opposed separatism and sectarianism with all energy.

[32] *Ibid.*, p. 105.
[33] *Ibid.*, pp. 105–6.

"Nothing could have been further from their intention . . . than to throw open the door for the system of sects. . . . Their object . . . was not to emancipate the individual to uncontrolled freedom, but to bend him to the definite objective authority of God's truth and grace." Far from being "the last necessary consequence and unavoidable fruit"[34] of the Reformation, the sect system was "a prostitution and caricature of true Protestantism," a bastard or "pseudo-Protestantism."

Schaf's diagnosis of the pathology of sectarianism deserves careful reading not only for its significance in his general historical conception, but also because it represented his assessment of the challenge he faced in America. At times Schaf seems to resemble many other European visitors to America who immortalize their first few weeks of cultural shock by writing deep cultural critiques. One feels a certain sympathy with Hodge, who found in this section the greatest concentration of erroneous fact and principle in the whole tract. To many Americans it must have sounded impertinent. But one may suspect that Nevin encouraged him in this unfavorable analysis of the sectarian propensities of the main stream of American religion, Puritanism.

Schaf had three major faults to find with sectarianism, all of which had their beginnings in Puritanism. Puritanism had been spiritualistic, unhistorical, and unchurchly. As the dominant religious tradition in America, Puritanism had also contributed these traits to the American religious character.

Spiritualism, first of all, is an exaggerated hostility to form in religion. Even in the Reformation itself the French and Scottish Reformed had reacted too violently against various harmless traditions in worship, but Puritanism went further. Schaf conceded that Jacobean Anglicanism had degenerated "into mere external formalism" so that "there was reason" in the Puritan "war against the tyranny of false forms." But Puritanism had gone on to attack form in every shape and had sacrificed "many beautiful customs by which religious ideas were sweetly interwoven with common life, and outward opportunity continually supplied for

[34] *Ibid.*, pp. 120, 118.

the favorable application of truth to the heart. . . . All this it is much more difficult to recover than to cast away." Schaf pointed out that forms provided some security through the periods of religious collapse, against which in themselves there was no protection, so that afterward when life returned it could find "its established church channels by which to flow forth among the people." Puritanism, by contrast, both in England and America, had collapsed without remedy in large sections under rationalist pressure into out-and-out Unitarianism. And the formalism into which the Quaker protest against form had congealed was "an involuntary argument for the necessity of outward embodiment." [35]

On this issue of form Schaf generally preferred the Lutheran to the Reformed attitude. He referred to the iconoclasm of the Seventh Ecumenical Council of 754 as "fanatical," and accepted the position of the Council of 787. He commended the Anglo-Catholic interest in church art and in "beautifying sanctuaries and altars" as the "natural expression of childlike love." By such action Protestantism might hold some who would otherwise leave "through dissatisfaction with the usual nakedness and barrenness of its worship." [36] Schaf approved the liturgical movement widespread in the Prussian church, concerned to eliminate the "watery" revisions of the rationalist era and to restore the ancient liturgies and chorales.[37] In the spring in which the *Principle of Protestantism* was published, Schaf insisted on an official observance of Good Friday at Mercersburg, the first such occasion there. In theory the German Reformed had maintained the church year in America, but in practice it was largely ignored.[38] Schaf was distressed that pulpit gowns and bands had been so generally abandoned in America. For all this kind of emphasis, even before the days of controversy over the liturgy, Schaf was severely criticized by many. It was a great triumph for Mercersburg when someone

[35] *Ibid.*, pp. 112–13, 84.
[36] *Ibid.*, p. 123–24.
[37] *Ibid.*, p. 148, Cf. thesis 64.
[38] T. Appel, *Recollections of College Life at Marshall College* (Reading, 1886), pp. 165 ff.

turned up an old picture of the colonial pioneer of the Reformed, Michael Schlatter, wearing gown and bands. Berg thereupon retired with as much dignity as he could, from the position that such attire was the rags of popery, to the view that it was in the category of the *adiaphora.*

Closely related to spiritualistic hostility to form was the second sectarian trait of Puritanism, its lack of respect for history. In contrast to the continuity with the genuinely catholic elements of the medieval church in the Reformation, Puritanism "would restore pure, primitive Christianity, with entire disregard to the many centuries of development that lie between, as though all had been labor in vain, and the Lord had not kept his promise to be with the Church always to the end of the world." [39] Lutheranism here also had kept more respect for tradition, was more conservative of what was old. The Puritan violence and contempt for history, on the other hand, furnished occasion, in part at least, for the multiplication of sects. In Germany Schaf belonged to the United Church, Lutheran and Reformed, and he still stood on this ground in America.[40] In its conservative attitude to history and its attitude to external forms, especially in worship, he preferred the Lutheran tradition. In this connection the Mercersburg movement was to signify an approximation of the Reformed type to the Lutheran in worship and ceremonies.

The third weakness of Puritanism, beside its spiritualism and unhistorical bent, was its unchurchly character. The church is both the medium through which the faith is brought to the believer, and the society in which he is to live out that faith. But Puritanism concentrated on the conversion of individual souls to the point of neglecting both these truths. Few in America seemed to have comprehended the depth and glory of the communion of the church as the Body of Christ. Rather "the principle of Congregationalism . . . leads legitimately to full Atomism." Schaf granted that in the colonial period Congregationalism sought to secure "a subordination of the individual to the general" by

[39] *Principle of Protestantism,* pp. 113.
[40] *Prinzip des Protestantismus* (Chambersburg, 1845), Vorrede.

means of the state. With the separation of church and state, however, there was nothing left to hold the system together. "It includes no limitation for the principle of sect." [41]

Such were the three weaknesses of the central Puritan stream of American Christianity which rendered it vulnerable to the sectarian tendency. External circumstances increased the pressures in this direction. The European migration brought great religious variety and rebels from European constraints in religion. With American independence came the general acceptance of the separation of church and state, removing all external pressures from the civil magistrate such as still existed in Germany and England. Everything seemed to conspire to produce in America an unrivaled proliferation of sects, gaining from year to year.

"Every theological vagabond and pedler" may here persuade himself that "he is called to be a reformer" and proceed, "in his spiritual vanity and pride, to a revolutionary rupture with the historical life of the Church, to which he holds himself immeasurably superior." In Rupp's *History of the Religious Denominations* of 1844, Schaf read descriptions of "not less than forty-one protestant sects," and yet the list was by no means complete.[42]

Schaf's main criterion of the legitimacy of a Protestant church in America, as Tayler Lewis pointed out, seemed to be the transplantation of a European state church. The one ground of separation from a previously existing institution which he justified was the Reformation plea—the necessity "to preach the pure word of God with freedom, and to administer the sacraments according to Christ's appointment." For this cause the Reformers had been forced out of the Roman church organization and had established the various national churches. In none of these, whatever other weaknesses or errors there may have been, was the freedom denied to preach the Word or administer the sacraments correctly. None of the bases of separation alleged from within the Puritan movement, consequently, would be adequate. Schaf thus listed as legitimate churches the Lutheran, Reformed, Presbyterian, and

[41] *Principle of Protestantism,* p. 115.
[42] *Ibid.*, p. 116.

Episcopal bodies. He pointedly did not include in his list the Congregationalists, whose influence in America he accounted the greatest of all; or the Baptists, the most numerous of all; or the Quakers.[43]

One surprising exception in this classification of churches and sects was the Methodists, who were treated by Schaf as legitimate beside the national churches. Schaf admired Whitefield and the Wesleys, who in contrast to the Puritans, "never laid aside their respect for the mother Church, but notwithstanding its degeneracy labored in its communion and died within its bosom." The Methodist movement, to be sure, pressed on to a divorce which was "unnatural and wrong," yet Schaf would still account it an orthodox body.[44]

This classification of churches and sects must have been rather startling in some respects to Schaf's hearers. Nevin, for example, had hitherto appealed to classical Congregational divines, such as Owen, Howe, Flavel, and Edwards, as much as to Presbyterians. The fault of the most recent Congregational divinity taught at New Haven, according to him, was precisely its approximation to Methodist synergism. The great cause which the Triennial Convention should strengthen, in Nevin's mind, was the cause of divine sovereignty against Arminianism, whether Methodist, United Brethren, Albright, Church of God, whether expounded by Charles Finney or Nathaniel Taylor. Nevin had suspected Congregationalism in so far as it leaned toward Methodism. Schaf, in contrast, gave virtually a clean bill to Methodism, but attacked Congregationalism for being unchurchly, spiritualistic, and lacking respect for tradition.

It is hard to avoid the suspicion that part of the explanation of the divergence here lay in the realm of political ethics. Schaf had forborne an exposition of the third manifestation of Protestant subjectivity, its tendency to political revolution, doubtless realizing that his Prussian monarchist views would find little sympathy in America. For him, however, there would have been a world of

[43] *Ibid.*, pp. 119, 117.
[44] *Ibid.*, pp. 113, 117.

difference between the loyal Tory John Wesley and the representative Congregationalist Cromwell, "who overturned in such stormful style the ecclesiastical creations of an older time and even stained himself with the blood of a king and an archbishop."[45] For Schaf Congregationalism would be the type case of pseudo-Protestant insubordination and revolution.

Even among the legitimate Protestant churches, in any case, Schaf observed a painful weakening of the church spirit. They stood "for the most part in such hostile relation to one another," and showed "so little inclination or impulse towards an inward and outward union in the Lord that one might weep to think of it." The religious press in particular—and Schaf may have been thinking of such samples as Kurtz's *Lutheran Observer* or the *Christian Intelligencer* of the Dutch church—seemed in their mutual attitudes predominantly hostile, contentious, malicious. The denominations in America habitually disparaged each other and declined to subordinate or even postpone their selfish advantage for the sake of a great common object. "To the man who has any right idea of the Church as the communion of saints, this state of things must be a source of deep distress."[46] Even orthodox Protestantism seemed to have largely lost the biblical and Reformation concern for church unity.

In all these tendencies to subjectivism or autonomy, however, Schaf's theory of development recognized some limited justification. Protestant rationalism, for example, while theologically deficient, had made enduring contributions to biblical study and church history. It had pruned traditional views of unjustified exaggerations, fanciful elaborations, illegitimate claims.[47] The sects, similarly, are not to be accounted pure error. "On the contrary, we suppose them to play an indispensable part in modifying and determining the development of the orthodox church itself."[48] Sectarianism and rationalism are justified in so far as the main body of the church has become diseased. Sects had often

[45] *Ibid.*, p. 113.
[46] *Ibid.*, p. 117.
[47] *Ibid.*, p. 132.
[48] *What Is Church History?* p. 82.

protested against real faults, such as dead formalism, evangelistic faithlessness, the failure of Christian nurture, and had recalled the church to its vocation in these respects.[49] But having so served the church, the sect had no justification for its further existence, and unless it could return to the church, it would remain petrified in the forms of its obsolete and irrelevant protest. The church is the historical bearer of Christian life and truth in its totality and in the long run, but at any given moment it may fail in its witness and need correction, even from a heretic or sectarian. They, too, had work to do for God in his providential economy and guidance of his church.

Schaf found some traits of enduring worth in the Puritan type. "The deep moral earnestness, the stern self-discipline, the unbending force of character, exhibited in Puritanism," he wrote, "must fill the unprejudiced historian with high admiration." Puritanism had contributed these qualities to American religious life, also its Sabbatarianism and biblicism. Unlike many Continentals, Schaf admired even these last aspects. Altogether he felt that American religious life compared favorably with that of the countries of the Old World. It had rescued thousands of immigrants who might have died in unbelief had they remained in their homelands under less vigilant church care. "Puritanism has a zeal for God," Schaf concluded, "but not according to knowledge." [50]

In still a fourth respect, Schaf found Protestantism an antithesis to the catholic tradition—the relation of the faith to society and culture, the theme of Richard Niebuhr's *Christ and Culture*. Schaf would have vigorously championed the position of "Christ transforming culture," although perhaps one might raise some questions as to whether in practice it would not have meant instead the "Christ of culture." In any case he had no respect for the asceticism of "Christ against culture" as found in the flight from the world of monasticism or some pietism. This was "contrary to the spirit and power of the gospel." Christianity means

[49] *Principle of Protestantism,* p. 134.
[50] *Ibid.,* pp. 112, 114.

rather the renovation of the world; there is no sphere of natural life which may not be glorified. It is a demonstration of the "catholicity" of the church that it aspires to convert the totality of life. Specifically Schaf considered four spheres: politics, intellectual life, art, and the social and economic order. "The Church," he postulated, "cannot be said to have completed its career, till the whole world shall appear transfigured with its divine spirit, and states, and sciences, and arts, with all their glory, shall fall down before the altar of the Most High in full, free worship." [51]

From this perspective Schaf paid homage to the religiously integrated culture of the Middle Ages. All aspects of the life of medieval society, he affirmed, were explicitly related to the faith and church. It was just this which "renders the Middle Ages so grand and venerable." All the arts, sciences, and philosophy were handmaids to theology and the church. Princes bowed to the pope and at his bidding warriors gathered from all over Europe to crusade to Jerusalem. The thought of liturgical music, the poetry of Dante, and the cathedrals raised Schaf to romantic eloquence. Their builders, he informs us, "were so occupied only with the honor of God in their work, that with a divine carelessness they have left even their own names to perish in oblivion." In all this Schaf mirrored the medievalist enthusiasm of the German romantics—of Goethe, Tieck, Novalis, the Schlegels; of Moser, Leo, and von Mueller. The general American ignorance and complacent contempt of the "Dark Ages" stirred him to indignant sarcasm and comparisons with American cultural achievements.[52] Protestants should not resign to Rome their interest in this legacy, especially since the richest charm of the period was the slow gestation over centuries of the coming Reformation.

There was, to be sure, a radical fault in the manner of Chris-

[51] *Ibid.*, pp. 135, 137. Cf. Nevin, "Catholicism," *Mercersburg Review*, 1851, p. 17. The penetration of American civilization by Christianity, "of the art and literature of the country, its commerce and science and philosophy as well as its politics," would be a greater advance toward the final redemption than the conversion in "the religious sphere" only of all India and China.

[52] *Ibid.*, pp. 137–39.

tianizing culture in the Middle Ages. The world was "overwhelmed" rather than "assimilated." "The papacy in the Middle Ages conducted itself tyrannically toward the State, and trampled on the rights of the nations"; it had constrained science, inquiry, and the arts arbitrarily. When these several forms of activity came to their maturity, the church refused to recognize the change or to put away the rod at the proper time. "The world then revenged itself on a large scale, by breaking away from the Church entirely, and entering upon a new course of development for itself. This took place with the Reformation." [53]

The significance of the Reformation, in this whole perspective, was then that of retreat from Christian cultural responsibility, of a major turn in the direction of the secularization of the west. The whole development from the Middle Ages displayed Protestantism at some disadvantage. Its cultural role, as Schaf saw it, was merely negative, that of assisting the emancipation of society from the church. Modern Roman Catholicism, by contrast, had continued to exercise "a much greater power than Protestantism over the consciences and spirits of those who stand in her communion." [54]

Since the sixteenth century, to be sure, the progress of the arts and sciences had been freer and richer on Protestant soil, but all this has been largely emancipated from the church. The only great modern art which he considered distinctively Christian was the religious music of the sixteenth and seventeenth centuries. The great modern composers, while they used Christian materials, were scarcely to be counted Christian artists. So it was with the poets; Milton and Klopstock [in one breath!] were pious, but tedious second-raters; while Goethe, Schiller, and Byron were not Christian. Modern church architecture had no relation to the "true idea" (read "Gothic") of a Christian house of worship. Schaf saw some promise in the contemporary Düsseldorf school of painters, but as with the Renaissance painters, his criterion of Christian meaning reached no deeper than nominal subject mat-

[53] *Ibid.*, p. 141.
[54] *Ibid.*, p. 140.

ter. The chain of modern philosophers in Protestant countries, from Leibnitz down, he noted, was vastly more profound and varied than the continuing Roman Catholic scholastic tradition, but who could call the leading figures "Christians," as one should do with the medieval scholastics?

Schaf wrote more fully and enthusiastically on these aspects of "higher culture" then he did in the more external political and socioeconomic realms. In this emphasis he reflected his German training. When he thought of the bearing of religion on politics, the image in his mind was obviously that of the paternalistic Christian monarchy of Prussia. Despite his Swiss roots, Schaf's references to republicanism, American or otherwise, were usually rather backhanded. He could not accord to the American separation of church and state more than a provisional and temporary acceptance.

In the socioeconomic sphere, similarly, he did not really come to terms with modern industrial society. He had grown up in economically retarded Germany and moved to an isolated American village. In neither was he stimulated to develop his idealist social ethics as a Maurice was doing in London, a Theodore Parker in Boston, or a Caleb Henry in New York. In such a setting Schaf's basic orientation might have contributed substantially to the American social gospel. His very postulation that a social transformation was desirable contrasted with the prevailing American view as Nevin had previously argued it.

That American view, as Schaf discerned, was not that of "Christ against culture" but rather that of a compartmentalizing of life's interests. "The idea seemed to be that a man's piety is deposited in one corner of his spirit, his politics in another, and his learning in a third. All good and necessary in their place, but having nothing whatever to do with one another." [55] Church and state were to remain segregated, worship and art, theology and the intellectual life of the country. The correctness of Schaf's analysis here is in part documented by the fact that the bulk of his readers evidently did not grasp what he was talking about.

[55] *Ibid.*, p. 136.

The one recognition which should be accorded to Protestantism in this connection, in Schaf's opinion, was that secularizing state and culture more completely had opened the possibility for a free and voluntary future conversion to Christianity. Such a reconciliation would be more rich and profound than the clerical control of medieval culture. In this sense Protestantism had been "only an apparent regression." Indeed Schaf at least hints that modern culture, apparently secularized as it is, is still "carried throughout on the shoulders of Christianity, draws from this constantly its most substantial life" and in this hidden contribution Protestantism is more important than Roman Catholicism.[56]

In any case, the whole historical development is brought under the same rubrics as the history of the doctrine and organization of modern Protestantism, of "objectivity" and "subjectivity."

> The better tendency of the time is indeed toward *objectivity;* not towards that of the Middle Ages, however, that could be upheld only by violently crushing, or wilfully restraining, the rights of the individual subject; but it seeks the objective rather in a higher form, *in which it shall be enriched and spiritualized by all that has been gained on the part of the subjective, the good fruits of the development of Protestantism through a period of three hundred years.*[57]

With modern Protestantism, thus, the extent and variety of subjectivist tendencies, practical and theoretical, gave evidence of serious trouble. Subjectivity or autonomy was manifest in the secularization of culture, in the rationalist disintegration of orthodox doctrine, in the sectarian and schismatic fragmentation of the corporate body of the church, in the revolutionary rage for political liberty. Yet the case was not hopeless. "There is still sufficient salt in the system, with all its diseases, to save it from corruption, full as much certainly as belonged to the Catholic Church toward the close of the Middle Ages; material enough therefore, for a new Reformation." [58]

[56] *Ibid.*, pp. 145–46; theses 98, 99.
[57] *Ibid.*, p. 146.
[58] *Ibid.*, p. 98.

With his "new Reformation" Schaf gave Baur's dialectical scheme a radically different outcome. The Hegelian dialectic is notoriously unstable; with Hegel and his disciples it was used alternatively for the most revolutionary and the most conservative of purposes, as either an ideology or a utopia. Baur had been a "left-wing Hegelian," standing on the antithesis. Schaf utilized much of his historical analysis but changed the whole intention by looking forward to a new synthesis, that of "evangelical catholicism."

There is an unexplained gap in Schaf's argument. He never tells us just how the two parts of his work fit together. What, for instance, is "the Protestant principle" of the title? Part I sets it forth in conventional fashion as the Bible and justification by grace in their interrelationship. Part II, however, makes it clear that this principle is inadequate for the modern situation and proposes an alternative. The appeal to the Bible alone provides no defense against disintegration into sectarianism. Reverence for tradition and devotion to the church—"with due subordination always to the written word" [59]—these are the objective and heteronomous authorities within which alone evangelical freedom can be safely fulfilled and restrained.

The "Protestant principle," we are told in Part II, "is the principle of movement, of progress in the history of the Church, progress not such as may go beyond the Bible and Christianity, but such as consists in an ever-extending knowledge of the Bible itself, and an ever-deepening appropriation of Christianity as the power of a divine life which is destined to make all things new." The principle of Protestantism, if we may compress the formula, is the principle of a growing, corporate, biblical tradition. Although some Protestants [60] agreed with Roman Catholics and Puseyites in a static orthodoxy, Schaf took it to be the distinctive Protestant insight to realize that we are not *fertig*, our church form is not yet perfect.[61] Catholicism regards the church as a

[59] *Ibid.*, p. 120.

[60] *Ibid.*, pp. 160, 130. (Princeton and Seceder Presbyterians, Old Lutherans.)

[61] "Katholizismus und Protestantismus," *Literarische Zeitung*, December 16, 1843.

given, complete, and perpetual structure. It "looks backwards; we look forwards. . . . We move toward Jerusalem, the new, the heavenly, the eternal." [62]

For Schaf, moreover, this eschatological note was urgent and decisive. In the English-speaking world, at least, it would be hard to equal the intensity of Schaf's expectancy with regard to the ecumenical church. Only F. D. Maurice comes to mind as sharing the prophetic conviction that all about him the sects were breaking up and that the one catholic church was manifesting itself ever more distinctly. Schaf confessed himself as in the tradition of Joachim of Fiore, the prophet of the Third Age. A new and greater Reformation was impending, and its signs were already in the heavens to be read by the weatherwise. No note in the *Principle of Protestantism* was more distinctive than this eschatological one. Referred to repeatedly, it was sounded in full and eloquent tones at both the beginning (in the German edition) and the end of the book. Schaf's enthusiasm contrasts with Nevin's guarded caution on this theme.

Schaf closed his work by borrowing from Schelling's *Philosophy of Revelation* the picture of the three ages of the church: Petrine legalism and authority, Pauline grace and freedom, and finally the synthesis of these two in Johannine love, of freedom in law, in the age now opening. Schaf did not hesitate to prophesy the festival of reconciliation for the nineteenth century and for the American people.[63]

This would mean reconciliation not merely of the various Protestant churches, but of Protestantism generally with Roman Catholicism. For Schaf Eastern Orthodoxy scarcely entered the picture: it was but a fossil without life. But of Rome he believed confidently that "even for this Church, which once thrust out our fathers with terrible ban from its bosom, the Lord has still great things in store. Why should we despair of another reformation? . . . This is wished and hoped for, by many even of its own best members." Neither Protestantism nor Roman Catholicism could

[62] *Principle of Protestantism*, p. 128.
[63] *Ibid.*, p. 176.

be consummated apart from the other. "The consummation of both will be at the same time their union." [64]

Such a union would be realized concurrently with the new and deeper conversion of society and culture to Christ which Schaf also prophesied. For Schaf conceived the world to be standing on the edge of the reversal of the trend to secularization which he had traced historically. "The day must come," he affirmed, when all the realms of culture must feel the need of reconciliation with the Church and would voluntarily return to the Lord. The new synthesis would be more internalized and profound than that of medieval Christendom.

> For the end or scope of all history is this, that the world may resolve itself into the Kingdom of God, reason into revelation, morality into religion, and earth into heaven. All sciences must be raised and refined into theosophy, all government into theocracy, all art into divine worship, and the whole of life into a joyful proclamation of the glory of God.[65]

> Away with human denominations! Down with religious sects! Let our watchword be: One Spirit and one body! One Shepherd and one flock! All conventicles and chapels must perish, that from their ashes may arise the One Church of God, phoenix-like and resplendent with glory, as a bride adorned for her bridegroom.[66]

Indeed this

> revivification of the spirit of John the Evangelist in the Church will open the way directly for His second coming, to establish the Church absolute and triumphant.[67]

With a proleptic celebration of the final consummation, Schaf declared:

> Yes, Christ and his body, the Church, are to be born again among us; . . . The stars have already risen in the East which will guide the wise men to the place of the holy nativity. . . . When the dawn breaks forth and the larks on high voice their song, then the dark spirits of the night which have held us captive will vanish, the

[64] *Ibid.*, pp. 173–74.
[65] *Ibid.*, pp. 145–46; cf. theses 9, 10, 57, 58.
[66] *Ibid.*, p. 121.
[67] *Ibid.*, p. 175.

sleepers will awake and greet the never ending day as one family joined in eternity.[68]

Thus Schaf rounded out his scheme of the development of the Christian church. Precisely what was the synthesis foreseen in these ecumenical prophecies? Just what was this *media via?* It was scarcely a synthesis of Reformation Protestantism and Roman Catholicism, as Schaf seemed to be saying. For the subjectivist errors of modern Protestantism were not those of the Reformation itself. As Schaf himself had pointed out, the Reformers explicitly and vigorously opposed all tendencies to the three chief forms of later subjectivism, doctrinal rationalism, sectarianism, and political radicalism.[69] All these "diseases" were caricatures of genuine or Reformation Protestantism, and Schaf was confident that the Reformers would have opposed them in their nineteenth-century form more sharply than they would have opposed Roman Catholicism. It had not been the Reformation, either, which had furthered the secularization of culture. On Schaf's own showing, and despite Baur's scheme, the Reformers were, in principle, objective, heteronomous, churchly, sacramental, historical, orthodox, catholic. The synthesis Schaf was urging, consequently, seemed rather to be a synthesis of pseudo-Protestant autonomy and of arbitrary Roman Catholic heteronomy, and in fact to be very close to the original intention of the Reformers. Thus, as a program for the German Reformed Church it was less radical than it sounded. To recover the full catholic dimensions of the Reformation would still leave some serious issues with Rome. Yet it is not wholly clear whether in Schaf's mind his new formulation may not have gone beyond the Reformation principle and perhaps been intended as an olive branch to Roman Catholics and Puseyites (who, after their fashion, also reverenced tradition and the church). Since Schaf never explicitly corrected Baur's misleading interpretation of the Reformation, there are some unresolved contradictions in his exposition.

On the whole, however, Schaf had opened to American Protes-

[68] Schaf, *Prinzip des Protestantismus,* inside cover.
[69] Schaf, *Principle of Protestantism,* p. 120.

tants vast historical perspectives, by which they might learn to know themselves better and understand better their relations to other Christians. He was recovering for Americans their own legacy from the Middle Ages and the Reformation, a legacy which they had neither understood nor valued. All this was calculated to break down isolation and provincialism and to further ecumenical understanding between Americans and Europeans, Protestant and Roman Catholic alike. The principle of historical development, with all its ambiguities, was cast as a bridge of understanding across otherwise unbridgeable chasms to other forms of Christianity.

6/ The Second Adam and the New Humanity

The Mercersburg men produced no formal systematics, at least not until Gerhart's *Institutes of the Christian Religion* [1] of 1891, which does not qualify in all respects for this role. Nevin's theology lectures, like Dick's textbook,[2] followed the order of topics of the Westminster Confession. He spent most of his time in class arguing with his text, but he never reorganized his theological views around the themes which he held fundamental. Just at the time when one might have expected him to pull his theology together systematically, he suffered a "nervous breakdown." His theology (had it been worked into a system) would probably have stood closest to the speculative Christological theologies, such as those of Dorner, Liebner, and Martensen or, in some respects, to the views of Moehler and Wilberforce.

The organizing principle of Nevin's theology is unmistakably the Incarnation. The whole gospel, he held, is comprehended in the phrase "the word became flesh." [3] He and Schaf characterized their distinctive orientation as Christocentric or Christological. As such it contrasted sharply with the two major American theological camps of the day—the scholastic confessionalism of Princeton and the old-school Presbyterians, and the New England theology in its various nuances at Andover, Yale, and Union. The characteristic themes of these rival schools—human depravity and inability, election and reprobation, imputation, the atonement, regeneration—had become stale and worn-out, at least as conventionally treated. Nevin was convinced that this whole habit of thought was "doomed to pass away." Even in New Eng-

[1] E. V. Gerhart, *Institutes of the Christian Religion* (2 vols.; New York, 1891, 1894).

[2] J. Dick, *Lectures on Theology* (American ed.; 2 vols.; Philadelphia, 1838).

[3] J. W. Nevin, *The Mystical Presence* (Philadelphia, 1846), p. 199.

land he thought he saw evidences of a new beginning. "On all sides," it seemed to him, "the persuasion gains ground that the Christological Question, embracing the true idea of the Church and its relation to the Savior's living person, is in truth the great question of the age, and carries in itself a power by which all the interests of religion are to be moulded hereafter into new shape." [4] In some measure Nevin prophesied truly what was to happen in the following half-century of American theology, although his particular formulation of the Christological question was not to become the prevailing one. How did Nevin and Schaf define the Christological question? How did they relate it to the true idea of the Church? What were the implications for ecumenical undertakings?

The Mercersburg view of Christ and the church was defined in constant polemic contrast with the speculative predestinarianism of Princeton. Nevin himself had been trained in the latter version of "Calvinism," and from the time Hodge "lowered the visor" in 1847 [5] Nevin recognized in his former teacher his most formidable theological opponent.

Nevin's protest against a theology based on the eternal decrees was not a matter of sentimental humanitarianism, as was increasingly the case with American Presbyterians. This factor seemed to play a role, to be sure, in Schaf's speculations about "the middle state," with which Nevin came to sympathize; but Nevin's representative reproach against philosophical predestinarianism was that it was *abstract.* All things being decreed before time, the actual working-out of God's purposes was unreal. Hodge had no explanations for the crucial turns in the story. The imputation of Adam's guilt was quite arbitrary, and equally so was the application to this or that individual of the benefits of Christ's atoning death. No continuing connection between Christ and his church was recognized, or any real necessity for the church at all. All

[4] "Wilberforce on the Incarnation," *Mercersburg Review* (hereafter cited as *MR*), 1850, p. 169.

[5] In his review of Bushnell's *Christian Nurture,* in *Biblical Repertory and Princeton Review* (hereafter cited as *BRPR*), 1847, p. 538.

the crucial events in the process of redemption took place in the divine mind in eternity, outside the world, which was left to run on its own way mechanically save for occasional miraculous interventions. For Nevin, on the other hand, theology must stand within time and within historical and social relationships through which men are reached by God.

In the earliest writings of the Mercersburg professors (from *The Anxious Bench*, second edition, "Catholic Unity" and "Pseudo-Protestantism" to *What Is Church History?* and *The Mystical Presence*) the most characteristic formulation of the new view of Christ was based on Paul's teaching of the "Second Adam." "Adam was not simply *a* man, like others since born," it was said in the sermon to the triennial convention, "but he was *the* man, who comprehended in himself all that has since appeared in other men. Humanity as a whole resided in his person . . . the second Adam corresponds in all respects with the first. He is not a man merely, an individual belonging to the race; but he is *the* man, emphatically the *Son of Man*, comprising in his person the new creation, or humanity recovered and redeemed, as a whole. . . . Christ is the root of the Church."[6] The Incarnation seen thus is the key to the relation of creation and redemption and the basis of the understanding of the church. It is "the key that unlocks the sense of all God's revelations" and "all God's works," from the creation to the consummation of all things.[7]

The categories Nevin used to describe these social wholes were either those of a biological organism or the logical correlates of general and particular. Either analogy portrayed individuals as dependent upon, and conditioned by, the general nature in which they participate.

> Thus sin is not simply the offspring of a particular will, putting itself forth in the form of actual transgressions, but a wrong habit of humanity itself, a general and universal force. . . . the disease is organic, rooted in the race, and not to be overcome in any case by a force less deep and general than itself.

[6] Nevin, "Catholic Unity," in Schaf, *Principle of Protestantism* (Chambersburg, 1845), p. 200.

[7] *The Mystical Presence*, p. 199.

What is true thus of original sin is equally true of salvation. The restoration of man begins beyond the individual in human nature generally.

> Humanity, fallen in Adam, is made to undergo a resurrection in Christ, and so restored, flows over organically, as in the other case, to all in whom its life appears. . . . the particular subject lives, not properly speaking in the acts of his own will separately considered, but in the power of a vast generic life, that lies wholly beyond his own will, and has now begun to manifest itself through him, as the law and type of his will itself, as well as of his whole being.[8]

The whole of history is thus comprehended in the relation of these two social organisms, the humanity of Adam and the humanity of Christ.

Nevin used his biological metaphor to explain the imputation of Adam's guilt to his posterity. No longer was this a purely arbitrary "legal fiction" as in the Princeton theory. He quoted against Hodge the observation of the arch-heretic Albert Barnes that Calvin had grounded the imputation of guilt on a real identity, whereas Princeton made it purely arbitrary.[9] It would have been equally justifiable on Hodge's grounds, Nevin went on, to impute to the human race the guilt of the sin of the fallen angels, and thus to dispense with Adam altogether. In Nevin's view, on the other hand, guilt is imputed because the human race actually was in Adam. All men partake, not only of Adam's body, but also of his soul, "transmitted by ordinary generation" in one "identical organic life-stream."[10] This is not to say that the individual Adam is in any way blended with his posterity. It is in his generic character as progenitor of the race that his identity lives in them.

The parallel conception to explain the solidarity of the new humanity in Jesus Christ is that of the "mystical union," "the true and actual formation of Christ's life into the souls of His people."[11] The Christian is not in Christ by natural birth, of course,

[8] Nevin, *The Anxious Bench* (2d ed.; Chambersburg, 1845), pp. 124–25.

[9] *Weekly Messenger* (hereafter cited as *WM*), August 2, 1848. Cf. A. J. Stansbury, *Trial of the Rev. Albert Barnes* (New York, 1836), Appendix, pp. 65–78. Cf. also Nevin, *Antichrist*, p. 16.

[10] *The Mystical Presence*, p. 165.

[11] Nevin, "The New Creation in Christ," *MR*, 1850, p. 6.

but by a second birth, or a process of engrafting into a new stock. While contending that the resultant union is as real and deep-seated as a physiological union, Nevin maintains it takes place rather on the level of conscious personality. We are not conscious of our biological participation in Adam, but our life in Christ is the very basis of self-conscious existence. "It is only as he is consciously in communication with Christ as his life-center . . . that the believer can be regarded . . . as a new man in Christ Jesus." The Person of Christ is the *root* from which all Christian personality springs; He is "an all-present everywhere active personal life."[12] Only in union with this life is full free human personal life realized; yet it is a union of "substance" and "nature" rather than merely that consent and convergence of mind and will which we call a "moral union."

Mysterious and incomprehensible as it is, the mystical union draws together "all that is great and precious in the gospel." Nevin wrote:

> I have no hope save on the ground of a living union with the nature of Christ as the resurrection and the life. Both for my understanding and my heart, theology finds here all its interest and attraction. For no truth am I more willing to suffer contradictions and reproach if such be the will of God.[13]

Nevin wrote to Harbaugh two years later in a similar vein:

> How clear it is to my mind that the whole sense and power of Christianity turn at last on the fact of the Incarnation, as embodied with perennial life in the consciousness of the Church. Apart from this all doctrine is cold and all practice dead.[14]

The idea of the First and Second Adams is to be understood also in the sense of "recapitulation" as used by Irenaeus. The Incarnation is not a single isolated event in the Bethlehem cave, but "a series or chain of events, a living historical process."[15]

[12] *The Mystical Presence*, p. 169.

[13] *WM*, Oct. 8, 1845.

[14] Unpublished letter, May 18, 1847 (Library of The Historical Society of the Evangelical and Reformed Church, hereafter cited as Library of the German Reformed Church, Franklin and Marshall College).

[15] Nevin, "The Apostles' Creed," *MR*, 1849, p. 323.

Christ was subject to special temptation, like Adam, and had to settle the same question. He was subjected to several trials of choice between obedience to God and service of self. In the temptation immediately after this solemn consecration to his mediatorial work by baptism, He made full and prompt decision in favor of the will of God. His human nature subjected him to many trials which were completed and gathered up in His death. He obeyed the law in full and conquered.[16]

The Second Adam relived the life and crises of the first but made different decisions. In this sense the hypostatical union is a process, a reworking of the history of the race, so that the several steps of development in Christ's life are steps in the work of redemption.[17] In his earthly career,

the power of a divine life was always actively present, wrestling as it were with the law of death it was called to conquer, and sure of its proper victory at the last. That victory was displayed in the resurrection.[18]

When the Incarnation was conceived in this larger sense, it comprehended in itself a theory of atonement, the old Greek theory of "Christus victor." The Logos assumed humanity in order to combat the powers which held humanity subject, "death and the grave, as well as . . . the power of sin from which they come." [19]

The passion of the Son of God was the world's spiritual *crisis*, in which the principle of health came to its last struggle with the principle of disease, and burst forth from the very bosom of the grave itself in the form of immortality. This was the atonement, Christ's victory over sin and hell.[20]

Nevin's opponents, especially Berg and Hodge, recognized in this exposition something different from the familiar view of the cross as a substitutionary satisfaction. Berg accused him of deny-

[16] W. H. Erb, *Dr. Nevin's Theology* (Reading, Pa., 1913), p. 224.
[17] *The Mystical Presence*, p. 234 *, in reference to Kliefoth, *Theorie des Kultus*, section 188. Cf. Nevin, "Wilberforce on the Incarnation," *MR*, 1850, p. 172.
[18] *The Mystical Presence*, p. 223.
[19] "The Apostles' Creed," *MR*, 1849, p. 326.
[20] *The Mystical Presence*, pp. 166, 239.

ing justification. Nevil replied that this was sheer misunderstanding. "We are justified forensically, objectively, in the mind of God apart from all righteousness whatever previously our own, on the simple ground of Christ's merit." [21] Yet while Nevin maintains a forensic justification, he associated it with an infused grace. When God imputes righteousness, he taught, he also transmits it in that the sinner lays hold on Christ. Justification and sanctification, while not to be confounded, are inseparable.

> The new life lodges itself, as an efflux from Christ, in the inmost core of our personality. Here it becomes the principle or seed of our sanctification, which is simply the gradual transfusion of the same exalted spiritual quality or potence throughout our whole persons.[22]

When Hodge accused Nevin of denying propitiation by Christ's death, Nevin replied that, on the contrary, his argument was compatible with *any* version of the Atonement. He taught his students that "the atonement was not simply designed to make an impression on the world, as held by Grotius, but to make satisfaction for the justice of God." God was bound to punish the sinner, or his surrogate, "not because he delights in punishment, but because He is the absolute law and must require satisfaction." [23] As Tayler Lewis recognized, Nevin honestly held to the forensic emphasis of the Reformers. He could not be classed with the Swedenborgians, for whom the mere assumption of humanity by the Logos constituted redemption, nor with the Coleridgeans, who admitted only an atonement of moral influence.[24] Nevin was actually maintaining side by side two explanations of the Atonement which involve rather different presuppositions.

A related tension between these presuppositions came out at another point of Nevin's exposition, the question as to whether there would have been an incarnation even without a fall of the

[21] *WM*, August 11, 1847.
[22] *The Mystical Presence*, p. 168.
[23] W. H. Erb, *op. cit.*, p. 94.
[24] *New York Literary World*, April 7, 14, 1849.

first Adam. The contention that the Incarnation was continuous with the creation had been injected into modern theology chiefly by Hegel. Similar views, however, had been held by some of the Greek fathers, by Alexander of Hales and Duns Scotus, and by Osiander at the Reformation. The suggestion had been picked up from the Hegelians by more orthodox theologians and reinterpreted. Nevin and Schaf had probably derived it from Dorner, who united the patristic and idealistic interest in the idea.

The theme, which had been stated in *The Mystical Presence*, reappeared in a series of three review articles which Nevin contributed to the *Mercersburg Review* late in 1850 and early in 1851. The first dealt with two publications of R. C. Trench, who like his colleague at King's College, F. D. Maurice, was much under the influence of German idealism. "Oftentimes it would seem," Trench had written, "as if our theology of the present day" held too inadequate a grasp of man's creation, "beginning, as it so often does, from the fall, from the corruption of human nature, instead of beginning a step higher up with man's creation in God's image." Consequently, the Incarnation was usually seen merely as a device to make the atoning death possible "while some of the profoundest teachers of the past, so far from contemplating the Incarnation in this light, have rather affirmed that the Son of God would equally have taken man's nature, though of course under very different conditions, even if he had not fallen —that it lay in the everlasting purposes of God, quite irrespective of the fall." [25] Thus the Incarnation was the climax of the whole creative work in which the pyramid of created nature aimed at conscious spirit, and all history, heathen and Jewish, prophesied a reconciliation of God and man.

Nevin's second article was the result of his reading the first part of the *Christologie* of Dorner's friend Liebner, of Kiel—a volume that was to eventuate in a dogmatics that found its focus in Christology. Liebner hoped to define the hypostatic union in such a way as to escape the Lutheran tendency to Docetism and

[25] Cited by Nevin, "Trench's Lectures," *MR*, 1850, p. 618.

the Reformed to Ebionitism. Contending that the soteriological orientation of the Reformers was no longer sufficient, he urged that the God-manhood must be seen "independently even of sin and its removal." God's aim in the creation of man was man's full communion with himself, and however the race might fail in the exercise of its freedom, "there was security still in the *head*." Humanity was made with reference to Christ and completed only in him. "These two facts go to make up one whole self-revelation of God in the world." [26]

In *The Mystical Presence* Nevin had similarly stressed the continuity between the First and Second Adam.[27] He was less interested in the contrast (that as by one came death, so by the other life) than he was in the completion of the first by the second. "The Incarnation then is the proper completion of humanity. Christ is the true ideal Man . . . the humanity of Adam himself, only raised to a higher character." The idea of humanity from the beginning required an incarnation, even apart from sin and the fall. "The object of the Incarnation was to couple the human nature in real union with the Logos as a permanent source of life." So viewed, the Incarnation constitutes as it were a seventh day of creation, bringing all the rest to a consummation without which they are incomplete.

Like Trench, Nevin was ready to supply a whole idealistic scheme of the natural order and of history, graded in a hierarchy of being and meaning to the summit of the God-manhood.

> The inorganic struggles towards the organic; the plant towards the animal; and the animal nature, improving upon itself from one order of life to another, rests not till it is superseded finally by the human. . . . All is dark till it has made its way up to the sphere of human consciousness. There all becomes light. Man is the centre of nature; the key to all its mysteries; the idea, which binds its manifold parts into one, and makes them complete as a single organic whole.

This human stadium is incomplete until it reaches the new humanity in Christ.

[26] Cited by Nevin, "Liebner's Christology," *MR*, 1851, pp. 63, 69, 70.
[27] *The Mystical Presence*, pp. 200–201, 167, 205, 165.

It includes in its very constitution a struggle towards the form in which it is here exhibited . . . a true and real union with the nature of God. . . . All is one vast prophecy of the coming of Christ.[28]

However similar it sounds, this language is not to be understood as evolutionism. Nevin shied away from that in the *Vestiges of Creation.* His references to the nisus upward through the hierarchy of being was to be understood only in the sense of meanings—that the several levels of being "find their own full meaning always in something beyond themselves." [29]

This kind of language becomes more readily intelligible, nevertheless, on the historical level. "History, like nature," wrote Nevin, "is one vast prophecy of the incarnation, from beginning to end." Human history moved forward according to the immanent law of its own nature toward its destined union with the divine nature. The ancient religions—Brahmanism, Buddhism, Parsism, the religion of Egypt, and the religion of Greece—all aspired vainly in various ways to unite humanity with God. Judaism alone marked a real approach to man on the part of God, but to the end it was "a revelation of God *to* man, and not a revelation of God *in* man." [30] The whole religion of the Old Testament was a prophecy of Christ and would be meaningless without fulfillment in a new humanity embodying an abiding union of divinity and humanity.

In his third article (reviewing writings by Julius Mueller) Nevin seems to have been shaken from this whole idealistic rationale for the Incarnation. On reading Liebner's defense of his similar position against Thomasius of Erlangen, he had apparently held his ground. But when Mueller attacked Liebner's position in two articles (entitled "The Question Examined, Whether the Son of God would have become man, if the human race had continued without sin"), Nevin summarized them for the *Mercers-*

[28] *Ibid.*, p. 200–201.

[29] *Ibid.* The Lamarckian evolutionary views of the anonymous *Vestiges of the Natural History of Creation* [Robert Chambers] occasioned considerable discussion in the religious journals in these years.

[30] *Ibid.*, pp. 201–3.

burg Review without any comment whatever. Mueller answered the question of his title with an unqualified negative, contending that only the fact of sin gave adequate reason for the Incarnation and that the contrary, idealistic opinion, was "unsound and unsafe." Mueller would not admit that the two interpretations of the Incarnation were complementary or harmonious. They really implied different and alternative views of the Atonement. If the God-man were the real head of the whole human race, it was difficult to maintain the propitiatory significance of Calvary. Mueller also warned against ideas of the union of man and God in their natures, as leading to "deification." When the union was seen in the personal terms of love, it implied the continuing distinction of substance.[31]

When Nevin summarized Mueller's articles, he was presenting a critique of a position he had himself been maintaining for half a decade. The complete absence of any hint of his personal evaluation of these arguments is puzzling. He states the points sympathetically but neither confesses that he is persuaded nor promises a reply. Did he hang on dead center, unready to decide? Was he already feeling the paralysis of will which was shortly to cripple his speculative interest? This whole aspect of the Mercersburg Christology ran out into a question mark and remained unresolved.

The second great phase of the Incarnation begins at the Ascension and will endure until the Resurrection and Judgment. This is the age of the church, which is the "new creation," "the new humanity," extending itself like a leaven in the lump of humanity fallen in Adam. In this sense the Incarnation is a "permanent" fact, an inexhaustible "fountain of immortality in our fallen nature." From the historical birth and death and resurrection of Jesus the Christ there proceed "the presence of the Holy Ghost, the power of a new creation in the world, the mystery of the Church, one, holy and catholic, and the whole process of salva-

[31] Nevin, "Cur Deus Homo," *MR,* 1851, pp. 221, 235.

tion from the remission of sins in baptism on to the resurrection of the last day." [32]

This immediate connection of Christ with the church makes it necessary to discuss the two themes together in Nevin. If one were considering the Princeton theology, on the other hand, or the New England theology, there would be no such tie; and the doctrine of Christ and the church would be most readily discussed in separate chapters.

A critic in the *New York Observer* (September 8, 1848), presumably Dr. Irenaeus Prime, flatly challenged the Mercersburg view of the mystical union and the new creation. With reference to an article by Schaff,[33] the critic said:

> The affirmation he makes that "the Lord is perpetually born anew in the hearts of believers" sounds strangely to our ears. . . . Again: "the *commencement:*" he says, "of Church History, is strictly the incarnation of the Son of God, or the entrance of the new principle of light and life into humanity." . . . What "new principle" has there been in humanity since the incarnation, that was not in it before? [34]

"His own idea of the Incarnation," Nevin observed, "is plainly, that it did not enter into the organization of the world at all, as a fact of permanent force." As he had once said of Hodge's idea of the Incarnation, we are to conceive of a Nestorian Christ let down like the sheet of Peter's vision and after received again into heaven, all things continuing as before. The world, "left behind by the transient apparition, pursues precisely its old course, including in its living stream nothing more than has belonged to it from the beginning." [35]

Hodge had contended that the Incarnation had introduced no "new creation" because this would imply an essential contrast of the new covenant with the old. Calvin, as Hodge pointed out, had not admitted such a contrast. Nevin frankly acknowledged

[32] Nevin, "Wilberforce on the Incarnation," *MR*, 1850, p. 172.

[33] "The Pelagian Controversy—a Historical Essay," *Bibliotheca Sacra*, 1848, pp. 205–42.

[34] Cited by Nevin, "The New Creation in Christ," *MR*, 1850, p. 1.

[35] *Ibid.*, p. 7.

a divergence from Calvin at this point, but he also remarked that Calvin had taken the mystical union with Christ as the basis of justification so seriously that he taught that the saints of the old covenant were saved in virtue of the *flesh* of Christ. Nevin had written *The Mystical Presence* "to reassert the old Protestant synthesis" and like Calvin to ground the Atonement "in the perennial presence of Christ's life."[36] But he was not ready, like Calvin, to extend this presence even to the Old Testament saints. He preferred to say that the new creation had begun in Christ, and that history ever since had contained a higher sphere of conscious existence in the church.

For Nevin the church is "the historical continuation of the life of Jesus Christ in the world"; "the only medium of his saving presence among men." There can be no church without Christ, but we can also say, "No Church, no Christ." "If there be no such supernatural constitution in the world as the idea of the Church implies, the whole fact of the Incarnation is turned into an unreal theophany." Faith in the church is thus properly confessed in the Apostle's Creed, following on confession of faith in the three persons of the Trinity. "Faith in the Church is the indispensable condition of all right faith in the only true God, and in Jesus Christ."[37] The article "I believe in the Holy Catholic Church" does not mean simply "I believe what the church teaches." To believe in the church is to trust that there *is* a truly divine church; bearing the life of Christ to the faithful through its ministry and sacraments. So Nevin wrote in the preface to his synod sermon of 1846 on *The Church*, "I believe—try to believe at least (Lord, help my unbelief!) in the holy, Catholic Church; and therefore I speak."[38] The church is "truly and strictly an object of Christian faith, as much so as the fact of the incarnation itself" and for the reason that it is "His body, the fulness of Him that filleth all in all."

[36] *WM*, July 19, 1848.
[37] Nevin, *The Church* (Chambersburg, 1847), pp. 16–17.
[38] *Ibid.*, Preface.

According to the view we have of Christ, in the end, will be and must be our view also of the Church. We come to the true conception of the Church through a true and sound Christology (as in the Creed) and in no other way.[39]

Salvation in Christ does not reach souls in isolation, as most American Protestants seemed to think.

As the human nature in its own constitution is social, and no individual man can be complete apart from his race; so Christianity, which is only the human nature made absolutely complete, includes pre-eminently the same character. In its very conception, it is the power of a common or general life; which can never appear therefore as something isolated and single, simply, but always includes the idea of society and communion, under all its manifestations.[40]

"A Bible Society, a temperance union, a benevolent association of any kind having Christians in its membership is no church." When we look upon the true church visible we may say not simply: the Church is here, but: this is the Church.[41]

Most American theologians, however, inclined to the opinion that the church did not belong to the essence of Christianity, but was "capable of being separated from it without serious damage to its life." [42] Two of Nevin's opponents in the German Reformed Church, the pastors Joseph Berg and E. Heiner, seemed almost to expect salvation normally outside the church. "Personal, individual piety," wrote Heiner "is to be preferred to any outward connexion with the church whatever. . . . There are thousands in the world who belong to Christ, and yet they have no outward or formal connexion with his visible church." [43] "Religion," agreed Berg, "is a personal matter from beginning to end." God deals with individuals separately, "here one, and there another, and thus we have the germ of the church. . . . The church does not make the believer. Believers constitute the church." [44] Nevin's

[39] Nevin, "Wilberforce on the Incarnation," *MR,* 1850, p. 196.
[40] Nevin, *The Church,* p. 10.
[41] *Ibid.*, pp. 19–20.
[42] Nevin, "Thoughts on the Church," *MR,* 1858, p. 191.
[43] "S.R.," *WM,* October 15, 1845.
[44] "Mercersburg Theology," *Protestant Quarterly Review,* 1846, p. 83.

opponents generally agreed that salvation meant some sort of union with Jesus Christ, but they contended that this was separable from the church—or at least separable from the visible church. The invisible church was simply the sum of such individuals redeemed by Christ.

Tayler Lewis had entered a shrewd *caveat* at this point. There was a great deal more real church feeling among evangelical Protestants, he argued, than Nevin or Schaf conceded. He urged that more attention be paid to the liturgical expressions most loved by the laity, the hymns of Wesley and Watts. The truest test was the feeling of the laity, and even New England had the sense of the church if not the articulated doctrine. Whence, after all, came the much beloved hymn "I love thy Kingdom, Lord"? What, on the other hand, was the content of a "church feeling" which embraced Portugal, Naples, and Abyssinia, but excluded Scotland, Germany, and New England? The point could be extended to the sacraments, where Lewis invited a comparison of Willison on the sacraments with various "companions for the altar." [45]

Nevin would not accept the usual distinction of the "visible" and "invisible" church. He preferred another pair of terms, the "ideal" and the "actual," which were related in quite a different fashion. By "ideal" Nevin did not mean an exemplary model or blueprint like a Fourierist social scheme. His analogy was again biological: the "ideal" was more like an Aristotelian entelechy, the *telos* conceived as the existing inner impetus, and thus the very substance of the real. Von Gerlach's terms, the "real" and the "palpable" church, as Nevin translated them,[46] help to interpret Nevin's intention. The church was an organism, sown in Jesus Christ, seeking to actualize its real nature. The real, "ideal" church is thus not the same as the palpable, empirical church. But it does not float above the confusions of history; it is rather within history, growing and struggling.

"Visible" and "invisible" church as used by Hodge, for ex-

[45] *WM*, January 28, 1846.
[46] *Ibid.*, October 6, 1847.

ample in his essay on "Theories of the Church,"[47] were static aggregates. Nevin and von Gerlach rather conceived the church dynamically, as a whole in process, something *becoming*. "In its very nature, the actual Church is a process, which has never yet become complete, but is always pressing forward to its completion, as this will appear in the millennium . . . when the ideal Church and the actual Church shall have become fully and forever one."[48] As "life," the new humanity is "an organic, regularly continuous development of the life of Jesus Christ." The new is engrafted into the old and is struggling to master it; the aeons overlap. "The old nature is not at once destroyed" in humanity any more than in the individual, "but the new nature of Christ is enclosed in it, as the papilio in the folds of the chrysalis."[49]

This struggle is, among other things, a thrust to visible externalization. "An invisible state, or invisible family, or invisible man, is not so great an absurdity and contradiction as an absolutely invisible Church. . . . The idea of the Church includes visibility, just as the idea of man supposes a body." This impetus to visible actualization may be considered in relation to the several attributes of the new humanity. "Its catholicity, unity, sanctity, all call for externalization." To believe in one holy catholic Church means belief in such a church under an outward, visible form. "For an invisible unity, catholicity, and holiness can never satisfy the requisitions of the case."[50]

The church can never be wholly invisible. Although at times it has been very corrupt, an actual interruption in its historical continuity would mean the interruption of God's redeeming work.

> If the Church should fail, all truth and holiness among men must fail irrecoverably at the same time. To suppose that it might take an entirely new start, under such visible organic character, in the fourth century, or the sixteenth, or at any time . . . is most assuredly

[47] *BRPR,* 1846, pp. 137 ff.
[48] Nevin, *The Church,* p. 12.
[49] Nevin, "Catholic Unity," in Schaf, *Principle of Protestantism,* p. 196. Cf. *The Mystical Presence,* p. 228.
[50] Nevin, *The Church,* pp. 10–11.

to belie its existence as a real Church entirely; as much so, as to imagine any similar void or break in our common human life, between its embryo formation in the womb and the full maturity of manhood, would be plainly to convert the whole process into a mere Gnostic phantom.[51]

This process, this living totality, then manifests phases or aspects. From one aspect, the actual church presupposes "imperfection and defect at every point of its progress." From another, the new creation is "complete and harmonious, and true to itself at every point from the beginning" even though all "may seem for a season to fail." [52] "The historical Church," in sum, "is always the true Church; but never a pure or perfect Church. It is by no means free, either from error or sin." The perfect church is struggling to actualization within the imperfect and exists only there. They are in the end the same. "The actual is the body of the ideal in *growth;* the process, constantly changing and flowing, by which it is externalized and so made complete, as the great world-fact of redemption." [53] To believe in the church is not to believe in either the actual or the ideal church separately considered, but the ideal *in* the actual, as the *real* church.

Two or three instances illustrate how this dynamic understanding of the church would apply to its attributes. "In her ideal character . . . as the article of the creed implies, the Church is absolutely holy and infallible, free from error and free from sin." The historical church has rarely claimed to be perfectly holy and free from sin, but important sections of the church have sometimes claimed to be free from error. This was, in fact, the substance of the ultramontane claim to papal infallibility.

Nevin translated an article by von Gerlach on the infallibility of the church, which argued against the ultramontane Munich organ, the *Historische-politische Blätter*.[54] Nevin himself attacked the ultramontanism of *Brownson's Quarterly Review* in America. Von Gerlach and Nevin agreed that infallibility was as much an

[51] *Ibid.*, pp. 18, 22–23.
[52] Nevin, "Catholic Unity," p. 202.
[53] Nevin, *The Church*, p. 15.
[54] *WM*, October 6 and 13; November 3, 1847.

attribute of the "real" church as holiness, unity, universality. "He who heareth you heareth me." They maintained, however, that this infallibility cannot be simply attributed to any particular part or organ of the historical church. Infallibility attaches to the whole and perfect church, "the sublime liturgy of the universal Christian world," in the sense of Vincent of Lerins and of "evangelical catholicity." The body of Christ was not to be sharply defined and legally demarcated. It was the mistake of Brownson and the men of Munich, with their "blind authority Christianity," to make the presence of the church a matter of observation rather than faith. "Romanism in this form is not Catholicism"; von Gerlach and Nevin alike denied that the ultramontanes represented genuine Roman Catholicism. To claim infallibility for a specific teaching office was magic and mummery, but to deny infallibility to the church was infidelity.

As with holiness and infallibility, so with the visible unity of the church. Division, like error and sin, is contrary to the idea of the church. As Calvin had said, there cannot be more than one church any more than one Christ. But again,

> the actual Church . . . is not . . . necessarily free from either heresy or schism. Its visible unity may be greatly marred by its distribution, more or less, into denominations and sects. This we are bound to lament; but we have no right to resort to the violence of unchurching all beyond some favorite communion, in order to remedy the evil. As it now stands especially, the Church, with its divine life-powers, is not confined to any one organization exclusively, as Romanists and tractarians believe, but extends its presence, with different measures of power, over different and divided communions. . . .
>
> . . . How far the Church life may reach in this way, we cannot say. There are sects, of course, that have no part in it whatever; and then there are others again, whose connection with it is sickly and imperfect, though still real. In all cases, however, the relation in question holds of the sect as an organization and not merely of some individuals that may happen to be living in it, as grains of metal in a heap of sand. To be satisfied with my sect, it is not enough to be sure that it includes some true Christians; I need to be sure, that the life of the Church is objectively present in its constitution *as a sect*, giving to its spiritual ministrations the force which belongs to the life of the

true Church, and to this life only. If I make no account of this point, I show my want of faith in the Church, and have good reason to tremble for my position.[55]

As for the system as a whole,

> We must believe that our sects, therefore, however necessary, are something wrong; a most defective, abnormal condition of the body of Christ; an interimistic abomination, in the Church but not of it, that is destined in due time to pass away, and which while it lasts all good men are bound to deplore.

How visible unity is to be attained we may not now see, but we may be confident it will be the actualization of the life of the church "organically creating for its own use the outward form which it needs in order to be complete." [56]

The last phase of the Incarnation would be found when the ideal church would become the actual church, the Lord would return, and the saints would be raised in glory to praise Him.

> The full and final triumph of the process is the resurrection; which is reached in the case of the individual, only in connection with the consummation of the Church as a whole. The bodies of the saints in glory will be only the last result, in organic continuity, of the divine life of Christ, implanted in their souls by their regeneration. . . . The resurrection body will be simply the ultimate outburst of the life that had been ripening for immortality under cover of the old Adamic nature before.[57]

Nevin laid more weight on the resurrection of the body than most of his opponents, who apparently would have been content with a Platonic heaven for "souls." With Nevin the same conception of soul and body which contributed to his distinctive views on the Eucharistic Presence and on the Incarnation came into play with regard to the final resurrection. We should not conceive of "a sudden unprepared refabrication of the body as an entirely new product of Almighty power at the moment, to be superadded to the life of the spirit already complete in its

[55] Nevin, *The Church,* pp. 14, 21 n.
[56] *Ibid.,* pp. 22, 13, 20 n.
[57] *The Mystical Presence,* p. 177.

state of glory." [58] No, the resurrection must also be seen in terms of the Incarnation, as the final culmination of the life of God in the soul of man.

Nevin had helped to bring to light long-neglected aspects of Reformation theology and uncovered a Calvin strangely different from the Calvin taught at Princeton. In his developed doctrine of the "new creation" he had gone beyond both Calvin and his German instructors, such as Sartorius and Dorner. He wrote,

> My sense of the church has not been borrowed in any direct or immediate way from German theology. . . . The later German theology has done much undoubtedly to promote right views of history, deeper apprehensions of the Christological questions, more realistic conceptions altogether of the new creation.[59]

Nevin, however, had gone further in the direction of "objective, sacramental religion" and made himself at home with Irenaeus, Athanasius, Basil, and the two Gregories.[60] With some justification Dorner called Nevin Eastern Orthodox in his orientation.[61]

In the synod sermon *The Church* Nevin had set forth systematically his conception of the new humanity struggling to universalize itself. There he had made it clear that the true church was distributed in many denominations and sects. Two years later he published an essay, *Antichrist, or the Spirit of Sect and Schism,* which analyzed the adversary of the true church within the gates. He had argued in "Pseudo-Protestantism" [62] that Antichrist could not be simply identified with the Papacy, but was also found within Protestantism. Now his application of the term to the sect spirit illustrates again the intimate connection of church and Incarnation, for the meaning of Antichrist to him, in the sense of I John 4:1–3, was the denial of the Incarnation.

[58] *Ibid.*, p. 228.
[59] *WM,* July 19, 1848.
[60] *Antichrist, or the Spirit of Sect and Schism* (New York, 1848), Preface.
[61] *Der Liturgische Kampf in der Deutsch-Reformirten Kirche von Nord-Amerika* (Philadelphia, 1868), p. 21. Nevin's conception of development, on the other hand, would not have been well received in those quarters.
[62] *WM,* August 13, 20, 27; September 3, 10, 1845.

Sectarianism was the Antichrist of nineteenth-century America because it denied by implication that Christ had come in the flesh, tending rather to Docetism and Nestorianism.

In describing his Antichrist, Nevin was not talking of any specific denomination or any particular theologian. He was describing an attitude, a tendency, which—when allowed to command the situation—developed into a whole system of sectarianism. It was, however, "capable of being associated also with forms of Christian character that are prevailingly sound and good," of insinuating itself "to a certain extent, into the thinking also of the truly pious and faithful." For "the conflict between light and darkness in the church is not simply that of system against system, outwardly opposed, but enters into the presence of the Christian life itself."[63] The sect spirit, like the true church, is distributed over many denominations, and there the two struggle together.

In Nevin's list the first mark of Antichrist was the denial of any real *mediation,* or union of God with man, as the basis of the Christian life. Christ might perhaps be honored as the Redeemer, but "no good reason appears why he should be a human Christ at all." The second mark was that his person is not felt in its full significance. "We are not saved according to this system by what He is, but by what He says or does." This work is arbitrary and outward in relation to men. Christ appears as a purely spiritual figure, not being really rooted in our common earthly life. Hyperspiritualism (mark 7) yields an unreal Docetic Christ.

When this hyperspiritualist, gnostic view is carried over to His body the church, the sect spirit is most clearly revealed. The sectarian has no faith in the church as a really divine constitution resting in, and in a sense continuing, the Incarnation throughout history (mark 3). His church is as spiritualistic and Docetic as his Christ. It is "invisible," leaving the empirical church "a mechanical aggregation of living atoms." In that empirical church the ministry has no divine consecration, sacramental grace is denied, worship has no objective character (mark 4).

[63] *Antichrist,* p. 32.

All sects boast of having the spirit in high degree, and claim to be thus freed of need for outward ordinances or tradition. Religion is a matter of intense, inward, particular experience. All this, however, cools off in time, and hyperspiritualism then tends to subside into its apparent opposite, rationalism and worldliness (mark 11). Nevin here was on his old theme of wildfire revivalism and its consequences. Or, to take another illustration of the convergence of apparent opposites, "What a difference apparently between the inspiration of George Fox, and the cold infidelity of Elias Hicks. And yet the last is the true spiritual descendant of the first."[64]

The sectarian mentality, again, is contemptuous of history and authority (mark 5), insisting rather on the freedom of the individual (mark 6). Though sectarians in fact acknowledge their own "tradition" and their own "fathers," they are limited by a narrow horizon isolated from the larger church. They claim the authority of the Bible, but only as interpreted by their private judgment and tradition. Sect theology is poor (mark 12); an inadequate conception of the church is usually indicative of related inadequacies with regard to God, Christ, and man. Lacking the steadying objectivity of churchly consciousness, the sect mind is spasmodic, irregular, running to extremes and fanaticism (mark 9).

In relation to church life, finally, the spirit of sect leads to endless separation (mark 10). Assuming that there is no actual holy church universal, the sectarian claims the right to leave the existing church according to pleasure and to form a new one with the help of the Bible. He usually admits that what he has made is not *the* church, but *a* church or society. Unfortunately, there is no power to heal divisions. Federations or alliances of sects only establish the principle of schism. Such is Nevin's portrait of the incubus he saw resting heavily on American Protestantism.

By the end of the forties the chief theologians agreed in condemning sectarianism. "All sects unite," Nevin observed wryly

[64] *Ibid.*, p. 66; cf. *The Mystical Presence*, p. 148.

in 1850,[65] "in deploring the misery of a divided Christianity and are ready on fit occasions to pass resolutions and make speeches in behalf of unity, toleration, charity and peace." He could remember when it was usual to defend the whole denominational system, on the analogy of distinct regiments in one army or instruments in an orchestra. They competed in good works, it had been urged, enlisting harmless rivalry in a good cause. These analogies Nevin rejected.

> Our sects do not love each other. Their relation to each other, at best, is one of indifference. To a fearful extent, it is one of quiet malignity and hatred. What sect takes any active interest in the welfare of another, rejoices in its prosperity, sympathizes with its griefs and trials, makes common cause with it in its enterprises and works? [66]

A limited amount of truth, to be sure, lay in the contention that the denominations represented an irreducible variation of temperament among Christians in different forms of piety and ethos. One might conceive of a denominationalism organized on such principles, Nevin admitted, but it would not look anything like American Protestantism. The existing denominations seemed rather the result of caprice, for other differences were as significant as those which had been made the occasion of schism. Most sects, forgetting the ground of their schism, were no longer real "confessions," but "ecclesiastical corporations simply," [67] carried on by institutional inertia in the absence of any compelling faith in the church universal or of any correlative sense of the sin of schism.

Among the several proposals afoot for combating sectarianism, Nevin found none satisfactory. He put no hope in the anti-sect movements, like those of the "Christians," the followers of the Campbells, or Winebrenner's "Church of God." This type of movement was so widespread in that generation as to provide a significant key to the prevailing American religious mentality. Man-made creeds and church traditions, it was argued, were to blame for the scandalous divisions of the church. The solution

[65] "Bible Christianity," *MR*, 1850, p. 360.
[66] "The Sect System" (second article), *MR*, 1849, p. 537.
[67] *Antichrist*, pp. 74, 80.

was to abandon all exclusively sectarian tenets so composed, and to unite on the simple, common platform of the Bible. "Where the Bible speaks, we speak," said the Campbellites; "where the Bible is silent, we are silent."

That such a self-contradictory scheme could have caught up thousands in this generation is an index of its extreme religious isolation and provincialism. As Nevin pointed out, Campbell, Stockton, and the rest were simply urging *their* understanding of the Bible as the basis for a church, as over against the theological traditions of Presbyterians, Methodists, Baptists. Whatever justification there might be for doing so, there was none whatever for supposing that they alone had got behind man-made creeds and traditions to the Bible pure. They had simply added another man-made creed and another sect.[68]

Not all the anti-sect crusaders became pioneers of new sects. Doubtless thousands of individuals and congregations remained nominally within this or that denomination but acknowledged no real authority in it. This was an example of something that has happened in hundreds and thousands of American congregations, where local independence and irresponsibility have been the outcome. Nevin took an interest in Stockton, a Methodist Protestant minister who campaigned for years against sects and at length cut loose from his Quarterly Conference to serve an independent congregation "in the bosom of the church general."[69] The whole movement of opposing sects in the name of Bible Christianity had further defeated church unity, either by still further reducing ties of church fellowship in local independency or by adding new sects to the existing Babel. There was no short cut out of the diverse theological traditions and the several denominations in which the church catholic lived.

A second ecumenical strategy was the reductionism proposed by "liberal Christianity." By denying or compromising their distinctive tenets, denominations could be brought to merge. Schaf protested,

[68] "The Sect System" (second article), *MR*, 1849, p. 530.
[69] Nevin, "Bible Christianity," *MR*, 1850, p. 356.

> To make room for union, peculiarities of doctrine are to be surrendered for which our fathers contended and made the greatest sacrifices. . . . Has the peculiar development of the different branches of Protestantism gone forward thus far, without meaning or fruit? After the toil of so many hundred years, must we go back again to the most indefinite beginning, the A B C we may say, of our church life?[70]

Nevin took a similar stand on this kind of "community church" catholicity. "It is a catholicity which stands wholly in negations; by which all that is affirmed as a distinguishing interest by the different denominations is either denied, or at least treated as something of no worth."[71] Such a church platform shut out nothing "just because there is nothing which it can be said effectually to comprehend and shut in."[72] An impoverished least-common-denominator Christianity would not be the church catholic. As with the restoration scheme of Bible Christianity, the cure was worse than the disease.

Probably the single development which most conspicuously embodied and furthered the new interest in church unity was the London Conference of 1846, which eventuated in the Evangelical Alliance. This movement caught up an earlier enterprise led by Samuel Schmucker of Gettysburg Seminary, looking toward a federation of evangelical denominations with a consensus creed. The London Alliance, however, did not aspire to be an actual federation. All previous efforts to bring together denominations as such had always failed, and it was thought wiser to form simply an interdenominational society of individuals who desired to manifest their unity with other Christians. It was not to be a church or even a council of churches, but it did intend to extend through the churches a sense of the sinfulness of division and an increased openness toward other denominations.

Schaf spoke for both Mercersburg men when he entered a "decided dissent" to the Evangelical Alliance movement. As a practical testimony of the sense of the great wrong of sectarian

[70] P. Schaf, *What Is Church History?* (Philadelphia, 1846), pp. 125 ff.
[71] "Bible Christianity," *MR*, 1850, p. 365.
[72] *Antichrist*, p. 82.

division, it was commendable; but its basis was not genuinely ecumenical. Instead, it was more nearly a partisan consolidation against "the encroachments of Popery and Puseyism." A pan-Protestant alliance represented "an altogether too contracted conception of union," as if all the elements of a perfect church were to be found in Protestantism, and the larger Roman and Greek communions were to be treated as a "gigantic spiritual zero." Schaf and Nevin were rather convinced that Rome at least would contribute truth and life, "not simply to the present posture of Protestantism (which no sound mind can hold to be itself complete), but to that last best state of Christianity in which full justice shall be done to the truth on all sides and the Church shall appear one and universal in fact." [73]

Even within Protestantism the Evangelical Alliance movement represented the unchurchly and unsacramental wing of individualist pietists and "puritans." Nevin considered it revealing that they had undertaken a new creed, without even considering the ancient baptismal creed and its characteristic order of doctrines.[74] (Had they affirmed the latter, they would have at once been committed to the implications of the Incarnation in the new humanity.) "Sects which have no faith in the church can never achieve catholic unity," [75] declared Nevin.

Suppose Schmucker had succeeded, either through the Evangelical Alliance or independently, in organizing a federal council of churches. "Would it be the visible catholic church?" No, it would be a human voluntary association. Federation implied the justification of the constituent parts and tacitly conceded the right to separate. It presupposed a merely instrumental view of church life with no sense of the meaning of schism. The whole procedure of approaching church unity through administrative devices as standing outside and over the church was futile. "A church is not to be fabricated in the study, by simply extracting, and putting together in an outward way, some propositions of

[73] *What is Church History?* pp. 123–24.
[74] Nevin, *The Church,* p. 20.
[75] *Antichrist,* p. 84.

apparently like sound, out of different symbolical books."[76] We cannot create church unity. It is a Rousseauist illusion that the fault is outside us in the institutions we have inherited, and that the powers to heal lie in our good will and ingenuity. On the contrary, unless God gave the church unity, no man or committee could advance it by calculation or stratagem.

These penetrating criticisms of the three most conspicuous types of ecumenical strategy of the day did not mean that the Mercersburg theologians were indifferent to the problem. On the contrary, as we have seen, Nevin flatly defined the actualization of catholic unity as "the most important interest in the world."[77] He was convinced, nevertheless, that the problem could not be approached directly on the level of administration and organization.

The first requisite of a sound ecumenical approach was religious and theological. The unity of the church, Nevin maintained, required an inner transformation of all constituent denominations as a precondition. Renewal and reform would be needed before separate organizations could really draw together. On the one hand, there must be a general realization of, and repentance for, the sin of schism, so widespread in America.[78] As Visser 't Hooft put it a century later, the ecumenical movement was first of all "a movement of repentance." The positive correlative to such repentance was "faith in the Church itself; the practical persuasion that there has always been since Christ, is now, and to the end of time will be, a real historical visible church in the world, which is the proper object of Christian faith and trust."[79] The text for Nevin's sermon on "Catholic Unity," Ephesians 4:4, does not say, he remarked, "Let there be one body and one spirit," but rather, "There *is* one body and spirit," and *therefore* are we bound to hold that unity. The only hope of church unity is in closer unity on all sides with the church's living Head.

In the absence of such growth into Christ the Head, the in-

[76] Schaf, *What Is Church History?* p. 126.
[77] "Catholic Unity," in Schaf, *Principle of Protestantism,* p. 203.
[78] *Ibid.,* p. 205.
[79] Nevin, *The Church,* p. 19 n.; cf. *Antichrist,* p. 88.

terdenominational debates over bishops and baptism would be sterile. Each tradition would seek to justify its usages, doctrine, and polity in legalistic appeals to Scripture, and there was no base for adjudicating such claims. Quoting Wilberforce, Nevin declared, "If the essence of the Church's existence be that certain men have a right to rule, and teach, and minister, whether they be chosen by the free voice of the congregation, imposed by government, or delegated by the Apostles, there is such large opening for cabal and dispute that love and peace and Christ's presence will soon be lost in the din of party strife." [80] In general, Nevin argued, the debates over church order, polity, and the ministry were less important than those over sacramental grace, for the sacraments were the sign and seal of whatever power was recognized to be in the church. Yet the sense of the church was more general and deep than even the right sacramental feeling. "The notion of grace-bearing sacraments, sundered from the sense of the Church as still carrying in it the force of its first supernatural constitution, would be indeed magical, and must prove quite as pedantical in the end as a supreme regard for bishops in the same dead way." [81] The first prerequisite for profitable ecumenical discussion was faith in Christ's active presence in his new humanity.

This position was not intended to defend quietism or inaction. The religious renewal of the church could not fail to bring about profound organizational changes. Nevin estimated that if the faith in the mystery of the church catholic in history were a powerful reality among Protestants in America, "half of our sects would be at once dissolved by it" and the range of division and debate among the rest would be reduced to less than half its present dimensions.[82] It was the duty of the church to observe and improve all opportunities to advance in a visible way the interest of catholic unity, as Nevin had once said with particular reference to the natural but ill-fated courtship of the German

[80] "Wilberforce on the Incarnation," *MR,* 1850, pp. 192–93.
[81] "The Anglican Crisis," *MR,* 1851, pp. 378–79.
[82] *Antichrist,* p. 88.

Reformed and Reformed Dutch churches. It could not be a matter of indifference "to pull down a single one of all those walls of partition,"[83] but churches were bound to follow where God led, not presumptuously to take the whole work into their own hands. We cannot know how or when He will complete this work; it is for us to do faithfully what is set immediately before us in the way of reconciliation. The unity of the church will not appear by administrative ingenuity, but only when generally believed in and earnestly prayed for.

[83] "Catholic Unity," p. 209.

7/ *Scripture and Tradition*

When Schaf's *Principle of Protestantism* was published in English in 1845, it reached American readers who were near panic with anti–Roman Catholic sentiment. The sudden and tremendous invasions of Roman Catholics into a hitherto almost exclusively Protestant society and culture had aroused violent reactions. Philadelphia was shaken by several days of rioting the summer Schaf first saw the city. The pope had declared Roman Catholicism opposed to the basic principles of the American political heritage of civil and political liberty.[1] He had attacked the dissemination of the Scriptures. Roman Catholic political pressures in certain centers were directed toward banning the Bible from the public schools. And all these alien ideas were made politically threatening by their embodiment in a new and massive immigration, of which the largest section, the Irish, were also socially undesirable in large numbers, bringing a high incidence of crime, violence, disease, prostitution. On social, economic, political, and religious grounds, Roman Catholicism seemed to large numbers of Americans the greatest danger. Anti–Roman Catholic feeling pervaded press and rostrum as it had not done since the French and Indian Wars.

On the specifically religious and theological level also, Roman Catholicism demanded attention. The church had become newly aggressive in the reaction after the Napoleonic Wars. There were rumors of conversions of distinguished Protestants on the European continent. The Puseyite movement in the Church of England was widely viewed as a Roman stalking-horse, an interpretation apparently confirmed by the submission of John Henry

[1] In the encyclical letters *Mirari vos* (1832) and *Singulari nos* (1833).

Newman to Rome in the year the Mercersburg controversy began. Even in the United States Rome seemed for the first time a spiritual rival, winning converts like Orestes Brownson and Isaac Hecker out of the very centers of New England culture. The American Episcopalians were infected with the same Romanizing virus as the Church of England. Here too a string of converts, or "perverts," as they were called, gave evidence that something was dangerously wrong. Roman Catholicism had succeeded Unitarianism and transcendentalism as the most pressing anxiety of American churchmen generally.

In the theological debate it was generally conceded that the crucial question was the rule of faith. Was the Bible the sole rule of faith and practice? Or was tradition also to be acknowledged as authoritative? "The recent publication in England of so many works on tradition," wrote Charles Hodge two years before Schaf's arrival, "indicates a new and extended interest in the subject; and their republication in America shows that the interest is as great here." [2] It was clear that the case for Romanism and Puseyism rested on the legitimation of extra-biblical tradition as an authority in Christianity. The appeal to tradition was the Pandora's box from which all their errors had poured forth. American Protestantism had almost universally taken the position that Christianity rested on the inspired Bible alone; all ecclesiastical traditions were human, fallible, and unnecessary. On this *scriptura sola* case all the leading theological centers were as one —Andover, Yale, Princeton, Union.

Against this background one can understand the violence of the reaction to Schaf's *Principle of Protestantism.* Despite the fact that in his commissioning sermon at Elberfeld, Schaf had identified Romanism as one of the dangers threatening America, he took what seemed in America a very irenic tone toward Rome. He urged that far from being the great apostasy and the mystery of iniquity, Roman Catholicism had been the main stream of true

[2] Hodge, "The Rule of Faith," *Biblical Repertory and Princeton Review* (hereafter cited as *BRPR*), 1842, p. 598.

Christianity up to the Reformation, and was still in some sense a part of the true church. He even looked forward to eventual reunion with Roman Catholicism. On the specific issue of the rule of faith, he maintained that tradition was too generally undervalued by Protestants and that extra-biblical tradition of some kind was indispensable. His colleague Nevin, in whom such arguments must have recently caused some extensive rethinking, backed him up at every point. To many good Protestants the Mercersburg Seminary must have seemed suddenly disclosed as a Trojan horse within the Protestant gates, like the University of Oxford and the General Seminary in New York.

To most American Protestants, indeed, Schaf's historical outlook must have seemed strange and almost unintelligible. His critics here were too disconcerted by the very idea of historical change and development to be able to enter into the new idiom and debate the specific case Schaf was arguing in these terms. But the old issues reappeared in different guise within the historical perspective. Modern historical thought rendered obsolete much of the current American debates about doctrine and polity on a narrow Biblicist basis. But one still had to have a criterion as to which historical changes and developments were legitimate and true to type. No one was ready to concede that there were *no* corruptions, heresies, syncretisms, or compromises in Christian history. Not all "developments" had been justified. One still had to come back to the question of the rule of faith. How did the new historical perspective affect the old issue of Scripture and tradition?

Schaf contended that the widespread American Protestant repudiation of all ecclesiastical tradition was not the Reformation position and that—far from being an impregnable defense against Romanism and Puseyism—it was indefensible and self-contradictory.

Tradition must be seen, Schaf argued, following Schleiermacher and Moehler, not merely as the objective aggregate of beliefs and practices handed down by the church, but subjectively, as the common apprehension or consciousness of the church of the substance of its faith.[3] The believer does not appropriate the Bible directly. He knows and reads it in the light of certain emphases, interpretations, perhaps omissions, which are the substance of his denominational perspective, or that of his generation, whether written as a confession or not. Those very Protestants who dismiss tradition in favor of Scripture, said Schaf, "in spite of their own theory . . . hold it [Scripture] only through the medium of tradition, and see and understand it too, only as mirrored in the present consciousness of the particular church to which they belong."[4] Every church, Protestant or otherwise, has a distinctive consciousness or apprehension, a tradition which it nurtures from generation to generation, into which the contents of the Bible are continually fed, and for each this tradition is the necessary vehicle and mediation of the Bible's contents. The true Protestant position, then, was not to deny tradition in the name of "the Bible alone," but to affirm that valid tradition must always be derived from Scripture and corrected by it. Valid tradition could never be, as with the Roman Catholics, a source of religious truth independent of the Bible and having different contents.

After all, what were the various confessional statements of the Lutherans, the Reformed, and the rest, if they were not ecclesiastical traditions? They expressed "the faith of Protestantism in the Scriptures themselves, and its apprehension of their contents." The Protestant churches enforced these confessions in various ways and degrees. What church could admit complete freedom to its members to extract whatever might seem plausible to any individual from Scripture and to maintain it? The very existence of a distinctive denomination meant a distinctive group tradition as to the substance of Scripture. To be sure, all ecclesiastical determinations of this sort on Protestant ground remained fallible and subject to correction. As Calvin said, "the Holy Ghost may forsake an entire synod." In Schaf's judgment, however, one did

[3] *Principle of Protestantism* (Chambersburg, 1845), p. 74 n.
[4] *Ibid.*, p. 90.

not need to stress among Protestants the fallibility of church authority. The Protestant curse of schism and sectarianism arose at least in part from "contempt of Church authority and the abuses of Protestant liberty." [5]

Schaf's opponents, however, resisted this argument for the necessity of a consensus in biblical interpretation. "The Scriptures are their own exponent" [6] said Berg, and he remained determinedly naïve about his own use of tradition. He and his supporters assumed that when they opened their Bibles, their minds were as a *tabula rasa.* They ignored the extent to which their understanding of the Bible had been shaped by years of sermons and hymns and prayers. "God forbid," wrote Berg, "that when we take up our Bibles to read what the Holy Spirit has indited for our instruction, we should stop at every sentence and every verse to ask, what interpretation does the church put upon this passage? . . . Must I have a book of canon law at my side for consultation?" [7] He was not aware that he already had the book of canon law in his head.

Nevin's brother William, professor of English in Marshall College, occasionally commented on the theological controversies by way of fictional dialogues in the *Weekly Messenger* between "Squire Schlosser" and "Solomon Trexler." He did not do much injustice to the *scriptura sola* party in the following exchange:

SCHLOSSER: In making out the meaning of the Scripture lessons for the class, do you not sometimes consult some other books than the Bible, by way of help?

TREXLER: No, indeed, Squire, I do not. I look at no other book but Barnes' *Four Gospels* and Scott's *Family Bible.* You'll never catch me off the track in that way. I would be very sorry indeed to look for instructions in any other book than in the Bible.[8]

Schaf, to be sure, had undertaken to rebut the Roman Catholic arguments that the Scriptures rested finally on the authority of

[5] *Ibid.*, pp. 89, 81–82, 92.
[6] *Weekly Messenger* (hereafter cited as *WM*), November 5, 1845.
[7] "Mercersburg Theology," *Protestant Quarterly Review* (hereafter cited as *PQR*), 1846, pp. 83–84.
[8] *WM*, February 25, 1846.

the church and its traditions. He conceded that the apostolic testimony had been maintained orally in the consciousness of the church before it became the New Testament, so that the church antedated the *written* word. But he quoted the "most important Roman Catholic theologian of the present age," Moehler, on the necessity of the Scriptures since the death of the living witnesses of Christ in the flesh. "Without the Scriptures," Moehler had written, "we could form no complete image of the Redeemer, as trustworthy material would be wanting, and all must be made uncertain through fables." [9] This was precisely the Protestant point: extra-Biblical tradition was not trustworthy.

To those, on the other hand, who tried to show the superiority of ecclesiastical tradition on the ground that it was the church which had determined the New Testament canon Schaf did not yield ground. The church did not make the Scriptures genuine by acknowledging them. The act of determining the canon was simply the recognition by the church that certain books had an apostolic authority which could not be gainsaid. Nor has the authority of the Scriptures since the determination of the canon rested on the authorization of the church. The final authority of the Bible for the reader has always been the inward testimony of the Holy Spirit that this is indeed God's word.[10]

The term "tradition" was used to cover a variety of elements, Schaf noted. The ancient traditions of the church included centrally the apostolic testimony which became the New Testament, then the earliest creeds, ethics, matters of church order, government and discipline, worship practices, and eventually the teachings of the fathers on all sorts of subjects. In its variety this tradition was even more susceptible of divergent interpretation than the Bible. Protestants conceded a greater or less degree of subordinate authority to these elements other than Scripture. For several of them Schaf urged more respect than American Protestants were accustomed to accord. With regard to the ancient creeds, indeed, Schaf insisted on their indispensability. He ap-

[9] Cited in Schaf, *op. cit.*, p. 91 n.
[10] *Ibid.*, pp. 92, 84–85.

pealed here to the Reformers. The Lutheran and Reformed churches, he wrote, "appropriated to themselves unhesitatingly the ecumenical symbols as true expressions of this Church consciousness, that is, as agreeing with the Scriptures." On the most central issues of doctrine the Reformation not only affirmed the necessity of tradition beside Scripture, to determine the sense of Scripture against heresies, but affirmed the *same* tradition as Roman Catholicism. The Reformers insisted "that all reformation . . . must maintain essential unity with the collective consciousness of the Christian church as it had stood from the beginning." [11]

Current American opinion, however, disagreed with classical Protestantism in this matter. Evangelicalism, the dominant religious tradition, in fact declined to use this creed. Children were not taught the creed; it was not used liturgically, or in families, in religious education or as a standard of orthodoxy. The *Puritan Recorder* spoke for New England in disavowing the creed.

> The experience of two centuries has shown that the Creed and Puritanism have not a kindred spirit. The first Puritans did not discard what is called the Apostles' Creed, but expressly allowed its use. . . . It even had a place in the *New England Primer*. But its life and spirit never entered into the life of the Puritan churches. . . . We are free to confess, that this Creed has forsaken the Puritans and gone over to become the idol and strength of all branches of antiPuritanism.[12]

Congregational churches commonly used covenants drafted by the individual congregations, but it would scarcely occur to one to use the Apostles' Creed in this way. When American Board missionaries in Constantinople organized a church, they concocted a completely new creed by original deduction from the Bible, systematically excluding any historical creed of the church. Similarly the Evangelical Alliance Convention, Nevin observed, "found it necessary to ignore the Apostles' Creed in full, and brought in a new set of articles altogether." [13] The heirs of the Puritans did not feel at home with the creed as the Reformers had

[11] *Ibid.*, p. 88.

[12] Cited in Nevin, "Puritanism and the Creed," *Mercersburg Review*, (hereafter cited as *MR*), 1849, pp. 581–88.

[13] "The Apostles' Creed," *MR*, 1849, p. 126 n.

felt. They did not recognize the internal logic of its structure; of the several articles they considered some of little importance or perhaps tending to superstition, and missed others that should have been deemed indispensable.

The *Puritan Recorder* did not speak only for Congregationalism in its repudiation of the creed. A Presbyterian periodical reprinted the articles on the subject from the *Recorder*, as did Kurtz in his *Lutheran Observer*. Princeton and New Brunswick joined the opposition when the *Princeton Review* published a monograph against the authority of the creed, composed by Dr. John W. Proudfit, Nevin's former college classmate who had now become perhaps his bitterest opponent in the Dutch Reformed church.[14] One might have expected the Unitarians, Baptists, and such sects as Campbellites, Cumberlanders, and Winebrennerians to dismiss the creed, but here were the spokesmen of the central Reformation tradition in America similarly declaring their emancipation from "the primary Protestant symbol, of more sacredness and force, assuredly, than any catechism." [15]

The bulk of Proudfit's article was presented historically, to substantiate the thesis that the Apostles' Creed was a late, post-Nicene tradition and that the Reformers, the pre-Constantinian fathers, and even those of the fourth and fifth centuries considered the Scriptures to be the sole rule of faith and practice to the exclusion of the creed. That Hodge and his colleagues ever permitted the piece to be published under the auspices of the *Princeton Review* is a startling indication of the level of patristic scholarship in the faculty of Princeton Seminary.

Berg, on the other hand, having failed in the attempt to prove the Mercersburg men unfaithful to Protestant standards, frankly turned against the Reformation. "In attaching so much importance to the authority of the church of the third, fourth, and fifth centuries," said Berg,[16] the Reformers themselves committed

[14] "The Apostles' Creed," *BRPR*, 1852, pp. 602–77.
[15] Nevin, "Puritanism and the Creed," *MR*, 1849, p. 600.
[16] "The Reformation," *PQR*, 1846, p. 164.

a well-nigh fatal error. For as soon as any authority was acknowledged to tradition, one would be pushed on irresistibly to Roman ecclesiastical infallibility. "There is no consistent middle ground," he wrote, "between the infallibility of the church, and the absolute indispensableness of tradition." [17]

Proudfit would have been wise, like Berg, to relinquish the historical argument. As with the arguments over the sacraments, the Mercersburg men had the Reformers on their side. Sixteenth-century Lutherans, Anglicans, and Reformed had all retained in authority the ancient creed in its three chief forms: the Apostles', the Nicene, and the Athanasian. Whatever else they had said theologically had been erected on this as a necessary foundation. The Reformed churches, for example, had used the creed at baptism, in the liturgy of the Lord's Supper, and in the preaching service, as well as in their catechetical and theological instruction. And not merely the first-generation Reformers, but men like Ursinus, Heidegger, and Vossius (as Proudfit had to admit), maintained the authority of the creeds on the ground that their substance was wholly scriptural.[18]

A similar debate over the authority of the ancient catholic creeds in Protestantism had been proceeding in Prussia, and almost certainly the Mercersburg argument was influenced largely by it. The whole doctrinal basis of the United Church of Prussia had been discussed at the synod of 1846 with Schaff's former mentors playing a leading role. Von Gerlach's *Kirchenzeitung* had led the opposition to modernized formulas for ordination, baptism, or confirmation. The three ecumenical creeds, it was urged, were the common bond of Christians in all lands and generations, and no regional church body had the right to tamper with them. The creed was, moreover, an organic whole; one dared not pick out links in the chain merely because they were embarrassing to the current world view. Recognition of the creed was a crucial point of distinction between church and sectarian

[17] "The German Controversy," *PQR*, 1846, p. 309.
[18] Proudfit, *op. cit.*, 1852, p. 615.

consciousness. Nevin, similarly, argued that it was one of the touchstones of the sect spirit "to have no taste for the Creed,"[19] but rather to depend on one's separate private judgment.

In the introduction which Nevin wrote for his English translation of Schaf's *Principle of Protestantism,* he restated Schaf's case to try to save him from being misunderstood. The crucial issue as Nevin saw it was the proper relation between private judgment and the authority of the church as embodied in tradition. It was a false alternative to oppose tradition to Scripture, for the Bible cannot interpret itself.

> The only fair alternative lies between the bible as apprehended by the Church, and the same bible as apprehended by an individual, or by some party or sect to which he may happen to belong. . . .
>
> It is indeed an abominable usurpation, when the Church claims to be the source of truth for the single christian separately from the bible, or the absolutely infallible interpreter of the sense of the bible itself; and so requires him to yield his judgment blindly to her authority and tradition. But it is a presumption equally abominable, for a single individual to cast off all respect for Church authority and Church life, and pretend to draw his faith immediately from the bible, only and wholly through the narrow pipe stem of his own private judgment. . . . Neither side of the alternative separately taken is true; and yet neither is absolutely untrue. . . . Private judgment, or if any one please, the use of the bible in this form, is a sacred right, to be parted with for no price by those whom the truth has made free; but it can hold only in the element of true Church authority. . . . The case requires a reconciliation of these unhappily divided interests, in such form that the truth which each includes may be saved in the union of both. . . . What is to be reached after, as the true normal form of the Christian life, is such an inward marriage of the two general tendencies, as shall be sufficient to make them one.[20]

The program Nevin set for Mercersburg was thus that of a middle way, a reconciling way, a synthesis which would do justice to the sort of institutional heteronomy represented by Romanism and Puseyism on the one hand, and the personal appro-

[19] "The Apostles' Creed," *MR,* 1849, p. 124.
[20] Schaf, *op. cit.,* pp. 14, 13.

priation of biblical truth sought by Puritanism on the other. In this area Mercersburg undertook the responsibilities of a *via media* at a deeper level than Oxford had done.

How was a due respect for the authority of the church to be combined with the right of private judgment? Nevin's general approach to such issues was laid down in a baccalaureate address in 1849 entitled "Faith, Reverence and Freedom." His argument was that true freedom, far from being simply opposed to authority, is only possible within the recognition of objective law, and reverence for it. Such law is the expression of the divine creative Spirit, in whose image men and angels are created. And the intuition or apprehension of such revelations of the divine is what is called faith.

Nevin agreed with Kant, in a related essay on "Human Freedom," [21] that the very nature of conscious action requires autonomy of will. Freedom is indispensable to the life of spirit. If then the individual will is to obey freely the Law or Will of the intelligible universe, it must do so as recognizing therein *its own* true constitution. It must be self-determined precisely in being bound to the structure of the moral universe. Autonomy is reconciled with heteronomy on the basis of their essential harmony of nature.

The structure of the moral universe was described by Nevin in terms of the three orders—the family, the state, and the church. In each of these sets of relations irresponsible individualism and tyrannical authoritarianism are to be avoided by an inner reconciliation of freedom and law. The task of education is to raise children and citizens and Christians to self-government in due reverence for the Divine Will in the moral orders.

This was a conservative Hegelian ethic. Nevin opposed the natural rights theory in politics as he did abstract private judgment in the church. Like his friend Tayler Lewis he admired Burke. "Radicalism and red republicanism" [22] were the political

[21] *American Review,* 1848, pp. 406–18.
[22] Nevin, "Faith, Reverence, and Freedom," *MR,* 1850, p. 107.

equivalent of sect and schism in Christianity, or for that matter, of Fourierism, agrarianism, or the emancipation of women in Frances Wright's style in the family.[23] Although Nevin and Schaf found themselves most of the time opposing excessive individualism and irresponsibility, they were aware also of the opposite danger of authoritarianism.

Nevin's exposure of Charybdis on this side was set forth in the course of an extended debate with the writer whom the American Roman Catholic episcopate designated as their quasi-official spokesman, Orestes Brownson. In Nevin's judgment Moehler was worth twenty Brownsons as a Roman Catholic champion, but Brownson as an ex-Puritan addressed himself more effectively to the American mentality.[24]

Brownson's own career, Nevin remarked, illustrated the attraction of the two opposite poles. Brownson had reacted from the extreme of Unitarian or transcendentalist individualism to that of Roman Catholic authoritarianism without ever coming in sight of the higher unity of evangelical catholicism.[25] Now he was an ostentatious ultramontane, making extravagant claims for the infallibility of the pope apart from the church, and parading his servility to the hierarchy. He was become a "Puritan Romanist"; he would swallow a camel. Nevin's description reminds one of "Ideal" Ward, who would have liked a new infallible utterance from the pope each morning with his breakfast egg.

Nevin did not believe that blind submission to either priest or king could again be restored. The Reformation had won modern liberty, religious and political alike, and it was not conceivable that the new ground could ever be surrendered. There could be no infallible authority in church or state if man was to "fulfil his true moral destiny. . . . The man who is truly master of himself . . . by inward union with the Divine Law . . . is prepared

[23] Nevin, "The Moral Order of Sex," *MR*, 1850, pp. 569–73.

[24] Brownson had declared it his intention to discuss the Mercersburg movement at his earliest opportunity three years before (*Brownson's Quarterly Review*, 1847, p. 134), but Schaf had written him personally, urging him to wait until he had read *The Mystical Presence* and *What Is Church History?*

[25] "*Brownson's Quarterly Review*," *MR*, 1850, p. 33.

to brave all tyrannical authority . . . whether it be exercised by singlehanded pope or hydra-headed mob.[26]

For Brownson, however, there was no third alternative to private judgment denying church authority, or authority overriding reason arbitrarily. He presented Catholic truth as a "heteronomic supernatural," to be received on mere authority by a passive believer. It was beyond natural knowledge and could only be accepted on the authority of the teachers or witnesses. The creditability of such witnesses, however, was to be authenticated by natural reason. In this way, as Nevin observed, his theology came out as a sort of prudential rationalism.[27]

In Nevin's judgment the truth of revelation was not to be established by authority any more than by rational argument. It is not because the church tells us to, that we believe in Christ. Nor is it by proving his miraculous conception or resurrection "that we prove him to be the Son of God; but we must feel him in the first place to be the Son of God, with Peter, before we can truly believe, on any evidence, either the first of these facts or the last. . . . Christ authenticates himself for faith. . . . Because we believe in Him we believe also the Holy Catholic Church; and not in the reverse order." [28]

Nevin's objections to Brownson's apologetics would have held equally against those of Princeton and the New England theology, and indeed against the whole prevailing American reliance on the arguments to the truth of Christianity from miracle and prophecy. The assumption usually made in this case was that the ordinary course of nature was mechanical and fixed, and that miracles were divine interruptions, violations of natural law. But this was to misunderstand the ordinary processes of nature in a deistic way, and to conceive of miracle as mere magic.[29] Conceived as marvelous events, miracles proved nothing of the divinity of their agents. "A miracle does not prove the truth of a doctrine, or the divine mission of him that brings it to pass. . . . The doctrine

[26] "Faith, Reverence, and Freedom," *MR*, 1850, p. 115.
[27] "Brownson's Quarterly Review," *MR*, 1850, pp. 50, 51, 54, 59.
[28] *Ibid.*, pp. 69, 71; cf. "*Brownson's Review* Again," *MR*, 1850, p. 324.
[29] *Ibid.*, pp. 310, 311.

must first commend itself to the conscience as being *good,* and only then can the miracle seal it as divine." Jesus Christ, the crucial case, "authenticates himself," and is not authenticated or proved true by any external evidence or argument. "It may be more truly said that *we believe the miracles for Christ's sake,* than Christ for the miracles' sake." [30] What need then of the miracles? They are a confirmation, a manifestation of the power of the present divine. Christianity must have both miracles and prophecies, as external seals, but "taken by themselves, they can never form a valid, full, and final reason for faith." [31]

Nevin's insistence on the authority of the creed is to be understood in connection with this view of the intuitive recognition of God's self-revelation. For him the creed was not understood as a series of doctrinal propositions. He distinguished it from those later, elaborate confessions of faith which are the product of theological reflection and debate. As its name indicates, the creed does not belong to the realm of theology so much as it represents the unreflective voice of faith responding to God's self-revelation. To stand on the creed was in effect to claim that the ultimate appeal in Christianity is God made flesh in Christ, and that we know this God only in the fellowship of those brought into communion with Him. The creed was not a theory of divinity in miniature, but "a direct spontaneous witness with the mouth" to the felt realities, "the direct immediate utterance of the Christian faith itself," "the free spontaneous externalization of the Christian consciousness." The creed speaks from faith to kindle faith. "Its object is, not to lodge its articles as so many points of Christian orthodoxy in the mind; but so to bring this rather into the consciousness of what they affirm, that they may be appropriated by it, and made one with it, as a part of its own life." [32]

The archetype of the creed and its germ article is to be found in Peter's confession: "Thou art the Christ, the Son of the Living

[30] Nevin, "The New Testament Miracles," *MR,* 1850, pp. 578, 584.
[31] Nevin, "Trench's Lectures," *MR,* 1850, p. 607.
[32] *Ibid.,* "The Apostles' Creed," *MR,* 1849, pp. 214, 205, 219, 215.

God." Here was the spontaneous reply of faith to revelation, and obviously prior to any consideration of the theological implications. Peter acknowledged the only partly comprehended presence of God in Jesus. Yet implicit in that manifestation of God Incarnate was the whole Trinity. The basic Trinitarian architecture of the creed was thus no accident but a matter of intrinsic necessity. "The Creed was not made; not manufactured like a watch; it grew, self-produced," like a biological organism.[33] All the later additions were involved potentially in Peter's confession. It was still the same faith—in one article, in three, in twelve, in all its local variations. For centuries the baptismal creeds of local churches or church provinces varied in detail, as did their liturgies. Yet the substance of these variant formulas was felt to be the same, and to be the same as the substance of the apostolic preaching. That is why we may legitimately speak of "the Creed" as well as "the creeds," and why also it may be truly described as *apostolic*, even though it was not composed by the Apostles, as the Roman Catholics generally held. The creed was a prime instance of a valid development which remained true to type.

Nevin's opponents, such as Hodge and Proudfit and the editor of the *Puritan Recorder*, did not understand or accept this conception of a *developing* creed. They maintained that since the creed as we have it is not older than the fifth century, it is therefore neither apostolic nor authoritative. Nor did they concede the intrinsic necessity of its developing structure and exfoliation. In their view the creed *was* "manufactured like a watch." It was simply a selection of theological affirmations, and not necessarily the best selection.

Nevin's opponents were also cool toward the creed in general, partly because they disagreed with him on the affirmations for which he found it most useful—those of Christ and the Church. With regard to Christ, to be sure, they did not actually deny anything the creed said, but the recognition of the incarnate Lord was not for them the germ article of their faith and the-

[33] *Ibid.*, p. 219.

ology. Nevin represented here the prevailing method of German theology since Schleiermacher had labored to be consistently Christocentric, but American Protestant theology did not in the 1840's generally proceed from the Incarnation. Epistemologically it usually began from Scriptural Inspiration, and materially the key doctrine was that of the Atonement. The doctrine of the person of Christ in relation to the Trinity and to the church was an unfamiliar point of orientation.

Even Schaf had not been so consistently Christocentric as Nevin. He presented the formal principle of Protestantism as the inspired Scriptures. Nevin, however, pressed behind the Scriptures. The substance of revelation was not letter but life, not a body of doctrines, but God, His "being, and presence, and glory." [34] Faith was spiritual vision, the immediate apprehension of God manifest in Christ; and the revelation was self-authenticating, not assured because it came through an inspired book or by an accredited authority. Nevin was thus resting the authority of the Scriptures on the fact that they contained Christ, rather than believing what the Scriptures had to say about Christ because they were inspired. In so doing, Nevin was again returning to the position of the Reformers. But the position of the Reformers was unfamiliar to most American Protestants, who had lapsed again into the mechanical Romanist theory of verbal inspiration.

Much more obvious and explicit were the objections to the creed as being too churchly—the very point on which Nevin had been most emphatic in his exposition. "The new creation," he wrote, "commences with the Father, enters the world through the Incarnation of the Son, and runs its course in the world's life subsequently, by the Holy Ghost constantly present and always active in the Church." [35] It was the declarations about the work of the Holy Spirit in the church which brought the *Puritan Recorder* and the *Princeton Review* to open rebellion against the creed. It was the current "Puritan" conception that the Holy

[34] *Ibid.*, p. 210.
[35] *Ibid.*, p. 320.

Spirit communicated with *individuals*, who might consequently attach themselves to churches. In these quarters "the holy catholic church, the communion of saints," savored of ecclesiasticism and incipient popery.

For Proudfit the valid basis of a creed was that faith is the assent of an individual mind, requiring expression in a testimony or confession. By nature such faith must be individual. Proudfit could find no basis for a *corporate* faith. For Nevin, in contrast, the creed was the response of the community *as a whole* to the manifestation of God. In good romantic style he compared its origin and development to that of language, or the common law. (This was not to say, he warned, that the creed was but a myth, as Strauss contended.) He considered it a recommendation rather than a liability that the creed had no such definite authors as the New Testament books. "No man can be said to have composed it," he wrote, "it is no work of bishops or synods; it must be taken rather as the grand epos of Christianity itself, the spontaneous poem of its own life."[36]

The church as Nevin expounded it was not simply one possible object of the activity of the Holy Spirit, but the definition of the total scope of that activity. No place was left for the Puritan notion of the salvation of individuals prior to their relation to the church. "To a vast deal of our modern thinking," Nevin commented, "the order here observed by the Creed must appear careless at least, and ill-advised. It would be led far more naturally to say: I believe in repentance and conversion, then in the communion of saints, and finally in some sort of holy catholic church." In the creed, however, the process of salvation is specifically through the church; furthermore, it is inseparably related to the sacraments of the church. Nevin did not interpret the "communio sanctorum" in this sense, but the "remission of sins," he said, is doubtless to be read in the sense of the Nicene article "one *baptism* for the remission of sins." Again he states, "The religion of the Creed is, throughout, sacramental and churchly."

[36] *Ibid.*, p. 217.

Nevin conceded, "All this was liable to be greatly abused, and, as we all very well know, was so abused in fact. But still, rightly understood, it expresses deep and sacred truth." [37]

It was possible, to be sure, to reinterpret the creed into Puritan individualism. "The article may be indeed construed to mean an invisible church simply, where grace works without sacraments." And presumably this was the interpretation put on the creed by Hodge, for example, who is said to have used it in family worship. "But then it is forced out of its historical sense. . . . The Church here spoken of is a real mystery derived through the Holy Ghost from the fact of the Incarnation." [38]

Proudfit, for the Dutch Reformed (like the Congregationalists generally), simply gave up this article and the creed as essentially Roman. With a characteristic flourish, he protested:

> That single article, "I believe in the Holy Catholic Church," with the Papal interpretation, is a gate large enough for an army with banners to pass through. What an interminable line of shaven monks, begging friars, lying Jesuits, and inquisitors keen on the scent of heretical blood—what rites, orders and ordinances ("which the Lord commanded not, neither came it into his mind"), interdicts and indulgences, anathemas and canonizations have already emerged through that ample portal . . . all under the sacred auspices and unquestionable sanction of "the *holy* Catholic *Church*." [39]

Nevin observed:

> Everything like a churchly, priestly, sacramental religion, is for him [Proudfit] the abomination of Romanism itself. He believes in no descent to hades, no continuation of the glorified resurrection life of Christ *en mysterio* here below, no supernatural church, no remission of sins, no communion of saints living and dead, *in the sense of this primitive symbol.*

Being thus out of harmony with the creed, the Puritanism of Dr. Proudfit did not see this as the "necessary matrix of all true Christian theology" but was ready to read another sense into the Scriptures.[40]

[37] *Ibid.*, pp. 333–34.
[38] Nevin, "The Anti-Creed Heresy," *MR*, 1852, p. 615.
[39] "The Apostles' Creed," *BRPR*, 1852, pp. 626–27.
[40] "The Anti-Creed Heresy," *MR*, 1852, 615–16.

Nevin would not allow the Puritan individualistic and unsacramental exegesis of the Bible, through which they arrayed the Bible against the creed and church as he interpreted these. What they set forth was not the Bible, he declared, but their misinterpretation of the Bible. Nevin was ready to supply passage after passage to substantiate his churchly, sacramental view. "The sixth chapter of John, the terms employed in the institution of the Lord's Supper, the foundation of the Church on Peter, the Apostolical commission, the giving of the keys, and the numerous passages which directly or indirectly ascribe the power of a new birth to baptism and make the church the organ and vehicle of salvation, may be noticed as instances." [41] The Puritan was forced by *his* tradition to misinterpret all such passages outrageously.

What conclusions did Nevin come to, through this study of the classic creed of Christianity, on the question of Scripture and tradition? On the face of it, he seems to have moved some distance from the *Principle of Protestantism.* One might even guess that if the York Synod had had Nevin's articles on the creed before them when the charges of heresy were made, the outcome might have been different.

Nevin had transferred the locus of authority from the Scriptures to Christ, so that the Bible was revelation in a derived and secondary sense. The creed, on the other hand, could no longer be contrasted (as merely human tradition) to the inspired word. The creed also has a derived and secondary authority co-ordinate with the New Testament. It did not "spring from the Bible" as Schaf had said, but "from the living sense of Christ's presence itself." [42] In fact, Nevin seems at least by inference to exalt the oral transmission of the creed over the written word of the Bible. The creed was not, he says, "an outward dead *traditum* or deposit" put together by some of the Apostles [43] and handed over to the keeping of the church. He did not apply this latter description to the books of the New Testament, but they would seem

[41] *Ibid.*, p. 619.
[42] Nevin, "The Apostles' Creed," *MR*, 1849, p. 337.
[43] *Ibid.*, pp. 201–2.

to fit. In any case the creed antedated the New Testament, it was independent of it, and as mediating the revelation of Christ it could likewise be called a "divine tradition." Creed and New Testament seemed to be co-ordinate, independent testimonies and vehicles of the same revelation.

These two authorities, according to Nevin, are in continued reciprocal influence. The Bible, as we have seen, is to be interpreted from within the orbit of the creed, on the basis of faith in Christ and from within the communion of the church. Just what might be implied here is not clear. Nevin did not undertake to show "when and how precisely this ecclesiastical tradition must be allowed to rule the interpretation of the Bible." [44] At least it would require a Trinitarian reading of the Bible, for without the guidance of the creed to the apostolic testimony, as Nevin replied to the *scriptura sola* party, the Bible alone was capable of a Unitarian exegesis.

The church, on the other hand, must also be "ruled by the Bible." The consciousness of the church, while starting prior to the Bible, "becomes the living stream into which continuously the sense of the Bible is poured, through the Holy Ghost, from age to age." Being ruled by the Bible evidently left room for the role of private judgment in exegesis, within the community of faith in Christ. "Will it be said that this is a circle? Be it so. In such circle, precisely, is it the divine prerogative of faith at all times firmly and serenely to move." [45]

The point was not, said Nevin,

> the Creed against the Bible; this last we all allow to be supreme; but the Creed against the inward habit and tradition of Puritanism. . . . We go for private judgment too, and Protestant independence; but for this very reason we wish to secure the conditions that are most favorable to their rational exercise. . . . Why may not private judgment stand in the bosom of the old faith, as fully as on the outside of it? [46]

[44] "Dr. Berg's Last Words," *MR*, 1852, pp. 287–88.
[45] Nevin, "The Apostles' Creed," *MR*, 1849, pp. 339–40.
[46] "Puritanism and the Creed," *MR*, 1849, p. 598.

Nevin does not need to be reminded, he declares, of the "vast achievements and high merits of Puritanism." In a rare admission of human weakness, he confesses, "The hardest Puritan we have to do with always is the one we carry, by birth and education, in our own bosom. But the misery of it is, for our quiet, that the Catholic is there too, and will not be at rest." In the reconciliation of these two he sees the vocation of his theology. Here too Mercersburg is romantic and idealistic in its hope of ecumenical and theological synthesis.

> We are deeply persuaded that the sense of authority and the exercise of free thought go hand in hand together, and cannot be disjoined in the moral world without deep prejudice to truth. We are deeply persuaded too, in the case before us, that Catholicism and Puritanism both enter of right into the constitution of Christianity, and that neither can legitimately exclude the other. The problem of their true and proper union, is indeed one of no common difficulty; the great problem, as it would seem, for the new era of Christianity which is now so generally supposed to be at hand. . . . Blind outward authority, and mere private judgment, are alike insufficient as a key to the Bible. What we desire is, that this should be acknowledged, and a true conciliation at least aimed at between the great tendencies, which are here placed in opposition and conflict. It is not by the simple assertion of its own life, but in *so* asserting this life as to leave no room for the other side of religion that Puritanism seems to us to be too often in fault. . . . Puritanism is bound to acknowledge the rights of other tendencies, the Catholic, the Lutheran, the original Reformed, for instance, if it would have its own acknowledged, and so cooperate efficiently in the great task of bringing Christianity to its last universal form.[47]

To the great majority of his readers, however, Nevin's argument must have seemed disastrous to Protestantism. By acknowledging the authority of a tradition separate from the Bible he seemed to accept in principle the position of Trent and the Puseyites. To be sure, he had spoken only of the creeds, and he had argued effectively that the Reformers also had acknowledged the creeds. Many Protestant theologians had held the creed in-

[47] *Ibid.*, pp. 602–3.

spired as well as apostolic. But it was not clear why he must stop with the creeds if the Christian consciousness was the source of such "outbirths." Nevin had broken down the popular distinction between Scripture and tradition. One might assume that he would go at least as far as Moehler and agree that only through the New Testament does the church have reliable concrete knowledge of the character of the Incarnate Lord. But then how far would he permit the church to control exegesis of the New Testament in the interest of a received teaching?

Nevin had also in principle justified the development of ecclesiastical traditions other than the creed. Infant baptism, for example, was to be defended on grounds of tradition rather than Scripture since Scripture alone was not conclusive on the issue. It was intimated that the same principle should be applied to questions of liturgy and church festivals, which were at that time under debate in the German Reformed Church, and to the issue of episcopacy. On what principle could Nevin ever stop? What of papal primacy? Supremacy? Infallibility? What of the propitiatory sacrifice of the mass? Enforced celibacy? Indulgences? Such were the questions which arose in the minds of many readers. Nevin had been content to undermine the current Protestant argument. Many of his readers would have been reassured if he had shown more clearly how on his grounds some of the Protestant case against Rome could still be made.

In at least three ways, however, Nevin had insisted on Protestant ground. His account of the correlation of faith and revelation effectively ruled out "implicit faith" or faith on the authority of others as taught by Rome and Oxford. Every man must do his own believing, as Luther repeatedly stated. Then, too, within the church, there was no infallible organ of truth separately taken, whether papacy, episcopacy, or ministry as a whole. If the separate infallibility of the teaching office was the ultimate authority of Roman Catholicism, this was rejected by Nevin. Every given officer, council, or assembly was fallible. One could be confident only that saving knowledge would never depart from the church as a whole. In any case, and finally, one would believe the church only as discovering in it the Christ. One did not believe Christ because the church taught so, as Augustine had said.

Such was the substance of Nevin's effort to find a reconciling middle way, a new ecumenical synthesis, with regard to the problem of authority in relation to Scripture and tradition. He satisfied few Protestants and no Roman Catholics, but probably few on either side were willing even to face the questions he raised.

8/ Nevin's "Dizziness"

For five or six years the Mercersburg professors blocked out the main outlines of their "evangelical catholicism." In 1851 came a crisis. John Nevin, the theological leader, was caught up in the current of the more advanced Anglo-Catholics of England. Almost all his theological writing for a year and a half was devoted to the study of the ancient church, toward which he adopted much of the Roman view. His friends and associates watched anxiously as his articles showed increasingly a despair of Protestantism and a loss of confidence in the Mercersburg hope of Protestant development. Nevin resigned from his various offices in the German Reformed Church—as professor of theology, chairman of the liturgy committee, chief contributor to the *Mercersburg Review*, president of Marshall College. For months he weighed the question whether to submit to Rome. Having broken down physically and nervously, he felt the choice to be what church he should die in. The validity and continuance of the whole Mercersburg tendency, in the meantime, seemed to hang on the issue of his defection. An opponent later referred to this period as Nevin's "five years of dizziness." [1]

For an understanding of the situation, the practical difficulties of Marshall College and the Mercersburg Seminary are important. Under Nevin's presidency the college had achieved fame and distinction, but its finances had never attained stability. He had accepted the office at Rauch's death only provisionally and without remuneration. His personality and vigor had drawn and held an able faculty at miserable salaries, and his gratuitous service as president and professor had held the college above the level of a country academy. The *Mercersburg Review* and *Der Kirchenfreund* gave Marshall national distinction, and the life of the mind was vigorous in the village. The annual budget for the whole

[1] J. I. Good, *History of the Reformed Church in the United States in the Nineteenth Century* (New York, 1911), p. 312.

college, on the other hand, was only about $3,000 and the tendency was downward. In 1848, the science teacher resigned in discouragement, followed the next year by the mathematics teacher. Periodically, Nevin himself proposed resigning, to force the church to act responsibly to the college, but his colleagues always dissuaded him.

In 1849 emerged a new possibility for solving the grim and exhausting penury at Marshall: the proposal of a merger with Franklin College at Lancaster. Franklin College had property but only half a dozen students and two instructors, whereas Marshall College was a flourishing educational enterprise without financial resources. Nevin, as can be imagined, eagerly welcomed the opportunity, and his faculty and students all favored it. From local Mercersburg interests, however, there was so much resistance that Nevin won over his board only after a long struggle in the winter of 1849–50. Then he had to lobby at Harrisburg for empowering legislation from the Pennsylvania legislature.

The charter granted and the act of incorporation drafted for "Franklin and Marshall College," Nevin wrote a series of six articles in the *Weekly Messenger*, stating the case for "The Removal of Marshall College." [2] He confessed that he had "been meditating for at least two years the propriety of giving up the presidency for the purpose of setting things in their true light." The long-term prospect had been so hopeless that for some time he had not felt free to solicit liberal gifts to the college, but now adequate properties and endowment were a possibility for the first time. If this opportunity were rejected, Nevin would have nothing more to do with the college. He was using his threat of resignation as an ultimatum, since there was still opposition in the Mercersburg community. "We are so heartily sick," he explained, "of the whole business of trying to carry forward a College without proper means."

Nevin's burden through these negotiations had been extraordinary. He was preaching weekly at the broken-down congrega-

[2] *Weekly Messenger* (hereafter cited as *WM*), May 1, 8, 15, 22, 29; June 6, 1850.

tion in the town; teaching his seminary classes; filling about half of the *Mercersburg Review* with his debates with Hodge, Brownson, and other solid opponents; and warming up his long-disused mathematics to replace the instructor in that field. One can imagine the poor man's frustration as he sometimes wrestled a whole afternoon with an ordinary algebra problem! The insupportable strain was sufficient to explain Nevin's letter to the seminary board at the end of the summer term of 1850, declaring his intention to cease instruction in theology at the end of the next term.[3] The necessities of the college took prior claim on his time. This procedure seemed also the only way of forcing the board's attention to the arrears in his salary as theology professor.

At the end of the term, in the spring of 1851, Nevin not only discontinued theological instruction according to his notice but also submitted his resignation outright. Only twenty-six seminary students were in residence, and Schaff could hold the school together for a time, since he could now lecture in English as well as in German. Yielding to the pleas of the seniors, Nevin gave them private lectures in theology through the summer. It is from 1851 that most of our student lecture notes on his course come.[4] Though he had asked to be freed of the formal obligations of his theological chair, he remained president of Marshall College and apparently intended to do so until the move to Lancaster was effected.

In this resignation from the seminary chair we have the first definite indication of Nevin's theological vertigo. The direction of his mind was made evident by the publication in July, 1851, of "The Anglican Crisis" and thereafter by the series "Early Christianity" and "Cyprian." As Schaff put it, the resignation arose in part "from conscientious doubt whether he was, just now, the man suited to educate the theological youth for the service of a

[3] H. M. J. Klein, *History of the Eastern Synod of the Reformed Church in the United States* (Lancaster, 1943), p. 217.

[4] W. H. Erb, *Dr. Nevin's Theology* (Reading, 1913); and manuscripts in the library of the German Reformed Church, in the college library of Franklin and Marshall College, and in the Good Collection at Eden Theological Seminary.

Protestant denomination, while the whole Church question was undergoing a radical revision in his mind."[5] Like Newman a decade earlier, Nevin had seen a ghost, the serious realization that Rome might be right.

"The Anglican Crisis" shows Nevin engaged with surprising intensity in the affairs of the Church of England, with no evidence of any local incident to explain his shift of views in the preceding spring. He had evidently been following, for the preceding two or three years, the heated controversy over the Gorham case—the "crisis" of his title. Gorham was an Anglican vicar, whose bishop, Dr. Phillpotts of Exeter, had refused to install him at Brampford Speke on the ground that his doctrine of baptism was heretical. Gorham startled and dismayed many Anglicans in 1849, when, having lost an appeal to the ecclesiastical Court of Arches, he appealed again to the Judicial Committee of the Privy Council. That court of seven lay judges ruled that Gorham's views on baptism fell within the permissible bounds of Anglican doctrine and ordered that he be installed. This decision of March, 1850, was memorable both for its theological substance and for the fact that it was the Privy Council which had decided such an issue.

The Roman Catholics had pressed their advantage at this brutal exposure of Anglican captivity to the civil power. Wiseman wrote tellingly in the *Dublin Review* (March, 1850), and that summer Newman delivered his lectures on "Anglican Difficulties." There followed a wave of secessions to Rome greater even than that touched off by Newman's departure five years before, and across the Atlantic Nevin discussed the situation in much the same terms as Newman. "The constitutional deficiency" of Anglicanism, he observed, "its want of ability to assert and carry out in full the proper functions of a church," now forced Anglicans of Catholic sympathies to reconsider their relations to Rome. The whole Tractarian movement for half a generation had protested against civil supremacy over the church; now a theo-

[5] Letter to the editor, *Reformierte Kirchenzeitung,* quoted in *Christian Intelligencer,* December 16, 1852.

logical question of primary consequence had been settled for the Church of England by purely civil authority, "and the English hierarchy, with his Grace of Canterbury at its head . . . dutifully succumbs to the insolent and profane dictation." Chalmers had led the best men of the Church of Scotland out of the establishment on just such an issue. The outcome in England would probably be similar, for the wing which still took Catholic truth seriously leaned powerfully toward secession, "whether it be to form a new body or to fall into the arms of Rome." The number and quality of those who had already followed Newman and Manning were without precedent. Nearly two thousand ministers were reported to hold views which would hardly permit them to remain in the state church. "A great churchslide, which is destined soon to shake the whole world with its thundering sound," seemed imminent.[6] And Nevin evidently suspected that the geological fault under the Church of England extended also under the hills of Mercersburg village.

Far more than the Anglican establishment hung on the Gorham case. The state-church relationship involved was of course peculiar to the Church of England, but the theological issue was common to all English-speaking Protestantism. The various nuances of meaning regarding baptismal regeneration did not exhaust the issue; the question was whether sacramental grace was to be recognized in any form in Protestantism—English, Scottish, or American. Nevin had apparently been shocked at the extent and sweeping character of expressions opposed to such recognition both inside and outside the Church of England. The antisacramental, unchurchly "Puritan" party (Anglican, Congregational, Methodist, Presbyterian, Baptist, or Lutheran) seemed anxious to reject their Catholic and Reformation heritage, to get clear "of all such obsolete mystification as we find on the subject even in Luther, Calvin, and the English Prayer Book." In Nevin's mind loomed the "final deadly conflict for the mastery of Protestantism" between the churchly and unchurchly tendencies.

[6] Nevin, "The Anglican Crisis," *Mercersburg Review* (hereafter cited as *MR*), 1851, pp. 380–81, 388–89.

"How," he asked, "can Lutherans and the Reformed, Methodists, Presbyterians, or even Congregationalists of the old stamp . . . not be struck with some feeling of anxiety and dread at the thought of making Protestantism by its own voice and vote constitutionally baptistic and unsacramental, in any such open revolutionary style?" No previous crisis had so focused the issue for Nevin. This was life or death for Protestantism; and if the latter, what else was there but Rome? The issue was "the true sense of Protestantism, and its right to exist, over against the pretensions of the Church of Rome." [7]

Fallacies had been exposed and delusions brought to an end. The difficulties and contradictions in the present state of the church, hitherto passively accepted, were now brought out sensibly. The hollowness of the established order was disclosed, and in English Protestantism the idea of *the church* must now become either far less or far more. Protestantism in general was being winnowed, and all intra-Protestant controversies were dwarfed by the great question now set before all the heirs of the Reformation. Nevin's title might well have been "The Crisis of Protestantism," not merely "The Anglican Crisis." He did not attempt to resolve the issue, but his language about Protestantism was colored by disillusion and distaste, while he defended Roman Catholicism warmly from Protestant criticism and persecution. Taking the two as they stood, he clearly suspected that there was more to be said for Rome, and the only reason for remaining Protestant was the hope that Protestantism might be radically reformed.

In the great struggle between the churchly and unchurchly tendencies, episcopacy was a minor circumstance. The mechanics of an episcopal succession provided no such security as the Anglicans thought.

> No *jure divino* constitution in any such style as this, can uphold in a real way for faith the mystery of the one, holy, Catholic and Apostolical Church. . . . This does not imply that such organs and functions may be indifferently in any form, or in no form whatever

[7] *Ibid.*, pp. 372–73, 392.

. . . but it does mean certainly that the organs and functions make not of themselves the being of the body.

The crucial question concerns the divine character of the church, having its ground and force in the mystery of the Incarnation. For this reason the question of sacramental grace is more fundamental than any matter of polity or order, "for the sacraments are the standing sign and seal of whatever power is comprised in the Church." To be sure, it is possible to conceive of grace-bearing sacraments separately from the sense of a divine church, but this is mere magic. "We must believe in a divine Church, in order to believe in divine sacraments, or in a divine ministry under any form."[8] This, for Nevin, was the article of "the standing and falling church," not any particular order of the ministry, and on this basis Anglicanism shared the dangerous common ground of Protestantism generally. It would have been a great relief, Nevin declared, to be able to find in Anglican Episcopacy a truly rational and solid answer, but neither there nor in any other Protestant body was there such security. Anglicanism offered no option distinct from Protestantism generally.

Apart from formal reconciliation with Rome, the only position to which Nevin could seriously resort was that based on historical development. The very conception which had carried Newman to Rome was the only alternative Nevin opposed to Rome. Thereby

without prejudice to Catholicism first in its own order and sphere, or to Protestantism next as a real advance on this in modern times, though with the full acknowledgment of the faults and views [flaws?] of both systems, it is assumed that the whole present state of the church is transitional only and interimistic; and that it is destined accordingly through the very crisis which is now coming on . . . to surmount in due season the painful contradictions (dialectic thorns) of the Protestant controversy . . . and so to carry it triumphantly forward . . . in some form that shall be found at the same time to etherialize and save, in the same way, the last sense also and rich wealth of the old Catholic faith.

[8] *Ibid.*, pp. 387–89.

By this view Protestantism might be regarded as "the main though by no means exclusive stream" in which the true church was being carried forward.[9]

Nevin followed this delineation of the crisis of Protestantism with his series of seven articles on early church history—three articles on "Early Christianity" and four on "Cyprian"—published in the second half of 1851 and in 1852. The literary fruit of these years thus was some three hundred pages of patristic studies. Nevin gives us a clue to their theological and religious significance to him when he quotes from Heinrich Thiersch the following account, which evidently comported closely with his own experience.

It is a strange impression that the church fathers make on one who first enters on the study of them, under the full force of a merely Protestant consciousness. So fared it with the writer himself. Nurtured on the best that the old Protestant books of devotion contain, and trained theologically in the doctrines and interpretations of the orthodox period of Protestantism, he turned finally to the fathers. Well does he remember how strange it appeared to him in the beginning, to find here nothing of those truths which formed the spring of his whole religious life, nothing of the way the sinner must tread to arrive at peace and an assurance of the Divine favor, nothing of Christ's merit as the only ground of forgiveness, nothing of continual repentance and ever new recourse to the fountain of free grace, nothing of the high confidence of the justified believer. Instead of this, he found that all weight was laid on the incarnation of the Divine Logos, on the right knowledge of the great object of worship, on the objective mystery of the Trinity and of Christ's Person, on the connection between creation, redemption, and the future restoration of the creature along with the glorification also of man's body, on the freedom of man and on the reality of the operations of Divine grace in the sacraments. But he was enabled gradually to live himself into this old mode of thought, and without giving up what is true and inalienable in the Lutheran Protestant consciousness, to correct its onesidedness by a living appropriation of the theology of the fathers. He soon saw, that over against the errors of the present time, its pantheism and fatalism, its spiritualism and misapprehension of the

[9] *Ibid.*, pp. 396, 398.

significance of the corporeal, the church needs a decided taking up again of what is true in the Patristic scheme of thought, and an assimilation of her whole life to the ancient model—in spirit and idea first, as outward relations are not at once under human control. This old primitive church stood out to his view more and more in its full splendor, in its sublime beauty, of which only fragmentary lineaments are to be recognized in the churches, confessions, and sects of the present day.[10]

In this discovery and appropriation of the fathers Nevin and Thiersch alike found a suggestion and foretaste of genuine evangelical catholicism as it might be, repairing the inadequacies at once of Protestantism and Romanism.

But Nevin's presentation of patristic theology to his Protestant readers was more polemical than Thiersch's statement. His articles in this series were intended to substantiate for American Protestants the thesis of Newman's *Essay on Development*, that the type and genius of the ancient church was reproduced far more accurately by modern Roman Catholicism than by any Protestant body. "Few theological tracts, in the English language," wrote Nevin of Newman's *Essay*, "are more worthy of being read, or more likely to reward a diligent perusal with lasting benefit and fruit." [11] Most of the historical argument today would be conceded by Protestant historians generally. To understand the scandal it caused in the mid-nineteenth century, one must remember the curious image of Christian history then current in American religious periodicals and the teaching of even the chief centers of theological scholarship—Andover, Yale, Princeton, and Union. The same background is needed to comprehend the emotional wrench involved in Nevin's reorientation from his "Puritan" education to the appropriation of a catholic heritage he had been trained to scorn.

In his first article on "Early Christianity" Nevin reviewed the usual Anglican appeal to the authority of the fourth and fifth centuries and concluded that it was not tenable against the Roman Catholic position. Bishops in apostolic succession, but out of

[10] "Early Christianity," first article, *MR,* 1851, p. 555.
[11] *Ibid.,* third article, *MR,* 1852, p. 33.

communion with the bishop of Rome, would have been mere schismatics to Cyprian, Ambrose, or Augustine. By the criteria of the fourth and fifth century, Anglicanism, high or low, was simply schism. The historical arguments used by Anglicans to prove the necessity of episcopacy were equally cogent for papal primacy. As Newman had written, if Athanasius or Ambrose came suddenly to life, they would certainly feel more at home in Roman Catholic circles than among Anglicans or other Protestants.

The second and third articles in this series pushed the same argument back into the third and second centuries, constituting a rebuttal of Leonard Bacon's view that the martyrs at Lyons in the days of Pothinus and Irenaeus suffered for the same truths as those being preached in the pulpits of Connecticut and Massachusetts. Such fathers as Ignatius, Justin, Polycarp, Tertullian, and Irenaeus, said Nevin, were in no way Puritan, but churchly sacramentalists. The whole conception of a primitive evangelicalism, succeeded by a fall and apostasy of the church, was a "Protestant myth," as wildly unhistorical as the reconstructions of the Tübingen school. The early church, from the end of the first century, concluded Nevin, was "catholic" and not Protestant.

The four articles in the series on "Cyprian," which appeared in 1852, were somewhat inconsistent in form. Nevin obviously had intended to compose a monograph of the "life and times" pattern which Neander had established with his studies of such men as Julian, Chrysostom, and Anselm. He had worked through the whole Cyprianic corpus, arranged his materials clearly, and summarized or translated a substantial portion of the chief treatises and letters. Only a little editing of these articles would be needed to assemble a coherent, well-organized, historical account of Cyprian. The editor, however, would have to eliminate other matter—especially in the third article, which is really a sequel to the argument of "Early Christianity," seeking to push the Cyprianic doctrine of the church back into the second century.

Regarding church order and the ministry Nevin consistently preferred the Roman to the Anglican reading of Cyprian. Cyprian was not merely a champion of hierarchy and episcopal succession;

he found the virtue of the episcopal office dependent on the unity of the bishops, a unity signalized by their communion with Rome. The same insistence on the authority of bishops in apostolic succession and on the primacy among these of the Roman bishop was to be found in Irenaeus and Tertullian in the second century and in part even in Ignatius. "It is plain enough," Nevin concluded, "that the government of the church, in the second century, was in this [episcopal] form; and we think it sufficiently clear also, that the See of Rome was regarded as possessing a central dignity in the system, a sort of actual *principality*, derived from the original primacy of St. Peter." [12]

Although Nevin devoted fullest attention to matters of polity and the ministry, he also noted half a dozen other points at which the ancient church was more Catholic than Protestant. The fathers viewed the sacraments as mysteries, the Eucharist involving the real presence of the Lord's body and blood, and a participation in his propitiatory sacrifice. They lived by the creed and the doctrinal authority of the clergy rather than by the Bible as known to private judgment. Their sense of the communion of saints reached beyond the grave, leading to sacrifices and prayers for the dead, and the belief in the intercession of saints and angels. They venerated relics and reported frequent miracles. They set a high value on celibacy, voluntary poverty, and the monastic life.

In developing his case Nevin drew not only on Newman, but also on the work of scholars who arrived at very different conclusions from the same facts—Rothe's *Anfänge der christlichen Kirche*, for example, which he is reported to have described as the most stimulating book he had ever read.[13] Although radically unchurchly, Rothe identified his own conception of the ancient catholic church as a footnote to Moehler. Isaac Taylor similarly argued in his *Ancient Christianity, and the Doctrines of the Oxford Tracts for the Times* that church life from the second to the

[12] "Cyprian," third article, *MR*, 1852, p. 428.

[13] W. M. Reily, "John Williamson Nevin, D.D., L.L.D.," *Magazine of Christian Literature*, II (April–September, 1890), 325.

fifth centuries was far more Roman than Anglican. Taylor, however, was out to undermine the Tractarian notion of an ancient golden age of the church. The widespread ascetic practices, he contended, were expressions of gnosticism, the cult of saints and martyrs was a relic of polytheism, many of the miracles were fraudulent, and public morals in the Christian Empire of the fourth and fifth centuries were appalling. Medieval popery was, on the whole, an improvement on Nicene Christianity.

Nevin's own attitude toward his Romanizing fathers was ambiguous. He adopted the form of a descriptive historian, but at times he wrote actually as an advocate. Periodically he reminded his readers that his points were historical, not doctrinal, and that he was not *defending* the fathers. Yet he often did defend them. Occasionally Nevin also intimated that he could conceive of valid alternatives to patristic views, or at least improvements on them. The prevailing tone, however, was warmly sympathetic, and the comparisons with modern Protestantism were almost always to the disadvantage of the latter. With a view to Puritanism at least, Nevin declared, "we choose to go here with the early church. . . . Come what may of the Reformation, there are certain general maxims of faith here which we can never safely renounce." [14]

"Puritanism" had been the object of Nevin's criticism, of course, for years, on the general subjects of church and sacraments. In his patristic studies he seems to have made several specific changes of view even further away from the Reformation, to have shifted ground, for instance, on the ministry and on Eucharistic sacrifice (both of which will be discussed later). Other topics showing this change of attitude include prayers for the dead and the intercession of the saints, which he now treated with gentleness and sympathy. From this feeling for communion with the church triumphant he could also understand the ancient veneration for relics. Personal experiences of bereavement had given several of the Mercersburg leaders special sensitivity in this connection. The Schaffs had lost several children, some in especially

[14] "Early Christianity," second article, *MR,* 1851, pp. 561–62.

distressing ways. Nevin had been deeply affected by his father's death in 1829. Harbaugh, who eventually became sainted throughout the church, chiefly because of his series of works on heaven and the sainted dead, had turned to these subjects after losing several children and his wife. Nevin's discussion of the views of the fathers on these themes was definitely warmer than the usual Puritan attitude. (He later was attracted by Swedenborgianism because of this interest.)

Nevin also sought to explain and apologize for, if not actually to defend, the inadequacies of Cyprian and the early fathers on original sin, justification by faith, and human merit. The early fathers generally, he observed, did not hold the Reformation view of justification by faith. But even the Bible, he declared, lacks the careful distinction between justification and sanctification which is made in the Protestant confessions. "Theology," said Nevin, "may require in a later stage of its history distinctions and determinations which were not called for in the period going before." [15] At least Cyprian had given no hope to the natural man outside baptism and had acknowledged no good works outside the means of grace. For him justification implanted in the believer the real principle of righteousness as the germ of sanctification. Hence good works in alms, celibacy, confession, and martyrdom grew from the faith nurtured by the sacraments. They were also, to be sure, understood to have real merit to atone for sin.

Nevin was now ready to defend in particular the religious value of celibacy, a theme in which he had shown no interest in his "Moral Order of Sex." [16] He opposed as "monstrous" Isaac Taylor's thesis that such asceticism was a gnostic, Buddhist, or Hindu corruption of Christianity. "It is not to be questioned," wrote Nevin of Cyprian's proof texts in this connection, "but that these passages, rightly considered, are of real force in favor of the principle which is here involved. They go to show, in harmony with the natural religious sense of the whole world, that virginity and continence are not a matter of indifference in the service of

[15] "Cyprian," fourth article, *MR,* 1852, p. 549.
[16] *MR,* 1850, pp. 549–73.

God." Nevin could not see how Taylor's theory of asceticism as a foreign ingredient could "be set in harmony with any sort of real faith whatever in the divine origin and true historical continuance of Christianity, as a revelation starting from Christ, and upheld by his Spirit."[17] Asceticism and celibacy, Nevin remarked, did not suit the "worldly prudence, utility, materialism and common sense" of the American Puritan.[18] He liked to think of the bachelor members of the Marshall faculty as Christian celibates, and a few years later some of them actually talked of something like vows. He later expressed much interest in Muhlenberg's efforts to create Anglican sisterhoods on the Lutheran deaconess pattern.

In conclusion, the ancient church from the end of the first century was closer to Roman Catholicism, Nevin maintained, than to Protestantism, and Protestantism was related to the early church only through Roman Catholicism. The only possible way of vindicating the Reformation, apart from a notion of fall and apostasy immediately following the Apostles, which seemed to Nevin sheer infidelity, was through a theory of development which recognized the legitimacy of ancient and medieval Catholicism. "The only escape then is in the formula of the same and yet not the same, legitimate growth, historical development. If this cannot stand, if it be found at war with the true idea of a Divine revelation, we for our part must give up all faith in Protestantism, and bow as best we can to the authority of the Roman Church."[19]

Nevin was carefully hypothetical in his formulation of development in this connection, observing that the theories of Newman, Rothe, Schaf, Thiersch, Neander all differed.[20] He could not say whether or how Protestantism could be taken as a more advanced state of that ancient Catholic life. Whether "unity in the midst of change" could actually be made "the true key to the problem of Protestantism" he did not know. "We say merely, that if this interest be at all capable of rational apology, in the face of its

[17] "Cyprian," fourth article, *MR*, 1852, pp. 556, 559.
[18] "Early Christianity," second article, *MR*, 1851, p. 528.
[19] *Ibid.*, first article, *MR*, 1851, p. 482.
[20] "Cyprian," fourth article, *MR*, 1852, p. 562.

notorious disagreement with ancient Christianity, it can be in this way only and in no other." [21] The problem caused him anxiety and alarm.

Protestantism was so obviously "fast tumbling into ruins," a "chaos of dissolution," that it could be repaired only by the co-operation and help of Romanism, as "the proper and necessary complement of its own nature." Both traditions were "to be regarded as falling short of the full idea of Christianity." Their synthesis might be anticipated in any one of three patterns—with either of the two as dominant or with both meeting on even balance. Nevin declined to analyze the merits of these alternatives. To many readers, however, it must have been startling to find him even stating the hypothesis that Protestantism "must in the end fall back into the old Catholic stream in order to fulfil its own mission." [22]

Nevin warmly defended Roman Catholicism from the abuse and slander it received on all sides in America and in England. "It is not easy," he wrote, "to read the writings of Bishop England, glowing with the eloquence of noble gentlemanly feeling as they do on almost every page, and not be filled with indignation, as well as moved even to tears at times, with the gross and cruel wrong which has been heaped upon the Catholics among us." Sanctity and true godliness were not at all rare in that communion, and they rose from the inner life of the system rather than despite it. Borromeo, Fénelon, Philip de Neri, were cases in point. "Such an institution as that of the Sisters of Charity can never be transferred to purely Protestant ground; as no such ground either could ever have given it birth." Rome, "with all its supposed errors and schisms, has ever had power in its own way to produce a large amount of very lovely religion." [23]

"The Anglican Crisis" and "Early Christianity" broke the patience of some in the German Reformed Church. Dr. B. Schneck, editor of the *Weekly Messenger*, had hitherto incurred criticism

[21] "Early Christianity," third article, *MR*, 1852, p. 33.
[22] *Ibid.*, pp. 41, 48, 53, 49.
[23] Nevin, "Early Christianity," *MR*, 1851, pp. 480, 477, 478.

for apparent partiality to the Mercersburg professors. Now he had had enough. In an editorial of September 17, 1851, Schneck publicly protested against the course of affairs at Mercersburg, affirming that nineteen out of twenty ministers shared his objections.

When the synod met at Lancaster the next month, it was faced with some delicate decisions. It had to act on Nevin's resignation of the preceding spring. In view of this editorial, accepting the resignation would seem to be following Schneck's lead and voting no confidence in Nevin's theology. At the same time, Schaff offered to resign and accept a call to Salem Church in Philadelphia (the largest German-speaking congregation in the denomination), apparently intending to make it possible for the board to meet Nevin's salary obligations and thus retain him. Yet even some of Nevin's warmest friends had doubts about his position as they read "The Anglican Crisis" and "Early Christianity." Would they be right in urging him to withdraw the resignation? [24]

The case of Schaff came up first, and the synod voted forty-two to five to reject his resignation. They wished to retain Schaff at the seminary in any case. The debate on Nevin's resignation was protracted. Resolutions were proposed affirming confidence in his orthodoxy. A substitute motion, however, was finally adopted (forty-two to four) requesting Nevin to withdraw his resignation and—if he would not do so—declining to fill the chair in the hope that he would see his way clear to return to the professorship. Schaff spoke eloquently for this motion.

Nevin was deeply moved by this demonstration. He thanked his brethren for the expression of their confidence and promised to take their request under consideration. He had not resigned because he felt that he had lost the confidence of the church, but for quite other reasons. In fact he believed that he still held the confidence of the church generally. With great emotion and tears, he confessed, "I love this Synod from the bottom of my heart." From such a man of granite, this declaration moved many

[24] Schaff to the editor, *Reformierte Kirchenzeitung*, quoted in *Christian Intelligencer*, December 16, 1852.

others to tears likewise.[25] Without doubt most of the synod felt a profound admiration for Nevin as a theologian and as a man.

Would the course of the Anglo-Catholic movement have been the same if the Anglican bishops had responded to Tract 90 with a comparable demonstration of confidence in the Oxford Tractarians? No doubt, Tract 90 was in some ways more offensive than "The Anglican Crisis" and "Early Christianity." With Nevin, who was always candid, there was no suspicion of disingenuousness or sophistry. Whatever the differences, Nevin was touched to tears by the trust and gratitude of his church, whereas Newman had felt himself disavowed and discredited by his.

How much of Nevin's writings did this vote of confidence include? Was it an endorsement of "The Anglican Crisis" and "Early Christianity"? Jakob Helfenstein treated it as such[26] and issued a circular urging sister denominations to protest the synod's action. Doctors R. Porter and W. W. Halloway, delegates of the Dutch Reformed Church, reported the action to their synod as having this significance. The opinion expressed in Berg's *Protestant Quarterly Review* was doubtless more correct in estimating the vote as a testimony of personal confidence in the face of general disagreement with "Early Christianity."[27] In so far as the vote was by implication a trial of Mercersburg principles, it amounted at least to the judgment that heresy was not proved. And Schaff claimed that the synod had committed itself to the Mercersburg tendency more definitely than ever before.[28]

Throughout the winter following the Synod of Lancaster, Helfenstein's call to arms found a widespread response in the periodicals of several denominations, beyond the long-standing opposition of the *Lutheran Observer* and the Dutch *Christian Intelligencer*. The Congregationalist *Puritan Recorder*, for example, concluded a scandalized review of "Early Christianity"

[25] T. Appel, *Life and Work of John Williamson Nevin* (Philadelphia, 1889), p. 421. Cf. Good, *op. cit.*, p. 280, and *WM*, October 5, 1853.

[26] *Christian Intelligencer*, November 6, 1851.

[27] January, 1852. Cf. *Christian Intelligencer*, December 16, 1852.

[28] *Der Deutsche Kirchenfreund*, 1851, p. 431.

with the prophecy that Nevin would probably try to carry as many as possible with him to Rome. Although Berg's position in his *Review* had seemed less alarmist, he later suddenly seceded from the denomination in protest. His farewell sermon at the Race Street Church in Philadelphia, "Jehovah Nissi," was rather theatrical and forced. Taking advantage of this fact, Nevin responded with ferocious sarcasm in the *Mercersburg Review*, indicating that he was still ready to defend his position within the German Reformed Church.

Schaff, the sole member of the Mercersburg faculty in 1851–52, was having a very difficult year. In their theological society and informally, the students hotly debated such themes as papal primacy, celibacy, confession, and absolution, an intermediate state (with the related ideas of prayers for the dead), and the intercessions of the Virgin and saints.[29] Appel reports that Schaff had as much to do with upsetting them as Nevin by the books he recommended. The students were reading Moehler, Balmes, Wiseman, and England with the excitement of a new perspective ably presented. When Benjamin Bausman and a fellow student won a debate with the proposition, "Resolved, that Protestantism is essentially gnostic," they were called before a special meeting of the board. Bausman himself became uncertain about his Protestant position and sought help privately from both Schaff and Nevin. Nevin, he reported, admitted the difficulties, but Schaff tried to reassure him by repeating arguments he had himself previously called untenable.[30] Schaff agreed with Nevin's historical judgments about the ancient Catholic church but did not share his increasing despair of Protestantism.

The theological debates among the students became crystallized by fusion with student politics. The seminary body then included a large number of recent immigrants from Germany who

[29] W. W. Wetzel, "Debates and Discussions in the Society of Inquiry" (unpublished B.D. thesis, 1954, Lancaster Theological Seminary). Cf. Good, *op. cit.*, pp. 293–94.

[30] H. H. Ranck, *Life of the Rev. Benjamin Bausman* (Philadelphia, 1912), pp. 85 ff.

were already in some tension with the party of the "Americans." Schaff's attempt to reconcile the parties was unsuccessful and gave the Germans the impression he had sided against them. They spread stories of his Romanizing heresy and rebelled at his discipline. When he suspended the leader, the others went on a strike and appealed to the board. Nevin was much disturbed at what seemed to him the worst blow the seminary had ever received. The board did not wholly succeed in its efforts at reconciliation, and six students withdrew from the seminary. (Two or three of these "Germans" later founded the Mission House Seminary in Sheboygan, Wisconsin, in a very different spirit from the Mercersburg tradition.)

Roman Catholics as well as Protestants were watching the course of affairs in Mercersburg with close interest. Two Roman Catholic editors, who had been following Nevin's articles of the preceding year, wrote to him personally in 1852. Orestes Brownson, who had already debated with him, was joined by James Alphonsus McMaster, editor of the *New York Freeman's Journal*, Bishop Hughes's quasi-official organ and the most influential of the Roman Catholic weeklies. Both men were themselves converts, militant ultramontanes, and infallibilists.

McMaster wrote Nevin in May, 1852, proposing that they form a personal acquaintance, remarking that he had followed Nevin's writings from before his own conversion. Nevin responded to the overture and accepted McMaster's aid in securing Roman Catholic literature, including De Maistre's *Du Pape*, Audin, Newman's *Idea of a University*, and Wiseman's *Dublin Review* article which had so impressed Newman. He wrote McMaster that he read the *Freeman's Journal* regularly and sympathized completely with Bishop Hughes's struggle against "godless education" in New York.[31] He found the Pastoral Letter of the National Council of Roman Catholic Bishops "able and dignified" and carrying "quite an apostolical sound." It would be hard work, he thought, "for a Presbyterian or Episcopal Assembly to talk just in the same style." Of his personal religious position he wrote frankly.

[31] Brownson Archives, Notre Dame University Library.

It is plain enough indeed, that my sympathies have grown to be very strong towards Catholicism, in its general character and form. A great revolution in regard to it has gradually taken place in my mind. I would consider it now a great privilege, only to be *made inwardly sure* in any way that the Roman Catholic church is really what she claims to be, the true succession in full force of the supernatural constitution with which the Church started in the time of the Apostles. Such faith, with a truly correspondent heavenly reality, would be like life from the dead, amid the shadows and shams which make up too generally the life of the world at the present time. But, alas, how many difficulties be in the way of such faith for a Protestant mind, in the Catholic system itself and in the present state of the Catholic world.[32]

McMaster, who had earlier reprinted excerpts from "The Anglican Crisis" and "Berg's Last Words" gave more than four columns to "Cyprian," especially those passages arguing for the Roman primacy.[33] He editorialized that the views there expressed "convince us that the day is not distant when another triumph will be added to the faith in the conversion of this profound and learned scholar." He asked the prayers of all his pious readers toward this end. Such an editorial could hardly escape notice in the German Reformed Church, even while the personal interchanges that lay behind it were unknown.

Orestes Brownson was among those who joined the campaign of prayer. He also wrote Nevin directly late in the summer and received an extended reply.

I am glad to know that you and others in the Catholic Church take an interest in my welfare and pray for my conversion to what you consider to be the truth; for it is my own daily cry to God and to his Son, Jesus Christ, that if this way of yours be in fact the glorious vision which gladdened the hearts of saints in the beginning it may not remain hidden to me as it is to those who are lost, but that I may have power before I go hence and be no more fully to see it and courageously to acknowledge it before the world. Some Protestants are praying for me too in their way. All round I have no objection to this; and I may add that I would most gladly enjoy also the intercession

[32] June 9 (?), 1852, Brownson Archives, Notre Dame University Library. (Question marks in parentheses indicate uncertain transcription.)
[33] *Freeman's Journal*, August 14, 21, 1852.

of the saints in the upper [?] world and particularly of the Blessed Virgin, if such benefit be at all possible [?] for the exiled children of Eve in this valley of tears.

My article on Cyprianic Christianity I have meant to be merely historical, though it breathes throughout, I know, a strong sympathy with its subject, over against the reigning Protestant theory of the Church at the present time. In my next article, already in type, the matter is made still worse [?] by the general admission that this Cyprianic doctrine was not peculiar to him or to the third century, but goes back to the time of the Apostolic Fathers and underlies the whole structure of the Creed. You ask, how I am to set this in any rational harmony with the cause of the Reformation. My answer is frankly, I see not how it can be done in a fully satisfactory way; and it is no part of my plan or purpose to attempt anything of the sort. My object is merely to hold up facts, to bring home if possible to others the actual difficulty of the case, to challenge as it were our explanation, from whatever quarter it may come. My own position is that of an anxious inquirer, far more than that of a dogmatic teacher. I write generally indeed under no inconsiderable pressure and pain [?] of spirit.

My Protestantism, you will see thus, is of the poorest sort. I am no longer fit for the defence of its interest in any vigorous style. For this reason, any controversy of a public sort in its behalf, either with yourself or any other champion of Romanism, ought to be in other hands. I find so much of the truth and right on your side, and so much of falsehood and wrong on ours as usually held, that I have no heart for any controversy of the sort, and dread being betrayed by it into the misery of making common cause with principles and tendencies which all good Protestants no less than Catholics are bound to oppose and hate.

If Protestantism is to be upheld, it can be only in the view of it being the historical succession of what Christianity was in ancient times—a Providential development, not without necessary violence, which is to be regarded as itself a process only still, (not by any means pleasant) towards a better state of things to come. It would be much, if our American thinking could be forced to see and feel this alternative. You will observe, that I do not venture of late to commit my own mind to it with any absolute assertion. It is presented only hypothetically. *If* our cause may stand, *then* must it be in this general way and no other.

But all this negative difficulty with Protestantism is no positive conversion to Catholicism. I wish at times it were so, and that it were possible for me to be fully and firmly assured that this, in its modern form carries in it still the powers and privileges claimed by the Early Church. If asked at the same time to say precisely what considerations stand in the way of such an acknowledgement, I find it not so easy to return any clear answer. The difficulty rises sometimes in one form, and sometimes in another. Where a whole habit of thought, kept up for many years, is to be set aside, in favor of another altogether different, it becomes very hard to distinguish between intellectual conviction and the force of mere custom as such. My general posture is not so much that of any distinct issue with Catholicism, the solution of which might carry the whole question for my understanding, as it is one rather of inability to bring the question to any such issue, a state of perplexity and doubt which I am not prepared yet to bring to an end.[34]

Nevin could isolate two or three specific difficulties. Among them were the Roman views of Mary. He had "vast respect for the Virgin, and would be greatly pleased to have the aid of her intercessions, if they are to be reached in any way"—a point which had seemed to him unlikely. But Liguori's *Glories of Mary* had confounded him with its extravagances.[35] "If this worship of the Virgin be so necessary—the medium some say of *all* grace to the world—why do we not find it in Cyprian and the fathers of the second century?" Similarly with the article of the immaculate conception. "If it has always been part of the explicit faith, why any hesitation or question about its proclamation at this time?" Had there not been a growth of doctrine here? Another difficulty was "found in the supposed degradation of some Catholic countries, Sicily for instance, and part of Italy. The force of this objection has been somewhat broken indeed in my mind, but still I cannot shake it off entirely."[36]

In his reply Brownson had remarked that Nevin's articles could hardly fail to prepare many minds to follow him into the Catholic church[37]— an idea that had occurred to others. Two members of the editorial committee of the *Mercersburg Review* who had

[34] August 18, 1852, Brownson Archives, Notre Dame University.
[35] Cf. n. 32.
[36] August 18, 1852, Brownson Archives, Notre Dame University.
[37] August 28, 1852, Brownson Archives, Notre Dame University.

called on Nevin to discuss the issue left with foreboding after he had described himself to them frankly as "an enquirer after the truth." [38] Bausman, to whom Nevin confided that he did not wish to continue as acting editor of the *Review*, felt "pretty sure that Dr. Nevin will go to the Roman Catholic Church if he lives ten years longer. He is in a very critical state of mind." [39] In correspondence with Professor Gerhart of the Ohio Seminary, Bausman wrote:

> I am often pained to hear with what contempt Dr. Nevin speaks and writes about Protestantism. I have long since felt that he is a singular exponent of German Reformed doctrine, but I trust he has been the means of infusing to some extent, a healthy vigorous life into our Church.[40]

At the commencement that fall Nevin did withdraw from the *Mercersburg Review*, which published a notice to that effect in the November issue. He also announced his intention to resign as president of Marshall College and to remain in retirement in Mercersburg, instead of going with the college to Lancaster.

When the Synod of 1852 came to act on Nevin's final resignation as professor of theology, the situation had changed from that of the preceding year. Many of his friends were aware that he was threatening to do what Berg had always prophesied of him. The resignation was accepted while the synod "testified to the zeal and ability with which he discharged his duties during nearly twelve years," and promised to "continue to cherish for him sentiments of very high regard, and never cease to love and respect him." [41] This resolution, which skirted any reference to theology, was proposed by Dr. Heiner, who had long been an opponent, but still did not wish Nevin to feel any personal rejection.

During the winter Nevin seemed to hang on dead center. The *New York Freeman's Journal* and the Philadelphia *Catholic*

[38] A. B. Russell, *Fourscore Years and More* (Philadelphia, 1908), p. 91. Cf. Good, *op. cit.*, p. 311.
[39] Ranck, *op. cit.*, p. 79.
[40] *Ibid.*, p. 81.
[41] Klein, *op. cit.*, p. 220.

Herald continued to urge prayers for his conversion. Schaff was fearful. Mrs. Nevin, in some distress, sought out Professor Appel of the college faculty to ask whether he thought her husband was about to go to Rome and seemed somewhat surprised when he thought not. In answer to the direct inquiry of another friend, Nevin admitted that he was "greatly troubled with the claims of the Catholic Church. . . . It has become for me a question of life and death. One great object of disengaging myself from all past responsibilities has been that I might be more free to examine it." On the other hand, he did not anticipate any sudden submission. "For any such step, however, I am not prepared, with all my strong Catholic sympathies and tendencies." [42]

Early in 1853 Nevin received another letter from McMaster, and one from Archbishop Hughes. To McMaster Nevin replied [43] that the great problem with which he wrestled every day, indeed almost every waking hour, could not be resolved by logic or natural evidences. It was more a matter for meditation and prayer than for dialectic. He had lost interest in debate.

> I see so much of wholesale error and confusion in the world, that I never felt less disposition to be confidently dogmatic in any position that is not upheld by tradition in some form; and when it comes to this, I find it more and more difficult, I confess, to make account of any opinion or judgment in such view, that ventures to place itself in contradiction to the authority of the Catholic Church.

He was about to conclude his last official obligation—the presidency of Marshall College. Although this did not entail directly any theological obligations, it did carry some restraining force. For this reason and because of his desire for relief from the burden, he would carry out his notice of withdrawal when the institution moved to Lancaster.

> One great object of my withdrawal is [he concluded] that I may be able to deal with this great Catholic question as independently as possible of all outward restraints. . . . Should it become necessary for

[42] Heyser Diaries (unpublished typescript in the Library of Lancaster Theological Seminary), 1852–53, especially the entry for January 13, 1853.

[43] February 26 (?), 1853, Brownson Archives, Notre Dame University Library.

me to take the step you anticipate, I shall have opposition enough from a wide system of private relations, aside from all public connections, to make it a species of moral martyrdom. Already this is making itself felt with no inconsiderable weight. But God's grace is sufficient for all things. As regards outward worldly estate, I am happily independent.

When Professor Appel tried to persuade him not to retire as president, the two chief considerations Nevin mentioned were his theological position and his health. He commented that he "was not satisfied with the present state of Protestantism and much less so with that of Romanism," and did not wish to burden the college with the odium of his unpopular views. The main difficulty, however, Appel reported, was his physical collapse. "Manifestly he was in doubt whether he would live much longer." Further service, Nevin thought, would shortly be cut off by death anyway.[44] Thus for him the question between Protestantism and Roman Catholicism was largely the question as to which church to die in.

What was his illness? From his youth he had suffered from a chronic liver affliction such that, at least up to 1870, he had never passed a day without pain.[45] He had aged early. Although he was not yet fifty, he evidently looked and felt much older. The condition, however, was psychological as well as physical; he later referred to himself as "much broken in mind and body."[46] He distrusted his capacities and could no longer interest himself in theological speculation, which had previously been his meat and drink. He drew in on himself and took little interest in the world about him. Life seemed a dreary waste, and he looked to eternity to resolve his doubts.

One is struck by the parallel with the "dyspepsia" which had laid Nevin low immediately after graduation from Union College and incapacitated him for some two years. That disease also "lay as a cloud upon my mind, entered as a secret poison into all my

[44] Appel, *op. cit.*, pp. 439, 723. Cf. his *Recollections of College Life at Marshall College,* (Reading, Pa., 1886), pp. 302, 314.

[45] Appel, *Life,* p. 47.

[46] *Ibid.*, p. 723.

feelings, and undermined the strength of my will. . . . Study, or even reading, for whole weeks and months, was a weariness to the flesh."[47] So it was now, thirty years later, from 1852 on. The moral and intellectual leader of the Mercersburg movement was a broken man and out of the fight, threatening to declare evangelical catholicism bankrupt by submitting to Rome.

[47] *Ibid.*, pp. 40, 42.

9/ *Consolidation and Recovery*

For the cause of evangelical catholicism much hung on the outcome of Nevin's wrestlings in retirement, and in any case the movement could not be expected to develop further theologically without him. Apart from Nevin, however, there *was* a movement and a party which could be counted on to try to hold the ground already occupied. The closely knit group around Marshall College and the seminary—faculty, alumni, board members, students—were conscious of representing a distinctive position and intended to maintain it. They were the chief influence in the German Reformed Church, so far as the denominational agencies were concerned, and they could not easily be dislodged.

The party was internally diverse. Among the students, at least, some were inclined to move faster and farther than Nevin toward Rome. As Appel recorded, Nevin "disapproved of the writings of his romanizing students—Ermentrout in the *Messenger*—especially where they went beyond him and yielded vital points to the [Roman] Catholics, when they were not aware of it themselves. In conversation he restrained and corrected them."[1] If Nevin were to go over to Romanism, he would not go alone. After the Civil War some of these young men actually took the plunge (Ermentrout, Gans, Wagner, and the Wolffs).

Just what was the stand of the two theologians, Nevin and Schaff? On specific positions it was hard to draw a line between them. Appel thought Schaff did as much as Nevin to encourage "Romanizing" among the students, and Schaff seemed ready to

[1] "Extracts from the Notebooks of Dr. Theodore Appel," typescript in Library of German Reformed Church, Franklin and Marshall College, p. 80a.

defend all Nevin's publications. Even of the contentions of "Cyprian" and "Early Christianity," he had written that "in a historical view, so far as the main facts are concerned, [they] can scarcely ever be refuted."[2] On the other hand, Schaff did not share Nevin's deep emotional repudiation of Protestantism and showed no signs of attraction to Roman Catholicism. Hodge was probably right in his opinion that Schaff's total effect on Nevin had been to slow him down rather than to lead him, and that Nevin, Schaff's senior, was also much the stronger man personally and theologically. Schaff at this period was probably under the ascendancy of Nevin's powerful personality, identifying himself with Nevin's theology but anxious about an emotional disorientation he did not share.

The Marshall faculty—Thomas Appel, T. C. Porter, William Nevin—were a harmonious and effective group, committed more or less, according to their several academic departments, to philosophical idealism and churchly theology. Only Appel, however, was sufficiently aggressive in such matters to be reckoned a force. His conception of evangelical catholicity, like that of the leading pastors of this camp—Bomberger or Harbaugh, for instance—was rooted without any qualification in the Reformation. Among Marshall alumni and readers of the *Mercersburg Review* there must have been an indefinite variety of opinion in interpreting or accepting the views of Nevin and Schaff. Loyalty to the college and seminary and personal affection for the professors must have counted for much in holding together an effective party in the courts of the church.

The effectiveness of the Mercersburg party is illustrated by the fact that Joseph Berg and Jakob Helfenstein, after years of agitating heresy charges against the professors, both gave up and withdrew from the denomination. Further evidence of the party's effectiveness is given in the arrangements made to provide for the several offices from which Nevin successively resigned. With half a dozen such opportunities for introducing new personnel

[2] "German Theology and the Church Question," *Mercersburg Review* (hereafter cited as *MR*), 1853, p. 140.

with other tendencies, the positions were consistently won by Mercersburg men, in spite of some contests.

The series began with Nevin's resignation as chairman of the committee on liturgy. The Synod of 1851 promptly substituted Schaff, who proceeded vigorously to work (and achieved more, one suspects, than Nevin could ever have done in this capacity). This was the synod that had been so concerned not to appear to agree with Schneck's attack on Nevin, that it declined to fill the professorship of theology which Nevin wished to vacate. And it flatly refused to let Schaff leave the seminary for a pastoral charge. The next synod (1852) finally accepted Nevin's resignation, with generous acknowledgments of gratitude. The man elected in Nevin's place as professor of theology was Dr. B. C. Wolff, a Baltimore pastor, who had generally sided with the Mercersburg professors and could be counted on to support Schaff. The Mercersburg party would have no reason to complain of the theological orientation of a faculty composed of Wolff and Schaff. No scholar or original thinker, Wolff was not a man to produce theological novelties. He was an excellent administrator, however, and in view of the state of the seminary treasury, he wisely deferred his acceptance of the election.

The attitude of the Marshall alumni was even more definite in the fall of 1852. At the meeting of the Alumni Association Nevin had indicated his desire to withdraw as chief contributor to the *Mercersburg Review* and recommended that the *Review* be discontinued. (There were those in the church, like Heiner of Baltimore, who felt that such action was long overdue.) To the surprise of Nevin and Schaff, one after another of the younger men, led by Appel and Williard, arose to urge that the *Review* be continued as a bond of union of Marshall men. Nevin smiled and concurred, and so it was voted—with the understanding that Nevin's contributions would always be welcome.[3] The same publication committee would continue, with Appel as acting editor.

The new policy was defined by Appel in a long editorial in

[3] T. Appel, *Life and Work of John Williamson Nevin* (Philadelphia, 1889), p. 301.

the January, 1853, issue. It was not likely, he wrote, that the *Review* would receive contributions "of the same vigor and compass" as Nevin's, but the intention was to continue the same general policy in philosophy and theology. It would stand on Reformation ground against excesses of private judgment, sectarianism, or political radicalism. It would also aim at a "true catholicity." "Between the lines," Appel recorded of this editorial, "it said that it was not to Romanize. This was satisfactory and well understood." [4] The first two issues under the new quarterly format, moreover, carried articles by Bomberger defending Nevin against his antagonists and praising him even "more . . . than was called for or needed," in Appel's opinion.[5] Editor McMaster of the *New York Freeman's Journal* expressed his pleasure at the affectionate and respectful manner with which the editors treated Nevin.[6]

Since *Der Kirchenfreund* had no official tie with the Marshall alumni, Schaff was more vulnerable. His collaborator, W. J. Mann, briefly of the Marshall faculty and now a Lutheran pastor in Philadelphia, had been objecting to Mercersburg Romanizing. What if all the church fathers were for Rome? [7] Many inquiries had come in as to why Schaff felt it necessary to apologize for the Reformation.[8] Mann wanted *Der Kirchenfreund* to be unambiguously anti-Roman and not to concern itself with some ideal church of the past or of eschatology.[9] The publishers, too, felt that Schaff had become a liability as an editor. He survived this pressure for some time, however. Not until December of 1853 did he address to his readers his final "Abschied," in which he gave several reasons for withdrawal without mentioning the objections to his Romanizing.

The major effort of the anti-Mercersburg party was directed toward the control of the new Franklin and Marshall College.

[4] Appel, "Extracts," p. 74.
[5] *Ibid.*
[6] February 5, 1853.
[7] Mann to Schaff, August 2, 1852 (Library of Mt. Airy Lutheran Seminary).
[8] Mann to Schaff, September 20, 1852.
[9] Mann to Schaff, October 1, 1852.

This whole project had been despaired of by many, including Nevin. There had been months of doubt over whether the city of Lancaster would raise its stipulated contribution, and then it seemed problematical whether the German Reformed Church could raise the sum necessary to buy out the Lutheran interest in Franklin College. Finally, to the dismay of the Lancaster friends of the institution, Nevin announced, in the fall of 1852, that he would resign as president and would not move to Lancaster with Marshall. By this time the financial and legal arrangements for the joint venture had been completed (with some borrowing by the board during the winter of 1852–53) guaranteeing that there would be a Franklin and Marshall College. But who would control it in Nevin's place?

The new board, headed by the Honorable James Buchanan, former United States minister to England, met in March, 1853, and at once fell into a struggle for power. An anti-Nevinist caucus proposed Dr. Mesick, a thorough "Puritan" with recommendations from New Brunswick, as president, wishing also to replace at least Professor Appel of the faculty.[10] To block this proposal from Heiner's nominating committee, Nevin permitted his name to be presented and was thus elected president of Franklin and Marshall. His determination to resign and devote himself to the Catholic question was not so urgent as to allow him to let the college fall into the hands of his opponents.

Nevin held the call to the presidency in his hand for a month while the faculty and students were packing for the move to Lancaster. Then, when the Mesick party was disorganized, he declined the election. "Other claims and interests," he wrote the board, "partly of health, partly of taste and comfort, but most of all, I may say, in the form now of theological inquiry and religious conscience" stood in the way.[11] This letter was read at the board meeting in April, and then Schaff was promptly nominated and elected. He was given permission to hold the call until Oc-

[10] Heyser Diaries (unpublished typescript in the Library of Lancaster Theological Seminary), March 1853. Cf. Appel, *Life*, p. 441.

[11] J. H. Dubbs, *History of Franklin and Marshall College* (Lancaster, 1903), pp. 264 ff.

tober, when it could be learned whether the synod would release him from the seminary. The first catalogue of Franklin and Marshall College listed Philip Schaff as "President-elect and Professor." The anti-Nevinists had been outmaneuvered.

The attempt to break up the Nevinist faculty was also defeated, and it was voted to take Professors Porter, Appel, and William Nevin to Lancaster, assuring an unbroken continuity with old Marshall. Appel reports that Schaff urged him to go and "safe your pacon." [12] Appel took with him the management of the *Mercersburg Review*. He was the first son of the church and the college to hold a chair on the faculty and, as it turned out, the chief defender of theological and philosophical continuity. The two former Franklin College instructors were not re-employed, and the one new appointment, Adolphus Koeppen, was too eccentric to affect the orientation of the faculty ("I am a Lutheran," he declared, "but I believe what I please"). Franklin and Marshall inherited the faculty and the very textbooks of old Marshall. It too was to be Anglo-German, positively Christian, metaphysically idealist, and theologically "churchly." From 1853 Rauch's old courses in psychology and ethics, as continued by Nevin, were taught at Lancaster by Appel. Appel took pride in going beyond Rauch's notes and drawing directly on Daub, Rosenkranz, Steffens, and Schubert,[13] but his material was all ore from the same vein.

This review of denominational agencies that were retained in Nevinist hands perhaps should include even the *Weekly Messenger*. In August, 1853, at the Second Reformed Church of Lancaster, a secret conclave was held, which seems to have been aimed primarily at S. R. Fisher, the editor of the *Messenger*, for his allegedly pro-Mercersburg partisanship. Charges of such partisanship were presented at the synod in November by Dr. Zacharias and Dr. Heiner. But the synod rejected the charges almost unanimously and reproved the plaintiffs for their language.

The Mercersburg men had maintained their influence on the

[12] Appel, "Extracts," p. 169.
[13] *Ibid.*, pp. 96, 26.

liturgical committee, the college, the seminary, the *Mercersburg Review*, and the *Weekly Messenger*. Their fortress, however, was beleaguered by surrounding evangelical hosts. The synod of the Dutch Reformed Church voted to discontinue sending fraternal delegates to the German Reformed synod, in order to maintain unflinchingly "its opposition to the Romanizing tendencies of the Mercersburg theology." A learned quarterly, the *New Brunswick Theological Review*, was called into existence apparently for the sole purpose of explaining what was wrong with Schaff and Nevin. Jacob Helfenstein seceded to the old-school Presbyterians with his Germantown congregation, firing a final blast at "the Perverted Gospel." The little classis of North Carolina declared itself independent of synod until the latter should clear itself of Mercersburg heresy. The midwestern section of the church was unfriendly. The *Lutheran Observer*, the *Christian Intelligencer*, the *Baptist Recorder*, were all trained on Mercersburg village. The publisher Scribner warned Schaff that the incessant attacks of the newspapers would greatly injure, if they did not entirely blast, the commercial prospects of his English-language *History of the Apostolic Church*, then in the press.[14]

By 1854 the outcry was diminishing. As in the last scene of *Hamlet*, most of the principals on both sides were out of action. Berg and Helfenstein had seceded; Mesick, Heiner, and Zacharias had been defeated, if not virtually censured; Schaff was in Europe, and Nevin in retirement—occupied, supposedly, in prayer and meditation. Then in the January (1854) *Mercersburg Review* the recluse of Mercersburg fired off a "whole park of artillery" (as Professor Porter put it) in a fifty-page article, entitled "The Dutch Crusade." The "crusade" of the title was the "impertinent intervention" of 1852 and 1853 against the Mercersburg theology and the German Reformed Church, carried on in the columns of Porter's *Christian Intelligencer* and such other "outlaws of the so-called religious press" as the *Lutheran Observer* and the *Protes-*

[14] Schaff to Appel, June 23, 1853 (Library of the German Reformed Church, Franklin and Marshall College).

tant Quarterly Review. Nevin was determined to have the last word, and in no uncertain voice.

Nevin had not, to be sure, cut himself off completely when he retired. He had been willing to take part in a delaying maneuver to prevent his opponents from taking over Franklin and Marshall College. He was not in a hurry. In June, 1853, Schaff had reported of him

> no marked progress in the ominous direction; but no sign of a reaction either. His preaching is exceedingly solemn and shows that he has continually the possibility of a complete moral martyrdom before his eyes. He confines himself entirely to his study and seems more disposed now to prayer, meditation, and ascetic exercises, than to literary labor.[15]

That very month, however, Nevin had journeyed to Lancaster to sit on the platform with his old college tutor, now bishop, Alonzo Potter, and to give an address at the ceremonial opening of Franklin and Marshall College. This address (on the vocation of the college) [16] made no reference to the church question, but it did indicate that Nevin was still able and willing to identify himself with the educational interests of the German Reformed Church. He repeated the trip at the end of August when the first class to graduate in Lancaster requested a baccalaureate address from their former president.[17] Yet in the winter Heyser reported the same impression Schaff had noted six months before, that a transition to Rome was a live possibility.

"The Dutch Crusade" is thus particularly interesting as Nevin's first declaration on critical issues since his retirement. The article opened no new ground theologically and was marred by some polemic bitterness. Its striking aspect was the tone and attitude of the author, which showed no hint of the self-disqualification of one emotionally or theologically alienated. A casual reader would not guess that the author had retired. If Nevin had been

[15] *Ibid.*
[16] *MR*, 1853, pp. 395 ff.
[17] *Ibid.*, pp. 492 ff.

still the accredited and official theologian of the denomination, he could not have taken command with more confidence in his right to do so than this article manifests. On each of the five crucial issues of the controversy he took it on himself to speak the official position of the German Reformed Church, doing so several times in the form of direct address in quotation marks. And he ended each of these five sections with a rhetorical challenge, like "Let the people answer!" This was not the tone or stance of one who had lost faith in his church or in his right to speak for her.

In reviewing the aspects of the German Reformed Church which were most offensive to its attackers, Nevin was in effect summarizing the achievements of the Mercersburg movement in the preceding decade. The first issue was the assertion of the binding authority of the creed. "One great cause of controversy with the German Reformed Church, on the side of other sects," Nevin wrote, "is . . . just her regard for the authority of the Apostles' Creed, and the zeal she has exhibited of late for the resuscitation of its proper original life among Protestants." Similarly the sense of the Holy Catholic Church as the Mystical Body "has of late penetrated the general mind of the German Reformed Church with new force" in contrast to the views of surrounding bodies favoring the "sect system." To be sure, the German Reformed Church had not committed herself formally on this point, nor on that of the ministry and sacraments, nor that of the historical continuity of the church. On all these the church left liberty, both to the professors at Mercersburg and to their anti-papist "Puritan" opponents. Yet in recent years the Mercersburg attitude had come to prevail with regard to sacramental grace and the church. Similarly "a very marked progress has taken place in the mind of the Church on the question of liturgical worship, even within the last five years." On the matter of the continuity of the church as against the theory of the Roman apostasy, Nevin interpreted the synod's action of 1851 as preferring the Mercersburg view but not committing itself to either. The synod had passed no judgment on his articles on early Christianity and would probably have found no unanimity on them, but it was not to be held responsible for these any more than the Presbyterian General Assembly for the articles on the church question in the *Princeton Review*. Dr. Mesick had been free similarly to deliver anti-papist addresses at the meetings of the Eastern and Western synods in 1853.[18]

It seemed to Nevin that the German Reformed Church had found its specific denominational vocation through the Mercersburg movement. That vocation was to defend the claim of Protestantism to the attributes of the Christian Church, "one, holy, catholic and historical, by showing in its constitution a continual want and endeavor, at least, after their full actualization. . . . Now right in the midst of the critical pass, and at this time preeminent among its defenders, appears the small band of our German Reformed church heroically contending for the original principles and maxims of the Reformation."

On the delicate question of this ecclesiastical position's vulnerability to conversion to Romanism Nevin freely allowed that this view was "more exposed to it than any less churchly and less historical scheme. . . . As a body," however, he remarked, "the German Reformed Church has no difficulty whatever in maintaining her full Protestant consciousness. . . . It is certain, too, that if anyone should become a Catholic in this way, it would have to be in the end by giving up, not merely the general position of the German Reformed Church, but the whole so-called Mercersburg theology also."[19] And Nevin closed "The Dutch Crusade" with an expression of confidence in the steadiness of the church in maintaining her distinctive genius.

What Nevin had done in this article was to pass by his own more controversial views or to treat them as matters of private opinion, and to state the position of his more moderate supporters. He had laid down the platform of men like Appel, Bomberger, Harbaugh, Wolff, which was in fact that prevailingly heard in the schools and press of the denomination. He had served notice that if he should later submit to Roman authority, it would

[18] Nevin, "The Dutch Crusade," *MR*, 1854, pp. 84, 88, 94, 97, 106, 111, 105.
[19] *Ibid.*, pp. 112–15.

be by abandoning the Mercersburg *via media* or, more militantly, the heroic battle in the theological Thermopylae.

Should one not conclude from Nevin's first declaration after his retirement that he was occupied not merely with his evaluation of Roman Catholic claims and doctrines, but with the calculation of what he had accomplished and might accomplish for a truly Catholic Protestantism by remaining where he was? And must he not also have speculated as to how much of this achievement would be wiped out by the reaction which would certainly follow his own defection?

Nevin published another theological essay in March, 1854, although it was apparently written late in 1853—a review of R. I. Wilberforce's *Holy Eucharist*. Perhaps Wilberforce had sent him the book personally on the strength of Nevin's sympathetic review of his work on the Incarnation three years before.[20] In any case Nevin received a personal letter from him in the fall of 1853 and another "more full and confidential" in the early winter.[21] Wilberforce, it will be recalled, had been an early associate of John Henry Newman, and then the confessor of Manning until the latter seceded to Rome. He was probably the best theologian of the Anglo-Catholics and much influenced by Moehler and "organic" theory about the church.

Since in these points he seemed highly congenial to Nevin, it is most interesting to see where Nevin parts company from him. Wilberforce had begun, much in the vein of Nevin's "Cyprian," by trying to establish the consensus of the ancient church with regard to the Eucharist. Nevin accepted his conclusions that the fathers generally believed in the presence of Christ in his humanity locally in the elements, effected by consecration and made the basis of an act of oblation and sacrifice by a qualified priest as the main function of his ministry. But Nevin did not, like Wilberforce, simply take the ancient view so defined as authoritative. Wilberforce wished to revive such a Eucharist as the

[20] *MR*, 1850, pp. 164–96.

[21] Nevin to Schaff, February 22, 1854. (Library of the German Reformed Church, Franklin and Marshall College.)

daily service of the Church of England. "This construction," Nevin replied, "is not in reality the doctrine or practice of the Episcopal Church either in England or in this country." It would not be accepted by the denomination generally on either side of the Atlantic and was "too alien from the reigning make and genius of the Church altogether, to allow the supposition" that it could "ever be practically ingrafted into its life." [22] If Wilberforce wished to claim a direct and undeveloped continuity with the ancient church he must go to Rome. Anglicanism could not provide it.

Yet might there be in Protestantism a Eucharistic doctrine which maintained the substance of the ancient view in new form? Calvinism, for instance, asserts, "a real participation of Christ's Body and Blood in the Eucharist as a transaction; but denies their presence in the elements, and owns in the mystery no sacrifice. In these points it differs from the doctrine of the ancient church." The question is "whether the difference be essential or simply accidental." If Calvinism were a tenable position, it seemed "to mediate between the difficulties of the case as it actually stands on both sides." There was "no true middle position anywhere" between this Calvinist position and that of the Council of Trent. If Wilberforce must have unchanging orthodoxy he should go to Rome; if he would admit "development" he might find essential continuity with the ancient faith in conservative Protestantism.[23] Although Nevin spoke of a valid "development" tentatively still, his tone was more positive than in "Cyprian."

In a review of Cardinal Wiseman's essays on the Oxford controversy Nevin declared "the advantage to be completely on the side of the champion of [Roman] Catholicism. . . . Anglicanism, after the Oxford fashion, is here shown to be a system which cannot stand." On its own principles Anglo-Catholicism was but a schism. "The Anglo-Catholic controversy is fairly at an end," [24] he wrote, as if almost irritated by what seemed to him Anglo-

[22] "Wilberforce on the Eucharist," *MR*, 1854, pp. 180, 186.
[23] *Ibid.*, pp. 187, 177, 186.
[24] *MR*, 1854, pp. 155, 156.

Catholic obtuseness. The Episcopal Church was on the same footing as the other historical and churchly forms of Protestantism and, like them, could make its case for Catholic substance only in Protestant form and on the theory of development.

About the time Nevin was composing his two articles on the "Dutch Crusade" and "Wilberforce on the Eucharist," Schaff was on the high seas bound for Liverpool. His expectations and plans as president-elect of Franklin and Marshall had been upset by the synod, which declined to release him from the seminary in Mercersburg village. He had even requested a reconsideration, but when the synod declined the request, he reconciled himself to the decision. He then requested and secured a year's leave of absence for a trip to Europe before returning to the isolation of Mercersburg with his eight or ten students. He was in a state of near exhaustion and made this the basis for his request.[25]

The year 1854, or most of it, constitutes an interlude in the Mercersburg story. We have no clear evidence of Nevin's state of mind from February, when he wrote Schaff, to November, when he delivered a notable address. Perhaps much of his time was spent in moving his residence from Mercersburg to Carlisle and settling there near Dickinson College. Mercersburg village was deserted. The seminary perforce closed altogether for the year 1853–54, having scarcely the funds to continue. The college had moved to Lancaster, where it was now in its second year without a president. And Schaff was in Europe until November.

Schaff's trip was full of interesting meetings and conversations which proved of great value for his future activities as an ecumenical administrator and ambassador, but which have less bearing on the course of the Mercersburg tendency. He had long talks on the church question with Wilberforce, Maurice, Leo, Kahnis, Liebner, Hurter, Rothe, Metternich, Manning, Schelling. Only the last seemed still to cherish a hope of an eventual reconciliation of Protestantism and Roman Catholicism. In Berlin, where Schaff spent a long spring, the cause of the United Church

[25] D. S. Schaff, *Life of Philip Schaff* (New York: Charles Scribner's Sons, 1897), p. 171.

seemed to have suffered and that of confessional Lutheranism to have prospered, though Hengstenberg seemed more powerful than ever.

Schaff found that Wilberforce had the *Mercersburg Review* and *Der Kirchenfreund* in his library and that he took an especially lively interest in Nevin's writing. When he saw him again in the fall, Wilberforce was about to go to the Continent, where, Schaff expected, he would "probably take the last step to Rome." About himself Schaff wrote his wife, after attending mass and hearing a sermon at Trent, that he had seen nothing to lead him to change his views on Romanism and that he would write Nevin that he would return "a better Protestant and a better American" than he left.[26]

In England Schaff seems to have spent the most time with Wilberforce and Maurice, and with Bunsen at the Prussian embassy. He also devoted a whole day to the Irvingites. He attended the morning service at "their beautiful Gothic church on Gordon Square, the first of the seven churches of London, thronged with devout worshippers. The Lord's Supper was administered with great solemnity, an imposing ceremonial, many hundreds communing." This was "the most beautiful and perfect liturgical service" he had ever attended, surpassing that in the Roman cathedral. He dined with Mr. Heath, the "angel" of the church, and then attended the service for the congregation at four and the service for outsiders at seven.[27] This experience with the Irvingites was to have important consequences in the liturgy of the German Reformed Church.

On the Continent Schaff was very well received. In Berlin he delivered a series of public lectures on America, which were published in expanded form that same year; [28] he dined at the royal palace; and he was awarded a D.D. by the university, a rare

[26] *Ibid.*, pp. 176, 193, 188.
[27] *Ibid.*, p. 178.
[28] P. Schaff, *Amerika: Die politischen, socialen und kirchlich—religiösen Zustände der Vereinigten Staaten von Nord-Amerika mit besonderer Rücksicht auf die Deutschen, aus eigener Anschauung dargestellt* (Berlin, 1854).

honor which he deeply appreciated. In Zurich he was asked if he would accept a call to Lange's chair. Probably the climax of his trip was the great "Kirchentag" in Frankfurt, where among the two thousand in attendance were nearly all the leaders of German Protestantism. Here Schaff read a report on German Protestantism in America, similar to the one he had prepared two years before for the "Kirchentag" at Bremen, and he delivered an address, *Deutschland und Amerika*, which was subsequently published.

When Schaff landed in America again, on November 13, 1854, feeling—he declared—ten years younger, he was carrying baggage full of scholarly loot. His conversations with leading scholars had kept him posted on the most recent developments in pre-Nicene church history, on which he had a volume planned. He had accumulated materials and ideas in hymnology and liturgy for the work of the liturgy committee. He had many notes and vivid recollections by which to build up his *Kirchenfreund* series of 1852 ("Gallery of the most important living theological professors of Germany") to the volume of 1857, *Germany: Its Universities, Theology, and Religion,* with its sketches of numerous distinguished divines. He was the bearer of substantial contributions to the libraries at Mercersburg and Lancaster from European donors, and of an offer for an endowed tutorship at the seminary which involved a year of study in Germany. He must have won a fresh perspective on the whole struggle in the German Reformed Church and probably was measurably emancipated from the personal ascendancy of John Nevin.

The situation to which Schaff returned, thus invigorated, was also dramatically improved. Late in July the Franklin and Marshall board had at last agreed on his successor, or substitute, as president. The rival parties had been able to agree unanimously on E. V. Gerhart, then president of Heidelberg College and professor at its associated theological seminary. Though Gerhart would not arrive until the following spring (April, 1855), he had accepted the appointment in September, so that there were at last definite prospects for the effective organization of Franklin and Marshall College. As with the Westerners generally, Gerhart had felt many reservations about Mercersburg theology, but he actually gave the Mercersburg men few grounds for complaints in his conduct of affairs.

The bankrupt seminary had been rescued even more remarkably. With no professors in residence in 1853–54, the treasurer had been able to pay up arrears of salary and to clear off several other debts. The buildings had been repaired and put in good order. Two bequests had been received in 1854, totaling $15,000, putting the seminary for the first time in a position to carry two professors financially. Dr. Schaff and Dr. Bernard Wolff, his new colleague, were both now ready to serve. The treasurer paid Schaff's salary for his sabbatical year, which had been more than earned by the gifts he had solicited and received for the school. After the twelve-month recess, the seminary had opened on November 1, 1854, with the best prospects in years.

A fortnight after Schaff's return Dr. Wolff was inaugurated in Zion's Church, Chambersburg. Dr. Heiner had been announced as the preacher, but he may have refused to appear on the same platform with Dr. Fisher, his opponent of the year before, for the inaugural sermon was actually delivered by Nevin. Entitled "The Christian Ministry,"[29] this sermon was described by Professor Appel as long, very able and theological, "one of his best, but the full house became tired of listening." They were better pleased with the shorter and more practical statement from Wolff, which followed.[30]

This address by Nevin is remarkable from two different points of view. On the one hand, it is one of the most, if not the most, dogmatically unreformed pronouncements he ever made. That it was received by the immediate listeners and by the denomination generally with weariness rather than shock is itself a phenomenon. Had they perhaps all written off Nevin anyway as an old, retired oddity?

On the other hand, startling as the sermon is in substance, the

[29] *MR*, 1855, pp. 68–93.
[30] Appel, "Extracts," p. 139.

fact that Nevin made it is probably the first definite public indication that he had decided *not* to go to Rome. On this whole subject, to be sure, there is too little evidence of Nevin's thinking through 1853 and 1854 for more than a tentative conclusion. Yet the act itself is eloquent. It was one thing to speak at the opening of Franklin and Marshall College, or even to preach a baccalaureate sermon for a graduating class. It was something else to declare on behalf of the denomination the meaning of the installation of its official teacher of doctrine. What role could be more representative of the church? A year and a half before, Nevin had freed himself from the last of his official responsibilities, in part to be able to consider the Roman Catholic question unencumbered. In the intervening period he had not turned to Rome but had published two essays which showed him, if anything, more firm in his Protestant position than he had appeared in his writings of the year *before* his retirement. The point of final decision in this matter may have been that day late in November, 1854, when Nevin agreed to preach the inaugural sermon in Heiner's stead. Support for this hypothesis lies in the fact that the one clear reference to a definite decision of Nevin's not to go to Rome comes from Professor Wolff[31] and the one occasion on which Wolff would have been likely to have had inside information in this matter would have been in connection with the inaugural sermon.

If this hypothesis is sound, the inner crisis of Nevin's religious conscience was resolved in Carlisle at the same time that Schaff returned to Mercersburg with new resources, personal and material, and the most serious institutional and financial difficulties of the seminary and college were measurably overcome. Also on this hypothesis, Nevin decided in favor of Protestantism the same month in which his Anglo-Catholic correspondent, Robert Wilberforce, submitted to Rome.

In support of this conjecture it can also be observed that from the time of Wolff's inauguration there are no more references to

[31] J. I. Good, *History of the Reformed Church in the United States in the Nineteenth Century* (New York, 1911), p. 311.

inclinations toward Rome. Professor Appel called on the Nevins in Carlisle in the spring of 1855. His account reads like the description of a convalescent who has passed his crisis. He inferred, he said, "that the family were not likely to make Carlisle a place of permanent residence and that, if they moved, it would be most probably to Lancaster city or county." Appel heartily agreed with this plan, observing in a letter to Schaff, as if it were a matter of course, "Here he might still be useful to the Church and the Institutions. We would give him a seat in the faculty as our worthy ex-President, and let him perform whatever duties he might see proper to assume." [32]

Two months later Nevin was speaking at the Marshall alumni banquet in Lancaster along with Bomberger, Schaff, and Gerhart. He alluded to physical disabilities, but showed no signs of religious or theological inhibitions.[33] He felt free to suggest denominational policies in the *Weekly Messenger* that fall, urging that the synod cease its fraternal correspondence with the old-school Presbyterians rather than submit to a Presbyterian review of German Reformed orthodoxy. The Nevin family did move to Lancaster that year. Soon Nevin was actively engaged in the work of the liturgical committee, in addition to lecturing at Franklin and Marshall on moral philosophy.[34] Two articles which grew out of his liturgical studies, "The Church Year" and "Christian Hymnology," were published in the *Mercersburg Review* in 1856. From 1857 Nevin seemed to have recovered his full powers and energies. He shortly resumed his debates with Hodge and Bushnell and undertook the defense of the new *Liturgy or Order of Christian Worship*. The Mercersburg leaders had survived their most severe tribulations and were once again, if more slowly, in movement.

[32] May 14, 1855 (Library of the German Reformed Church at Franklin and Marshall College).

[33] H. M. J. Klein, *A Century of Education at Mercersburg, 1836–1936* (Lancaster, Pa., 1936), p. 356.

[34] Lecture notes by A. S. U. dated January 3, 1856 (Good Collection, Eden Theological Library).

10/Baptismal Grace

The Mercersburg theologians did not produce a comprehensive interpretation of baptism comparable to their Eucharistic theology. Nevin, and somewhat later E. V. Gerhart, his successor as president of Franklin and Marshall College, did take part in the debates on baptism in the periodicals; and Schaff's historical treatment was sometimes as much normative as descriptive. Certain characteristic themes were asserted, together with a recognition of great difficulties in the subject. To some extent these essays give the impression of being inferences from other more central concerns. They presuppose, for example, the whole controversy between the revivalist conception of religion and the Mercersburg adherence to the rival program of religious nurture, "the system of the catechism." From this point of view the debate on baptism is a delayed continuation of, or sequel to, *The Anxious Bench* controversy. From another point of view the Mercersburg contentions on baptism may be read as attempts to maintain on this subject also the general conception of a sacrament which had been fully worked out with regard to the Lord's Supper, as in *The Mystical Presence.* Most comprehensively, it was the Mercersburg doctrine of the church which seemed to require the sacramental understanding of baptism.

The relative caution and reticence of Mercersburg on this theme are brought into relief by contrast with the contemporary high-church movement in the Church of Denmark led by N. F. S. Grundtvig. Both movements found their greatest comfort in the sense of the church as an unbroken historical community down the generations, through which the work of redemption was done. They also shared a high estimate of the Apostles' Creed as the authoritative tradition of the church on the meaning of the Gospel. For Grundtvig, however, the whole conception focused in the confession of the creed by the living church at baptism.

The continuity of the church for him lay in an unbroken chain of baptized persons confessing the creed. From his new understanding of the meaning of baptism in association with the creed, Grundtvig had proceeded to increased appreciation of the Lord's Supper. With Nevin the order was reversed. His new and deeper understanding had begun with the Communion, and had then been extended to baptism. Continually under pressure from opponents of infant baptism, moreover, Nevin was aware of difficulties which seem never to have troubled Grundtvig seriously.

Nevin's first extended references to baptism came in *The Mystical Presence*, as parenthetical illustrations of the same antisacramental tendencies he observed with regard to the Lord's Supper. He found in American Protestantism a serious decline in the practice of infant baptism and attributed it to the inadequacies of the prevailing theology on the subject. The whole tendency seemed to Nevin to constitute the most sure criterion of the power of the *sect spirit* in the American churches. The Baptist bodies, which rejected infant baptism outright, were the largest denominational family in the country, and, Nevin declared, "the baptistic principle prevails more extensively still; for it is very plain that all true sense of the sacramental value of baptism is wanting in large portions of the church, where the ordinance is still retained." [1]

Neither Calvin nor Luther would have tolerated the conception of baptism which had come to be dominant in American Protestantism and powerful even in the churches which recognized the Reformers as authorities. The basic trouble was defection from the Reformation doctrine of the church and sacraments.

> If the sacraments are regarded as in themselves outward rites only, that can have no value or force except as the grace they represent is made to be present by the subjective exercises of the worshipper, it is hard to see on what ground infants, who are still without knowledge or faith, should be admitted to any privilege of the sort. If there be no objective reality in the life of the Church, as something more deep and comprehensive than the life of the individual believer separately

[1] *The Mystical Presence* (Philadelphia: 1846), pp. 107, 150.

taken, infant baptism becomes necessarily an unmeaning contradiction.[2]

As documentation of baptismal practice in American Reformed churches, perhaps the fullest analysis comes from the Presbyterians. Leading Presbyterians had been voicing concern over this situation for decades. In the mid-fifties finally, discussion was brought to a head by the publication of two statistical analyses, one in the *Presbyterian Critic* in 1855 and the other in the *Princeton Review* in 1857. The second of these, "The Neglect of Infant Baptism," by Charles Hodge,[3] was the more substantial.

The most impressive evidence Hodge set forth in support of his title was drawn from the statistics of the General Assembly of the Presbyterian Church. That church reported annually both the number of communicants and the number of children baptized. In the changing ratio of these two sets of figures (available for the half-century from 1807 to 1856) Hodge found his most startling evidence. The decline began in 1812. From 20 baptisms per hundred communicants in 1811, the number was down to 7 by 1830 and 5.1 for the period 1852–56. If these figures were reliable (and Hodge could find no grounds for doubting them) only about a quarter as many of the eligible Presbyterian children were being baptized at the end of the period as at the beginning. "Fifty years ago there was one child baptized for every five members; now but one for 20!" Hodge could not avoid the conclusion that in the last twenty years "more than two thirds of the children of the Church have been 'cut off' from the people of God by their parents' sinful neglect, and by the Church's silent acquiescence therein!"[4]

Comparisons could be made with other Reformed denominations. The Episcopalians were the least affected by the general debilitation, in 1855 and 1856 maintaining infant baptisms at 17 per hundred communicants. The Dutch Reformed ratio for the

[2] *Ibid.*, p. 149.

[3] *Biblical Repertory and Princeton Review* (hereafter cited as *BRPR*), 1857, pp. 73–101.

[4] *Ibid.*, pp. 84, 87.

same period was 6.6, only a degree better than the Presbyterian (old-school). At the other extreme were the Congregationalists, among whom infant baptism had become very rare in some associations—in 1856 only 1.6 infant baptisms per hundred members. The new-school Presbyterians were closer to Congregational practice in this matter than to the old-school Presbyterians, their ratio standing at 2 per hundred, which meant, Hodge calculated, that six of seven Presbyterian (new-school) children eighteen and under were unbaptized. Hodge also noted that at times of widespread revivals, such as 1831–36, great numbers had been received into the Presbyterian church by adult baptism, or on profession of faith, who did not have their children baptized. All this evidence seemed to bear out strongly the Baptist contention that the chief pedobaptist churches in America were rapidly coming to agree with them in sentiment and practice.

The strength of the whole trend could also be estimated in terms of Baptist conversions. Much Baptist growth in this period had been at the expense of various Reformed communions. In New England the backbone of the Baptist denomination consisted of former Congregationalists who had split off in the excitement of the revivals. To a considerable degree the "Christians" or "Campbellites" of the western flank of the Appalachians were Scots and Irish of Presbyterian antecedents who were caught up by the "restorationist" and Baptist movement. Winebrenner's "Church of God" was a similar schism from the German Reformed, opposing infant baptism and confirmation as unscriptural. Such out-and-out defections or schisms, of course, were only a partial manifestation of the extent of Baptist sympathies in these several Reformed communions.

What was the Mercersburg understanding of baptism, especially infant baptism? It is interesting, in the light of the twentieth-century merger of the Congregational and the German Reformed Churches, that Nevin first clarified his view of baptism in a debate with Horace Bushnell. Now known as the patron saint of modern religious education and the father of liberal Congregationalism, Bushnell was but an obscure Hartford minister in 1847, when his *Discourses on Christian Nurture* appeared. Nevin's young friend Henry Harbaugh called his attention to the booklet,[5] and Nevin reviewed it in four issues of the *Weekly Messenger*.[6] When Bushnell replied to his critics in his *Argument for the Discourses*, Nevin was the only one he took very seriously. And in the fall issue of the *Princeton Review*, Charles Hodge made it a three-cornered discussion with an extended critique of both writers.

The three theologians found an initial agreement in a distaste for the overemphasis on revivalism and what it was doing to Christian nurture and education. Bushnell and Nevin, who were almost of an age, had each been nurtured in a home oriented to religious education rather than a stereotyped "conversion"; each had in later years been converted under considerable pressure; and each had again reacted from the whole revivalist method in the 1830's. Hodge apparently had never had a conversion experience, and to him Finney's revivals were almost as horrifying as that New Haven theology in which Bushnell was—not very submissively—trained.

Princeton had warmly supported Nevin's plea for the "system of the catechism" against the "system of the anxious bench," and the same considerations led Hodge to welcome Bushnell's plea for Christian education. "The whole tendency of the last 25 years," Hodge had written the preceding year, "has been to rely more on spasmodic efforts, on exhortations from the pulpit, and appeals to the feelings of the people, as a means of building up the church, than upon the teaching of Christianity. What other science do men try to teach by declamation?" [7] The notion that the cause of Christ should be advanced "by sudden and violent paroxysms of exertion" often led to spurious conversions and to depreciation and neglect of the ordinary means of grace. Not revival preaching but Christian training, he declared, was "the

[5] Nevin to Harbaugh, July 3, 1847 (Library of the German Reformed Church, Franklin and Marshall College).

[6] June 23, 30; July 7, 14; cf. also August 11, 25, and September 1, 1847.

[7] *BRPR*, 1846, p. 347.

appointed, the natural, the normal and ordinary means" for the salvation of the children of the church.[8] All three of these theologians conceived the ideal Christian training to be one in which the child should grow up a Christian and never have to undergo a technical, datable conversion.

Bushnell argued historically that ever since the Great Awakening extreme individualism had governed the churches. He claimed that it was only the "New Lights" of the Great Awakening who had become virtual Baptists. They had generally adopted the Baptist conception that religion was a matter for conscious conversion of adults, each by himself. According to this view, children were "capable of sin, incapable of repentance"; they were expected to grow up in sin, unable to do anything acceptable to God until converted; there was nothing to do but "wait for the concussion." Bushnell claimed to stand on the older Puritan platform, current before Edwards and Whitefield. Nevin, on the other hand, maintained that the radical individualism of the contemporary Baptists and Methodists was derived from "the original tendency of Puritanism itself," from the seventeenth century. To him Bushnell seemed not wholly consistent: he was a Puritan at war with Puritanism.

Both Nevin and Hodge applauded Bushnell's "organic" interpretation of human society, a conception which none of the Congregational critics seemed to grasp. Bushnell had presented it as part of the new current of social thought, in relation to state, school, family, and church. He noted, to be sure, that in all these spheres American thought generally was radically individualistic. His own interest was the child, and the child's education, and here the family was the most important of these "organic" communities. The child's sympathies, attitudes, feelings, and habits, he pointed out, are shaped in countless ways by his family, as his personality gradually gains independence in this social matrix. His religion in particular is normally the product, in large measure, of parental influences, especially the early influences prior to

[8] "Bushnell on Christian Nurture," *BRPR*, 1847, pp. 519, 510.

formal instruction. No child can be understood as a separate individual, and no adult is ever fully an individual separate from "organic" relations.

The term "organic," however, had divergent connotations for each of the three men. Hodge and Nevin both used it theologically. Hodge's lifelong debate with New England over original sin and man's federal union with Adam led him to apply the organic analogy to this relation, and so he pronounced that Bushnell's argument had "very much of an 'Old school cast.'" Nevin also used the term habitually to characterize man's solidarity with Christ and with Adam. Bushnell's usage, on the other hand, was not theological; he was simply analyzing social psychology. He thought his analysis could be associated with any theology, Episcopal or Unitarian, Baptist or High Calvinist. What God brought out through faithful parental nurture was the point he wished to stress. He feared that if he put his case in terms of the covenant promises, then men would continue to slight their responsibilities for nurture under the covenant. Similarly he noted that Episcopalians neglected religious education, apparently trusting to the power of the ordinance by itself. In discussing these points, to be sure, Bushnell did not wholly conceal his own theological orientation. He had no notion of an organic church in Nevin's sense or of imputed guilt or righteousness in Hodge's sense. For this reason Nevin spoke of Bushnell's work as a radically unchurchly plea for the church, and Hodge stated that Bushnell had not worked out the consequences of his own principles.

The divergencies first became sharp and clear when the argument turned to infant baptism. No man ever objected to infant baptism, said Bushnell, who did not have wrong views of religious education. At the time of his ordination in 1833, he himself had run into difficulties over the meaning of infant baptism, and only after changing his views on child nurture did he recognize the significance of infant baptism. Although Hodge and Nevin similarly deplored the widespread neglect of infant baptism, each had his own distinctive view of the subject.

For both Bushnell and Hodge the children of the church were

understood to be in a peculiar relation to God because of their parents' faith, not because of baptism. For Bushnell they were potentially regenerate, since they were in communication through their parents with the spiritual life which indwelt the church. They were to be baptized as a badge of this status and relation. With adults and infants alike, baptism did not create the membership of the church but simply indicated a membership already existing by virtue of spiritual life. Thus, for Bushnell, baptism was not a sacrament but a rite representing facts and relations which were independently true and effective.

Hodge knew no one doctrine more needed in the church than that of the "intimate and divinely established connexion between the faith of parents and the salvation of their children," such a connection as might lead parents to expect confidently that through God's blessing on their faithful efforts their children would grow up in communion with him.[9] For Hodge, however, this connection was not merely psychological; it was based on God's repeated covenant promises. Infant baptism under the new covenant was equivalent to circumcision under the old, for in both the promise was to the believers and their seed. In this connection, as with Bushnell, baptism was not a sacrament, but a badge of a relationship and status otherwise established.

Nevin found Bushnell's parental influence and Hodge's birth into the covenant alike unsatisfactory. Bushnell's argument seemed to him rationalistic in tendency if not intention. Neither original sin nor the necessity of regeneration by the Holy Spirit was taken seriously enough. If the new man in Christ was to be nurtured by parental influence, from what initial communication with God was the development to spring? Was the Christian man evolved from the old creature in rebellion against God? Again, could one treat the role of the Holy Spirit in regeneration as a psychological mechanism to be calculated and manipulated? No, the presupposition of Christian nurture must be grace communicated, a relation with God constituted in baptism itself.

Hodge repeated Nevin's criticism of Bushnell's naturalism. "If

[9] *Ibid.*, pp. 508–9.

salvation comes through nature, Christ is dead in vain." [10] Regeneration, he insisted, is not just another instance of parental influence; it belongs outside the natural causal order—in the class of Christ's healings, opening the eyes of the blind, and raising the dead. But while Hodge saw the need of something more than natural, psychological processes, his recourse to birth in the covenant did not satisfy Nevin. The latter inquired,

> What do good men mean when they tell us, that the children of professing Christians are Christian likewise, members of the Church and heirs of all its grace by their mere natural birth? . . . Our birth relation to pious parents may give us a right to be taken into the Church; but it can never of itself make us to be in the Church as our *born* privilege.[11]

We are put in a saving relation to Christ in the church by baptism, Nevin declared. Hodge's appeal to biological birth in the covenant seemed to Nevin to stand also on the ground of rationalism. Hodge too, apparently, was making an *unchurchly* plea for the church.

Bushnell and Hodge were both severe against "churchly," "ritual," or "priestly" conceptions of baptismal grace or regeneration. Hodge supposed and Bushnell denied that the infant was burdened with a guilt to be removed, but they agreed on the main argument (which, they maintained, all experience showed) that the vast majority of baptized and supposedly regenerate children were still aliens from Christ and subjects of the kingdom of evil. The notion of regeneration by virtue of the ordinance of baptism alone, without reference to nurture by believing parents or the faith of the recipient, was simply magic and served chiefly to maintain the pretensions and power of the priests. Hodge considered this churchly doctrine essentially the same—whether at Rome, Oxford, or Berlin. With obvious reference to Mercersburg, he estimated that "the German philosophical form of the doctrine bids fair to be the popular one in this country." [12]

[10] *Ibid.*, p. 534.
[11] *Weekly Messenger* (hereafter cited as *WM*), July 14, 1847.
[12] Hodge, "Bushnell on Christian Nurture," *BRPR*, 1847, pp. 537–38.

In his review of Bushnell Nevin did not clarify his own doctrine in relation to such arguments, but a correspondent of the *Weekly Messenger* drew him out by inquiring whether his criticisms of Bushnell meant that he believed in baptismal regeneration. Nevin replied that he did not, in the sense of a change necessarily brought about at the time in the recipient of baptism. "But in baptismal grace," he declared, "I firmly believe." Whatever there be of force in the constitution of the church for our salvation, "it is by baptism that we come first regularly and fully within its range." [13] Baptism does not assure us of salvation, he explained, but it does assure us of an offer of salvation which may save us if we receive it in faith. This offer may, on the other hand, be frustrated by unbelief. With baptism, as with the Lord's Supper, Nevin evidently believed in an objective communication of grace which was not, however, effective apart from faith.

In 1850, three years after Nevin had argued his particular conception of baptismal grace with two other champions of infant baptism, he helped to develop the Mercersburg position against the Baptists. He wrote against the Baptists, or even more against the crypto-Baptists in the Reformed churches, in an article called "Noel on Baptism." [14] As a springboard Nevin took the work in which the Baptist Noel stated the (exclusively biblical) grounds on which he had left the Church of England for the Baptists. About the same time Schaff must have been at work on the section of his history on infant baptism, for there is a very close relation between the views and topics and references presented by the two men. (Schaff's history appeared in German the following year, and Harbaugh translated the chapter on baptism for the July, 1852, *Mercersburg Review.*) The two expositions may be treated together.

> The Baptistic system [Nevin reminded the American Reformed] in the beginning was held to be at war with Protestantism no less than with the faith of the ancient Church. . . . How does it happen then that it should now be met with such easy toleration, as a thing of

[13] *WM*, August 11, 1847.

[14] *Mercersburg Review* (hereafter cited as *MR*), 1850, pp. 231–64.

mere outward fashion and form? For the reason simply, beyond all doubt, that the view taken of the Church has undergone a material change.[15]

The debate with the Baptists fell customarily under the two heads of the proper mode and the proper subjects of the ordinance. As to the mode Nevin scandalized some of his colleagues, such as Samuel Helfenstein, Jr., with his concession that the New Testament and early church generally favored immersion over sprinkling. Schaff similarly declared that "immersion, and not sprinkling, was unquestionably the original, normal form." Departures from immersion were at first permitted

> only in cases of urgent necessity, such as sickness and approaching death. . . . Not till the end of the 13th century did sprinkling become the rule and immersion the exception, partly from the gradual decrease in the number of adult baptisms. . . . It is well known that the reformers, Luther and Calvin, and several old Protestant liturgies, gave the preference to immersion; and this is undoubtedly far better suited than sprinkling to symbolize the idea of baptism.[16]

Sprinkling was established in the Protestant churches only in the seventeenth century, Nevin noted. He himself deplored the nineteenth-century practice of merely wetting the fingers of the minister "instead of taking up, as the old formularies prescribe, at least his hand full of the element, and so pouring." [17] As to the mode then, the Baptists had the better of it. They only went too far, Schaff maintained, "in making immersion, after the fashion of Jewish legalism, the *only* valid form of baptism." [18]

Far more important than the mode of baptism was its nature. Was it a genuine sacrament or rather, as Noel and the Baptists thought, a mere outward rite enjoined by divine law but devoid of grace or power in itself? In the New Testament, said Nevin, baptism "is the washing of regeneration; it saves us; it is for the

[15] *Ibid.*, p. 235.
[16] *History of the Apostolic Church*, trans. E. D. Yeomans (New York: Charles Scribner's Sons, 1859), pp. 568–70.
[17] "Noel on Baptism," *MR*, 1850, p. 240.
[18] *Op. cit.*, p. 570.

remission of sins."[19] "The communication of the promised sacramental grace," Schaff adds, "is not magical or mechanical, but is dependent, as well in baptism as in the Supper, on certain conditions, viz., a scriptural mode of administration on the part of the officiating minister, and repentance and faith on the part of the recipient." It is with good reason that the Church adheres to the principle "that baptism—of course not without faith—is in general necessary to salvation; while on the other hand, she asserts with the same right, that not the defect of the sacrament . . . but the conscious contempt of it, condemns."[20] The Baptists, on the other hand, rejected the sacramental idea of the early and Reformation church altogether. "The true issue in the end," said Nevin, "is, Church or No-Church; sacrament or merely moral sign."[21]

The other great issue to be argued with the Baptists was the question as to whether infants were rightly to be baptized. Adult baptism certainly predominated in the first and second centuries at least, as a consequence of missionary activity. Where churches were established, however, was there not even in the first century a Christian infant baptism corresponding to circumcision? Neander denied the existence of such infant baptism in the apostolic church, representing it rather as a development of the late second century, when Tertullian opposed it. But Schaff took issue with his teacher Neander, contending that "the introduction and exercise of this ordinance is as old as the independent existence of any Christian community" and that it was actually practiced in the five recorded instances of household baptism in the New Testament.[22]

Schaff did not try to make his case by explicit biblical injunctions—there are none—but on general theological inferences. "The ultimate authority for infant baptism in the bosom of a regular Christian community and under a sufficient guarantee of

[19] "Noel on Baptism," *MR*, 1850, p. 245.
[20] *Op. cit.*, p. 566.
[21] "Noel on Baptism," *MR*, 1850, p. 258.
[22] *Op. cit.*, p. 579. Cf. Nevin, "Noel on Baptism," p. 254.

pious education—for only on these terms do we advocate it—lies in the universal import of Christ's person and work, which extends as far as humanity itself." [23] "Redemption and salvation are brought to pass for the race," Nevin argued likewise. We may not limit the scope of Christ's redemption, so as to include Caucasians but not Negroes, or only those of eighteen and older. Nearly one-half of humanity is cut off by death before maturity is reached. Is there no room for infants and children "in the concrete mystery of the new creation, in the communion of Christ's Mediatorial Life, in the bosom of the Holy Catholic Church?" No, answered the Baptist, Dr. Carson, "The Gospel has nothing to do with infants, nor have Gospel ordinances any respect to them. . . . None can ever be saved by the Gospel who do not believe it. Consequently, by the Gospel no infant can be saved." [24] If saved at all, according to the Baptists, children must be saved by uncovenanted mercies, outside the church and outside of Christ.

With infant baptism, Schaff continued the argument, "is closely connected the beautiful idea, already clearly brought out by Irenaeus . . . that Jesus Christ became for children a child, for youth, a youth, for men, a man, and by thus entering into the various conditions and stages of our earthly existence sanctified every period of life, infancy as well as manhood." [25] Nevin also was fond of Irenaeus' interpretation of the Incarnation as "recapitulation." "His manhood was a process, starting in the Virgin's womb, and in this character it took up into itself, as a power of redemption, the entire range of our existence. He sanctified infancy and childhood, says Irenaeus, by making them stages of his own life." [26]

To these arguments based on the person and work of Christ and the nature of the church as humanity redeemed, Schaff added two others. First was the analogy with circumcision. Although all objections to infant baptism also applied to the circumcision

[23] *Ibid.*, p. 572.
[24] *Ibid.*
[25] *Ibid.*, p. 573.
[26] "Noel on Baptism," p. 249; Cf. *WM*, March 1, 1848.

of infants, this was incontrovertibly enjoined by God. Schaff's second argument was based on the inclusion of children in the covenant promises on the basis of "an organic connection" between parents and their children. Thus Paul spoke of children as included in the covenant of grace, which argues that if they are not already baptized, they are entitled to baptism.[27]

Nevin seemed to glory in the fact that these chief arguments for infant baptism were not exegetical, at least in the proof-text sense. "There is no direct, positive appointment of infant baptism in the whole Bible," he told Berg, "and no clear and explicit example of its use." [28] He was fond of twitting the antipapal polemics, such as Berg and "Kirwan," [29] with the fact that they were really resisting the Baptist position only on the basis of an ecclesiastical tradition derived from Rome. Here was more ammunition for his plea for the necessity of *tradition*. The church had adopted infant baptism not so much from specific precept as from the Word living in the church in the way of divine tradition.

> If it could be clearly made out that the household baptism of the New Testament included no infants; nay, if it were certain that the Church had no apostolical rule whatever in the case, but had gradually settled here into her own rule; we should hold this still to be of truly divine authority, and the baptism of infants of necessary Christian obligation, as the only proper sense and meaning of the New Testament institution, interpreted thus to its full depth by the Christian life itself.[30]

The crucial arguments in this case lay "not in the letter of the Scriptures but in the life of Christianity itself."

The strength of the Baptist case, Schaff considered, lay in the argument that faith is the indispensable condition of salvation. This proposition he accepted. The Baptists, however, made too much of the faith prerequisite to baptism, understanding it to be

[27] *Op. cit.*, pp. 579–80.
[28] *WM*, March 1, 1848.
[29] Nom de plume for Nicholas Murray, a former Roman Catholic, now a Presbyterian minister, whose *Letters to the Rt. Rev. John Hughes* were reviewed by Nevin, "Kirwan's Letters," *MR*, 1849, pp. 229–63.
[30] "Noel on Baptism," pp. 249–50.

regeneration and conversion. With the apostles, he said, it was not so. "The apostles never demanded full and formal regeneration before baptism, but simply an honest longing for salvation in Christ, which salvation was then actually administered and sealed to them by baptism, and afterwards nourished and developed by the other means of grace." Faith has its different stages, and the incipient form and slumbering germ may be found in the child. A child is subject to the influences of grace and may be actually regenerated. "Faith begins with religious susceptibility, with an unconscious longing for the divine, and a childlike trust in a higher power." [31]

Schaff did not explicitly apply this old Lutheran speculation about incipient faith to the week-old infant, and Nevin apparently found this an unconvincing line of thought.

> We have carefully refrained [Nevin emphasized] from the question, What specifically is the power of baptism in the case of infants? . . . We meddle not with it here, any farther than to assert the fact of grace objectively present in the sacrament under *some* form. Allowing this, there is room still for a difference of view in regard to its precise nature, just as there is room for a similar difference also in regard to the specific power of the Lord's Supper. . . . We know that there are great difficulties attending the subject of baptismal grace. . . . Whether we can solve them satisfactorily or not, we are still bound, in the way of preliminary faith, to accept the mystery of such grace itself, since the only alternative to this, is to give up the doctrine of the holy sacraments altogether in the old church sense, and so to bring in another gospel.[32]

Both men were emphatic that baptism is not *complete* without religious instruction and self-conscious, free turning to God at maturity. "Infant baptism needs to be completed in the subject," Schaff wrote, "according to ancient custom, by catechetical instruction, and by confirmation, in which the Christian, arrived at the age of spiritual discretion, ratifies his baptismal confession, and of his free determination gives himself to God." [33] Nevin

[31] Schaff, *op. cit.*, pp. 574–76.
[32] "Noel on Baptism," pp. 264–65.
[33] *Op. cit.*, p. 575.

agreed on both points, further explaining that confirmation meant the necessary personal acknowledgment and response, which however was not to be viewed as "a new and independent transaction," but rather "as the natural and suitable close of the baptismal act itself." [34] The baptismal act alone was *incomplete;* without Christian nurture and the response of faith, it was emptied of meaning.

In his discussion of baptism Schaff had more than once founded himself on the views of Professor Martensen of Copenhagen. Henry Harbaugh, now in effect the college pastor of Franklin and Marshall at the First Reformed Church of Lancaster, took up this cue. In the *Mercersburg Review* of 1852 and 1853 [35] appeared his translation of Martensen's book, entitled "The Doctrine of Christian Baptism and the Baptistic Question." This proved to be the most developed treatment of baptism published under Mercersburg auspices and must have been congenial to Schaff and Nevin on several grounds. Mercersburg fought the sect spirit, and similarly Martensen was polemically oriented against Baptist activities in the established Lutheran churches of Denmark and Germany, and against the related pietist tendencies. He shared the speculative Christological outlook of Dorner. And his criticism of philosophical predestinarianism read as if written for the spiritual good of the Princeton faculty. Schaff apparently agreed with less qualification than Nevin, who seems to have reserved his approval of the distinctively Lutheran aspects of Martensen's exposition.

Baptism, Martensen taught, was the "sacrament of election." What Jesus' personal call signified to his disciples, the entry in time and history of God's eternal election, that baptism has meant for the church ever since. The grace of baptism predetermines and preforms its subjects for salvation, actualizing God's eternal decree in the gathering of the historical church. The mystery of predestination must be approached from this concrete situation *in*

[34] "Noel on Baptism," p. 263.

[35] H. Martensen, "The Doctrine of Christian Baptism and the Baptistic Question," *MR*, 1852, pp. 305–21, 475–85; 1853, pp. 276–310.

mediis rebus, rather than as an abstract metaphysical speculation—complete outside of time. The election and calling in baptism summon its recipient to decision and empower him to free action. Baptism is thus seen as the point of conjunction of the antinomy of God's sovereignty and human freedom.

So seen, every baptism, even of adults, is in a sense infant baptism, for those who receive it properly are children in the new world of Christianity. The apostles regarded none as regenerate before baptism; the church was founded by baptism and is ever anew founded so, in *unregenerate* men. Although Martensen conceded that adult baptism was the norm in the first century, he declared that the fulfilment of Christ's missionary injunction would mean the general establishment of infant baptism in the world.

The baptism given to the unregenerate meant their justification and regeneration. Not only was the righteousness of Christ imputed and the mystery of the incarnation and resurrection appropriated, but Christ himself in his glorified life was actually imparted, "in, with and under" the outward acts. These benefits were not, of course, received by faith; rather the infant recipients of baptism were to be conceived as "unconscious Christophers." Martensen urged the analogy of the presence of the divine nature in the infant Jesus when still incapable of faith. In some such way the Holy Spirit, as a principle of susceptibility for Christ and the germ of faith, was imparted at baptism. Human nature was not changed thereby, as Roman Catholic theology taught, but an essential communion with Christ was initiated. There might thereafter be lapses, but the inward possibility of faith and the capacity to reform remained as aspects of a *character indelibilis.*

On the basis of this high estimate of baptism Martensen warned against the overvaluation of confirmation. He denied Schleiermacher's contention, which Nevin had supported, that confirmation was the completion of baptism, forming with it one transaction. Confirmation dealt merely with the subjective side of faith and was not a sacrament. It represented rather the climax of the nurture of the church. With regard to such nurture, to be sure,

Martensen would have heartily applauded Nevin's plea for "the system of the catechism."

For half a decade thereafter the Mercersburg theologians were engaged with other problems than those of baptism. Then when an extended debate on the subject broke out among the Presbyterians, the Mercersburg view was injected into that discussion. Presbyterian comment in the mid-fifties about the decline in infant baptism has already been noted. About the same time a practical problem provoked widespread debate. The General Assembly of 1857 appointed a committee, chaired by Dr. J. H. Thornwell of Columbia Seminary, to prepare a revision of the Book of Discipline. One of the most troublesome issues turned up by the committee was whether, or to what degree, baptized children were properly subject to church discipline. Dr. Thornwell drafted the report, which recommended that none but communicants should be subject to judicial process. But Dr. Hodge spoke so effectively against this recommendation that the report was recommitted in 1859 by the Assembly. For several years the Presbyterian periodicals were full of debate about the status of baptized children in the church.

Dr. Thornwell's position was that church discipline should be applied only to those who recognized and accepted the obligations of the faith. Children did not meet these qualifications, even if baptized. Their baptism entitled them to a technical church membership but had nothing to do with their spiritual relation to Christ. Until they should be converted they were "unregenerate members," "of the world and in the church," dead in trespasses and sin and alien to God. "Are they not the slaves of sin and the Devil," asked Dr. Thornwell, "existing in a free commonwealth for the purpose of being educated to the liberty of saints?" [36]

Dr. Thornwell—and his colleagues Dr. Stuart Robinson of Danville Seminary and Dr. R. L. Dabney of Union Theological Seminary, Richmond—thus held a virtually Baptist conception of church membership. They admitted no real force either to the

[36] "A Few More Words on the Revised Book of Discipline," *Southern Presbyterian Review*, 1861, p. 13.

covenant promises to believers' children or to the act of baptism. Baptized children were not members of the real church.

The Princeton theologians, on the other hand, were strongly convinced that the children of the church were genuinely members of it and that their treatment should reflect this status. This was the main theme of Professor Atwater's essay "The Children of the Church and Sealing Ordinances." [37] Atwater acknowledged a widespread confusion among American Presbyterians in this whole area. He wished to find a position between the Baptist denial of infant baptism and church membership, and the "Romanizing" idea of a regeneration effected by the sacrament.[38]

Most of Dr. Atwater's argument was directed against the substantially Baptist view, which had been disseminated with the revivalist preoccupation with specifiable and datable gracious experiences. Many Presbyterians had come to look upon infant baptism merely as a dedicatory act of the parents, with the hope that these baptized children would later "join the church." Baptismal practice had become careless in the extreme. Hodge reported that ministers and sessions often did not know how many children of the congregation were baptized. Parents were not properly prepared for baptism by their ministers. Hodge declared he had never heard a Presbyterian sermon on baptism! Parents did not generally consider neglect of the baptismal sacrament sinful, as they certainly would have considered neglect of the Lord's Supper. And what distressed Atwater most was that the baptized children were not treated any differently from the unbaptized. Sessions no longer insisted upon family worship. The old examination meetings on the catechism were falling into disuse. The tendency was to neglect all the laborious, appointed means of nurture and to wait for the cheap conversion in a revival.

With all his emphasis on the church membership of baptized children and their due nurture and instruction, Dr. Atwater was

[37] *BRPR*, 1857, pp. 1–34.

[38] Possibly a reference to Mercersburg. Cf. p. 4 on the "rebound" to "transcendental theology" and "mystic ritualism."

not very clear as to the effect of baptism itself. Sometimes he seemed to treat baptism as a sacrament. At other times he repudiated as Romanizing any notion that baptism had "intrinsic efficacy" or conveyed grace.[39] Hodge was clearer and more definite in holding that the children of believers were church members in virtue, not of that baptism, but of God's covenant promise to the faithful and their seed. It was the Reformed view, he held, that the children of believers were federally holy and were baptized in recognition of the fact that they were *already* church members. For Hodge infant baptism was no sacrament.

President Gerhart of Franklin and Marshall challenged this Princeton reading of the Reformed doctrine of baptism and specifically of the standards of the Presbyterian Church. In so doing he sought to convict Princeton of deviation from baptismal orthodoxy as Nevin had so successfully done with regard to Eucharistic doctrine. Current Presbyterian teaching and preaching, said Gerhart, conflicted with the standards of the church and with Calvin on baptism. He proceeded to discuss the relevant sections of the Westminster Confession and Catechism, the biblical passages supplied with the standards, and Calvin's *Institutes*. "The symbols of the Presbyterian church take high ground" he argued, "on the subject of Baptism, as high as that of any other Protestant Symbol, that of the Episcopal Church not excepted." The Confession teaches that "the baptismal transaction assures the person baptized . . . that . . . he is as certainly engrafted into Christ, regenerated by His Spirit, and forgiven through his blood, as he is externally washed with water."[40] To be sure, this appointed collocation of grace with the outward ordinance does not mean that all that are baptized are undoubtedly regenerated, or that no one can be regenerated without it. But, in the words of the Confession (XXVIII, 6) "by the right use of this ordinance, the grace promised is not only offered, but really exhibited and conferred by the Holy Ghost, to such (whether of age or infants) as that

[39] *Ibid.*, pp. 21, 24.

[40] E. V. Gerhart, "The Efficacy of Baptism," *MR*, 1858, pp. 40, 17 n., 18.

grace belongeth unto, according to the counsel of God's own will, in his appointed time."

Gerhart noted that in one passage of the Larger Catechism (Question 191) it was denied that the sacraments became an effectual means of salvation by any power in themselves and that Calvin occasionally used similar language. But these were instances, Gerhart argued, of an inexact use of the term "sacrament" to refer to the external action considered separately from the work of the Holy Spirit. The basic teaching, he held, was exactly what Atwater had denied, that grace is intrinsic to a sacrament by its very nature under divine promise. Picking up an old theme of Nevin's, he contended that the Princeton baptismal conception was really "Nestorian," if not "Unitarian," and so was much other American theology. Such sacramental views could be held together with an orthodox Christology only by violence. Either the antisacramental conception would drag down the Christology to its own level, as seemed to be happening in New England Congregationalism, or, as might be hoped of Presbyterianism, the Christology would require a congruent sacramental doctrine.

In his reading of Calvin and the Reformed confessions Gerhart had missed the basis for the Princeton doctrine that the children of believers were members of the church in virtue of the covenant promise. This he found "a very novel doctrine." Like Nevin, he argued instead that the covenant promise gives the children of believers the right to membership, but leaves them outside of the church as long as they remain unbaptized.[41] The baptismal order of the German Reformed *Liturgy, or Order for Christian Worship,* published that year, made this understanding of the baptismal act clear. The thanksgiving prayer returned thanks to God "that it hath pleased thee, through the mystery of thy holy Baptism, to deliver this child [or: this person] from the power of darkness, and to translate him into the kingdom of thy dear Son."

Nevin read Gerhart's essay with great satisfaction. "Dr. Gerhart's article on baptism in the last *Review* is truly admirable,"

[41] *Ibid.,* p. 33.

he wrote to Schaff.[42] "It must puzzle Princeton, what to say about it." But Princeton still had much to say. Hodge accused Mercersburg of being so immersed in Lutheran thought as to forget the ABC's of Reformed theology. With some support from Calvin he asserted

> the doctrine that parents represent their children, and that, therefore, children of professing parents are born within the Church, and on that ground are to be baptized, is the distinctive doctrine of the Reformed Churches. In opposition to this view, Romanists and Lutherans place the duty of infant baptism on the ground that all children are born outside of the church, and by baptism are inwardly renewed by the Holy Ghost, and thus become members of Christ's body.[43]

Thus baptism was necessary to salvation for Romanists and Lutherans, but not for the Reformed.

Hodge once again produced the Consensus Tigurinus (as he had done against Nevin with regard to the Lord's Supper) as the "most formal and authoritative exhibition of Reformed doctrine on the whole subject of the sacraments." The superior authority of this document over the great national Reformed confessions, to be sure, seemed to rest on nothing more objective than its greater affinity for Hodge's view. This view was a flat denial that baptism was the sacrament of regeneration. He wrote,

> The Reformed admit that children are susceptible of regeneration, and that it may take place at any time God sees fit to effect it; but they deny that there is any divine promise that the outward act shall be attended by the inward change, or that baptism, in the case either of adults or infants is the appointed means of effecting that change.[44]

Perhaps the basic reason why Hodge rejected the sacraments as such was his metaphysical orientation. For Mercersburg the church was constituted by relation to Christ and the sacraments were vehicles of this mystical union. But Hodge explicitly rejected this reference to Christ in favor of a speculative construction of predestination.

[42] Nevin to Schaff, January 28, 1858 (unpublished letter in the Library of the German Reformed Church, Franklin and Marshall College).

[43] "The Church Membership of Infants," *BRPR,* 1858, p. 373.

[44] *Ibid,* pp. 381, 379.

> Membership in the invisible church [he contended] is *not* vital union with Christ, or regeneration by the Holy Ghost! . . . [The invisible church] consists of *the whole number of the elect,* that have been, are, or shall be gathered into one, under Christ the head thereof. It includes, therefore, probably millions of the unborn and millions of the unconverted. . . . It is not their vital union with Christ, nor their actual regeneration by the Holy Ghost, that is presumed, but their election.[45]

In this range of opinion on the doctrine of baptism, the point of crucial difference was baptismal grace. Here the philosophical predestinarians of Princeton came out with the Baptists and Southern Presbyterians. Even Bushnell stood on the same side of the line. Mercersburg never wavered on the reality of baptismal grace, even though Nevin was much less confident than Martensen, for instance, as to how to explain it. Both Nevin and Schaff endeavored to bring again to credit the baptismal teaching of the Reformation in churches which had largely abandoned it. For Nevin, however, there remained such "formidable difficulties on both sides"[46] that quick and confident resolutions were folly.

[45] *Ibid.*, pp. 375, 376.
[46] "The Old Doctrine of Christian Baptism," *MR.*, 1860, pp. 213, 215.

11/Church Order and the Ministry

With the doctrine of the ministry the Mercersburg men broke most definitely with the Reformers. No special controversy attended the subject at first such as those provoked by their views of the Lord's Supper and church history, but from the beginning they held a distinctive theory.

On this particular topic their kinship to the Anglo-Catholic movement was conspicuous. The Tractarians had stressed nothing so much as their peculiar view of apostolic succession in the episcopate, and in England this had been a major focus of controversy. In comparison with Newman and Pusey, the Mercersburg men had only a rather tepid interest in bishops as such. Yet was not a Puseyism without bishops an equally plausible possibility? If such a position seems anomalous in the English context, a more exact parallel might be found in Thomas Cranmer's uncle-in-law Osiander and clerical Lutheranism.

Osiander was the sixteenth-century ancestor of that whole group of high-church theologians noted in Schaff's background, from Gerlach and Stahl to Loehe, Kliefoth, and Vilmar.

> The really characteristic doctrinal mark of this group of theologians emerges as the Osiander-Löhe teaching on the ministerial office. The powers of the clergy are not those common to all Christians and assigned to the ministry for exercise, but those peculiar to Christ, conferred by him on the Apostolate and transmitted in the church through ordination up to the contemporary holders of the office. The dichotomy of church and ministry is thus fundamental, and the ministry possesses the power basic to all church government.

The reason for this is that the efficaciousness of the means of grace and the very salvation of the world are bound to the ministerial office.[1] The idea of the visible church as a divine institution out of which there was no ordinary possibility of salvation thus found its cutting edge in the prerogatives of the clergy.

In Europe practical considerations made this high doctrine of the ministry attractive in the early nineteenth century. Most of the theologians involved served state churches and were anxious to find a point of leverage in the church for opposing the tendency of the civil governments to intervene in church affairs. Several of these theologians, in fact, were ready for this reason to face disestablishment.

The absence of this church-state problem in America may be part of the reason why the Mercersburg doctrine of the ministry did not evoke lively controversy. An American parallel to the "ideological" aspect of the European clerical movements did exist, however. It is not completely cynical to observe that the Tractarians and high-church Lutherans were almost all political and social reactionaries and that their view of the place of the ministry in the church paralleled closely such characteristic Restoration political views as those of Haller. *Legitimacy* had in America a kind of equivalent in political conservatism and the desire to maintain an aristocracy of status. Although Andrew Jackson happened to be a Presbyterian, the Mercersburg movement, like Brownson's swing to Rome, may perhaps be seen as a reaction against Jacksonian democracy. It was certainly a reaction against irregular itinerants, vulgar revivalists, and lay exhorters in the church.

Even the ministers in America generally seemed eager, in the generation after the War of 1812, to minimize their special status and distinctions from the laity. The novels of Harriet Beecher Stowe record the passing of the distinctive street dress of the eighteenth-century gentleman cleric. These changes reached also into the meetinghouse. The Genevan gown and bands passed so completely out of fashion that people no longer realized that

[1] E. Hirsch, *Geschichte der neuern evangelischen Theologie* (Gütersloh; C. Bertelsmann Verlag, 1954), V, 194.

such had been the habitual garb of Congregational, Presbyterian, and Reformed ministers in the colonial period. When a church building was remodeled in this generation, the old high pulpit was almost always lowered. The impression given is that the awesome authority of God's Word preached was being replaced by a testimony of individual experience which any layman might supply. Henry Ward Beecher, the representative popular preacher, preferred a rostrum to a pulpit and entered it with calculated informality, removing his rubbers after mounting the platform.

The priestly functions of the ministry were especially deprecated. Worship and the sacramental life were slighted. Church discipline was falling into disuse. The power of absolution was coming to be denied altogether, and ordination, as the solemn induction into ministerial office, was treated more casually as the dignity and authority of the office itself was minimized.

The abuses of the ministry most prevalent in the mid-nineteenth century were at the opposite pole from those in the generation of the Reformers. In the sixteenth century the canonical requirements regarding examination for fitness for the office and the people's consent were both systematically disregarded. Calvin observed that in the light of the teachings and canons of the ancient church on the consent of the people in the election of pastors, there was not "throughout the whole Papacy in the present day, any canonical election." [2] Beza challenged the validity of the bishops of the Papacy. "Were you elected to the episcopate by the elders of your church? Did the people seek for you? Were inquiries instituted regarding your conduct, your life, your belief?" [3] The papal church was careful to maintain regularity in the selection and ordination of ministers by bishops on behalf of the larger church, but it was scandalously careless with the canons designed to insure that ministers should be genuine pastors of the

[2] *Institutes*, IV, v, ii.

[3] J. L. Ainslie, *The Doctrines of Ministerial Order in the Reformed Churches of the 16th and 17th Centuries* (Edinburgh: T. & T. Clark, 1940), p. 231.

faithful. The chief emphases of the early Reformed church by way of correction were on the adequate "trials" of candidates and the voice of congregations in establishing a pastoral relationship.

In early nineteenth-century America, by contrast, many Christians regarded nothing *but* the voice of the people in constituting a pastoral relation. Often no effective provision was made for an adequate sense of responsibility to the larger church, or for the participation of representatives of that larger church in the selection and ordaining of ministers. By way of correction Nevin laid emphasis on the necessity of ordination by representatives of the existing ministry.

Viewed in terms of function, the late medieval priesthood almost completely neglected its prophetic role of witnessing and teaching. It was a vast corporation of mass priests, the large majority of whom could give no persuasive or even coherent account of the faith they represented. They had memorized certain formulas and ritual actions which were understood to have magical virtue, but they could not declare the faith. Such men, said the Reformers, were no true priests. They acknowledged as priests none save those who declared forgiveness in Christ Jesus and no sacraments save those interpreted by the Gospel to the people. A priest unequipped or unwilling to preach Christ was not a valid minister and could not rightly administer the sacraments. By way of correction, the indispensable and chief qualification for a true minister in the early Reformed church was the capacity to preach salvation.

By Nevin's day, however, American Protestants were in danger of being talked to death. There was a great deal of "preaching" which had not been carefully and responsibly shaped by the Good News. Nevin and Schaff had little to say about this in comparison with the contention that the priestly and regal functions of the ministry were inadequately served and even formally disavowed in part. They were anxious to reassert the legitimate priestly aspects of Christ's ministry.

Their concern for the sacraments has already been described.

A related aspect of the priestly functions of the ministry was the exercise of "the power of the keys." Nevin maintained that ministerial absolution was sacramental, since God's grace was really associated with the ecclesiastical act. "The absolution which the Church pronounces," he taught, "is not a mere declaration that God will pardon sinners, but the medium through which God communicates the grace of pardon." [4]

This conception was embodied in the forms for general confession and absolution, and for public excommunication and restoration to communion, in the *Liturgy, or Order for Christian Worship*. Such forms, as Nevin remarked, were regularly used by the Reformed church in the sixteenth century. "On this point the Church has manifestly fallen away from the practice as well as the view of the Reformed Church of the Reformation." [5] There can be little doubt that those ministers and members of the German Reformed Church who were startled by the absolution of the new *Liturgy* would have been still more shocked if they had taken the trouble to read the corresponding form in their old Palatinate liturgy.

Like Luther and Calvin, Nevin also considered private confession and absolution valuable in some circumstances, "for there are cases which can only be reached in this way." The only error to be guarded against, in his estimation, was to make the confession of all sins necessary. The whole transaction must be voluntary; to treat it as something to satisfy the church was the road to indulgences with "all their horrible abuses." [6] Few if any of Nevin's followers, however, seem to have introduced the practice of private confession.

The case was the same with the forms for excommunication and restoration. In the order for restoration, for example, the minister says,

> And now, In the name and by the authority of Christ and His Church, I announce to you the pardon of your sins, I release you

[4] W. H. Erb, *Dr. Nevin's Theology* (Reading, 1913), p. 368.
[5] *Ibid.*, p. 369.
[6] *Ibid.*, pp. 368, 367.

from the bond of the excommunication which you have incurred; receive you and restore you to the fellowship of Christ.[7]

But as Gans, one of the younger Mercersburg men, wrote, "Where is the power of the keys practically believed?" Both the theological basis for church discipline, and its actual exercise had been melting away in American Protestantism. The duty to admonish, suspend, excommunicate, and restore sinners was no longer seriously attended to. The decline had been conspicuous in New England Congregationalism since the last generation of the eighteenth century,[8] and the other Reformed churches were moving, if more slowly, in the same direction. Tayler Lewis had pointed out the connection between this collapse of the power of the keys in American Protestantism and its sectarianism. For so many American Protestants church censures and excommunication meant no more than expulsion from a debating society and often resulted in transfer from one voluntary society to another; or even the creation of a new "church." [9] As Gans observed, both church officers and congregations had come to doubt whether they really possessed the authority from Christ to use the keys.[10] The affirmation of such authority by Nevin and Schaff startled and frightened them.

Even in Pittsburgh and prior to his churchly conversion, as already pointed out,[11] John Nevin had a high view of the prerogatives of the ministry. It was not merely that God was the author and end of the office of a bishop, but that the selection and recognition of ministers were prerogatives of the eldership, so that an unbroken line of ministers extended from the apostles to his day as a self-perpetuating corporation within the church. He believed that such an institutional apostolic succession was both a fact and a requirement.

[7] *A Liturgy, or Order of Christian Worship* (Philadelphia, 1857), p. 266.
[8] E. Oberholzer, Jr., *Delinquent Saints* (New York: Columbia University Press, 1956), pp. 239–43.
[9] *Weekly Messenger* (hereafter cited as *WM*), January 21, 1846, reprinted from the *Biblical Repository*.
[10] D. Gans, "The Office of Bishop," *Mercersburg Review* (hereafter cited as *MR*), 1859, p. 133.
[11] See chap. 1, pp. 25–26.

Although he had found support for this view in the Congregationalists Stiles and Lathrop, Nevin generally contrasted it with the more usual theory of independency, that the ministry was the creation of the congregation. He appealed more characteristically to certain seventeenth-century British Presbyterians as sanction for his aristocratic conception.[12] Although Nevin did not identify his sources, they probably included the *Jus Divinum Ministerii Evangelici* of the London Provincial Assembly of 1654. "Church-power," that statement declares, "is first sealed in Christ the head, and from Him committed to the Apostles, and from them to Church-Officers. And they alone who have received it from the Apostles can derive and transmit it to other ministers." [13] Similarly Nevin wrote, "Ordination does convey, in this sense, objective virtue or force, such as no man, in the ordinary course of things, can be allowed to possess without it." [14]

Dorner protested at this point, arguing that this view of the ministry was Anglican, not Reformed, and that it exalted ordination to a "third sacrament." Nevin replied that on this subject Dorner carried no weight for him. "In this respect, we freely admit, our theology is more Anglican than German." [15]

This conception implies a continuity from the papal priesthood to the Reformed ministry of Word and Sacrament. To quote *Jus Divinum* again, "Our Ministry is descended to us from Christ *through* the Apostate Church of Rome, but not *from* the Apostate Church of Rome." [16] Nevin posed the issue hypothetically. Suppose all Spain were converted from popery. Would the Spanish priests be reordained? The idea evidently seemed to him preposterous.[17] On the other hand, he assumed something that the Reformers would have found preposterous—that the Roman mass priest was by preparation or the intention of his ordination equipped to be a minister of the Word and Sacraments. Nevin

[12] *WM*, September 10, 1845.
[13] Cited in Ainslie, *op. cit.*, p. 217.
[14] *The Church* (Chambersburg, Pa., 1847), p. 25.
[15] "Our Relations with Germany," *MR*, 1867, p. 632.
[16] Ainslie, *op. cit.*, p. 218.
[17] *WM*, August 20, 1845.

gave no sign of being even aware of the Reformation doctrine of the ministry. His interest was focused, in a way more characteristic of Anglicans than of the Reformed generally, on institutional genealogy without regard to the purpose of the office.

Nevin also associated institutional genealogy with the validity or efficaciousness of ministerial functions. As a consequence of the widespread sect spirit in America, he wrote, "vast multitudes . . . would seem to be left, by such false connections, without a ministry and without sacraments altogether, or at least in a state of most precarious uncertainty and question with regard to so great a point." [18] Legitimate ecclesiastical connections, apparently, would transmit the proper validation of ministerial acts.

A specific instance of such "false connections" was provided in 1849 by an application for admission to the Mercersburg Classis from a preacher of the Evangelical Association, Jacob Albright's religious following. The candidate was required to submit to ordination on the ground that the Evangelical Association was not a church and had possessed no power to ordain. (His baptism, which had been Roman Catholic was not questioned, but apparently there might have been questions if it also had been given by the Evangelical Association.) "The Albright body," said Nevin, "never had any call to become a church; . . . its ministry started from nothing and was of no force." Christian fidelity to the Albright Brethren themselves required the Classis to bear witness against their delusion and "to warn them plainly of their danger." Otherwise people would be encouraged "to take it for granted that all religious connections are alike good and alike safe." If there was any such thing as real schism, there could hardly be better candidates than "such self-constituted upstart bodies as the Albright Brethren [and] the followers of John Winebrenner." [19]

In the course of the debate the question was raised whether the principle invoked against the Evangelical Association did not also

[18] *Antichrist, or the Spirit of Sect and Schism* (New York, 1848), p. 79.
[19] "The Classis of Mercersburg," *MR,* 1849, pp. 387, 383.

challenge the validity of the Reformation and the Protestant ministry generally. The vindication, Nevin said, was

> not by any outward succession in the case of the ministry, nakedly and separately considered, but certainly not by any theory either, which overthrows the necessity of a true historical succession in the life of the Church, and makes it competent for any body of Christians, under any circumstances, to start an entirely new church. If then we must admit some disturbance in the ordinary law of ministerial succession at the Reformation, it does not follow at once that the succession itself for this reason fell to the ground; the true succession lay in the life of the Church, as a whole, and if it can be shown that *this* gave birth to the Reformation, it must be allowed to have been sufficient at the same time to make good, in the way of inward reproductive force, any *unavoidable* defect that was found to attend, in this revolution, the outward genealogy of the Protestant ministry. After all, it is the Church, the presence of Christ's life in his Body, which supports the true line of the ministry and not the line of the ministry that upholds mechanically the being and authority of the Church.[20]

In this statement a strict legalism in ministerial succession is held in some tension with the high doctrine of the church as an organism. Nevin, and Schaff also, wished on the one hand to insist on an unbroken ministerial succession through the papal church and the Reformation, "the founders of which," Schaff declared, "derived their own ordination regularly from the Catholic Church." [21] On the other hand, if there *were* any irregularity in the transmission of orders through the Reformation, as Nevin at least suspected there might have been, he believed that the church as a whole had the reproductive powers to restore a damaged organ. Ministerial functions and powers had been communicated from the Apostles to the whole community of believers as well as to the special priesthood of those inwardly called and outwardly recognized. The image of a biological organism permitted a degree of flexibility in the order and structure of the

[20] *Ibid.*, p. 385.
[21] *Principle of Protestantism* (Chambersburg, Pa., 1845), p. 125.

church. The essence of the church, "the presence of Christ's life in his Body," was not something assured by the mechanics of structure.

Although the references are too scanty for any confident comparisons between Nevin and Schaff, certain differences of emphasis seem clear. Apart from the *Principle of Protestantism,* virtually all Schaff's references to the ministry are found in his courses on the New Testament, the articles on the same subject published in *Der Kirchenfreund* from 1848, and the *Apostolische Kirche* of 1851 (in which the articles also reappeared). Like Nevin, he talked of the transmission of valid ministerial orders from the papal church, but at least in one footnote Schaf raised a theological question which opens a radically different perspective. He quoted Calvin's comment on Roman claims to episcopal succession. "Their plea of uninterrupted succession," Calvin had written, "is a vain pretence, unless the truth of Christ, which was transmitted from the fathers, be permanently retained pure and uncorrupted by their posterity."[22] In fact, Calvin observed, this succession of bishops had "revolted from Christ himself," and was no longer part of Christ's ministry. It was not the Reformers who had effected a disturbance in the succession of the ministry. That succession had already been broken some time previously, and they were seeking to restore it. There was no valid episcopate or ministry in existence to which they could adhere by regular institutional succession.

If Schaf had taken this line of thought seriously, he could scarcely have accepted a definition of valid succession apart from theological intentions and religious meaning. He seems, however, not to have clearly resolved the two conceptions of validity. With Nevin the idea of "continuity of life" held them both in an undetermined relation.

The error of Rome and the Tractarians, Schaf contended, was to hold an "external and mechanical" view of the ministry and a low and inadequate view of the church as a whole. They confined ministerial functions and powers not merely to the ministry as a

[22] *Institutes* IV, II, ii, as cited *ibid.*, p. 127 n.

whole apart from the laity, but to certain distinct officers, such as diocesan bishops or the pope, whose offices had evolved in the historical development of the ministry, "as though they were specifically different in their nature, and were alone competent to transmit ministerial power." On the unproved and unprovable postulate of a separate succession of diocesan bishops since the Apostles, the Tractarians unchurched all Protestant bodies lacking an episcopal constitution. "The German Reformed, Lutheran, and Presbyterian bodies, with all their religious life, are flatly denied any such [church] character, and even their most godly and successful ministers are branded as ecclesiastical bastards, or mere hirelings privily smuggled into the sanctuary." [23]

"I have all respect for the episcopal system," Schaf declared. "It possesses in fact many undeniable advantages, and by its antiquity besides must command the veneration of all who have any right historical feeling." Of itself, however, it gave no assurance either of church unity or of the promotion of true piety, as the history of churches under episcopal government abundantly showed. No genuine renewal of the church would result simply from having all unbishoped clergy validated "by the hands of his Grace of Canterbury, or some diocesan Onderdonk on this side of the Atlantic." [24]

As Schaf thus criticized the Anglo-Catholic confinement of the power of ordination to the bishops, Nevin attacked the Roman restriction of doctrinal teaching to the ministry. He criticized Brownson, for example, who sharply distinguished the *ecclesia docens*, that part of the ministry with doctrinal authority, from all the rest of the church. This ministry, according to Brownson, was not to be conceived (as it was in the New Testament) as an organ of the new creation generally, through which the prophetic, priestly, and kingly functions of the whole were to be primarily exercised. In Brownson's ultramontane view, "the ministry rather is independent of the Church; it has a life of its own; it is a separate organization, through which the higher powers of

[23] Schaf, *op. cit.*, pp. 125–26.
[24] *Ibid.*

Christianity are carried forward by a wholly distinct channel."[25] The body of the church, Nevin pointed out, would then be purely passive in the process of interpreting and clarifying Christian truth, and would scarcely be the Body of Christ at all.

Nevin felt that Brownson's conception of the infallible teaching office of the ministry was more external and mechanical than Romanism needed to be. He preferred Newman's view, in which "the general mind" of the church also contributed to the definition of doctrine and was not a merely passive recipient. "Rome," Nevin observed, "is compelled to allow this to some extent in her own way. . . . The infallibility attaches, not to the ministers of the Church separately, but to the ministry as a whole; and so it is only in certain circumstances, and under certain conditions, that the Pope himself, the head of the corporation, is to be taken as its true voice."[26]

In support of this judgment Nevin referred to the reports of opinions of Roman theologians in Hobart Seymour's *Mornings among the Jesuits at Rome*. Seven requisites of an infallible papal decision were there laid down, including communication with all bishops, the possession of all available information on the point in hand, and, finally, universal reception by the church as an infallible definition. "This," Nevin commented, "is something wide away from a mere mechanical infallibility. There is no safety in the mind of the pope, any farther than it is found to hold in *living* communion with the mind of the universal church, and of this no assurance can be had by the common Christian, without active, waking, and earnest attention on his own part." "Let it appear," he proposed, "that the decisions of the Pope, though taken to be moved by the Holy Ghost, are the product in some way of the general life of Christianity, rationally working out the result through such central organ, according to the law of man's nature as otherwise known; and we can at least listen patiently to the plea that is put in for his infallibility."[27]

[25] Nevin, "Brownson's Quarterly Review," *MR*, 1850, p. 61.
[26] *Ibid.*, p. 73.
[27] "Brownson's Review Again," *MR*, 1850, pp. 321–22.

This conception of the role of the papacy in an organic catholicism was substantially Moehler's early view, and Nevin doubted that it was acceptable at Rome. Pius IX, in particular, had made a "pretty explicit claim to infallibility" in his encyclical *Qui pluribus,* of November 9, 1846. "This," commented Nevin, "is sufficiently bold and strong, it must be confessed." [28]

The order and functions of the church, in Nevin's own view, are both to be understood in relation to the Incarnation. As the Body of Christ, the church continues his threefold work—as prophet, priest, and king. The church possesses prophetic power to define and proclaim religious and moral truth; it has priestly power to present sacrifices, to administer sacraments, to intercede, to absolve; it has regal power to enforce discipline and establish rites and ceremonies. In all these functions the ministry is the chief organ through which the church acts.

Approached more abstractly, the church has various attributes which must characterize the Body of Christ because of its nature. It must be one and universal and cannot fail throughout history. It must be holy and apostolic. Once again it is pre-eminently through the agency of the ministry that these attributes are actualized. None are perfectly realized within history, but they are essential to the entelechy struggling to birth in history.

The relation between these functions and attributes of the church, on the one hand, and its structure and polity, on the other, is a flexible one. The church is a living and therefore changing organism. To some extent structure and offices are adjusted to varying circumstances, and each of a variety of forms may be legitimate in appropriate conditions.

Among the rival forms of church government which had occasioned so much controversy in church history, Nevin had least respect for congregational polity. The theory of independency, as held by Baptists, Disciples, many sect groups, and some Congregationalists,[29] appealed more than any other, he acknowledged,

[28] "Brownson's Quarterly Review," *MR,* 1850, p. 72 n.

[29] "The congregational system in this country is not Independency; it embodies many Presbyterian elements, which is its salvation" (Erb, *op. cit.,* p. 449).

to the common-sense rationalism of the common man.[30] The claim of the independents to the New Testament also had, to be sure, some limited justification. There was no established institutional authority over individual congregations in the first century, and the laity then shared in the exercise of church power more than it did later. On the other hand, first-century Christians thought of themselves as part of one universal visible church and accepted the catholic authority of the apostles over the separate congregations. Modern independency, in contrast, denied the unity and universality of the visible church; it was sectarian in principle.[31]

All three other forms of church order—presbyterianism, episcopacy, and papalism—have a legitimacy, Nevin claimed, which independency lacks. In all these, "the Church is regarded as a whole, individual congregations being subordinate to the Church in general"; and in all of them the ministry is understood as a necessary organ with divine commission and authority. No one of the three, however, is derived as such directly and unmistakably from Jesus Christ or the apostles, although each can find some biblical support. Presbyterians cite the parity of the presbyter—bishops of the first century and their participation in ordination. Episcopalians see in the superior authority of the apostles the principle of a hierarchy within the ministry and argue from analogies in the Old Testament. Papalists appeal to Peter's admitted leadership among the twelve. On the other hand, "There are facts in the New Testament," Nevin pointed out, "which cannot be made to harmonize with any system of church government in vogue since the days of the Apostles." [32]

Nevin and Schaff did not seek to defend presbyterianism by the historical arguments used at Princeton. They saw no reason to suppose that any system like modern presbyterianism was first established and then corrupted or violently constrained into

[30] Erb, *op. cit.*, p. 451.
[31] *Ibid.*, p. 453.
[32] *Ibid.*, pp. 446–48.

episcopacy. Although the rise of episcopacy remained clouded in obscurity, the system seemed to have come about naturally and without contention early in the second century. It met the needs of the church for many centuries. The case for presbyterianism must be made in terms of a variation on episcopacy to meet a new situation in the sixteenth century in conformity with the genius of the New Testament.[33]

Diocesan episcopacy, on the other hand, with all its substantial historical services, could not legitimately be made the article of the standing or falling church. "High and dry" Episcopalians who regarded episcopacy as essential to the being of the church were Judaizing legalists, like the Baptists with immersion, or the Seceders with their psalms. All such rigid legalisms betrayed a lack of faith in the church.[34]

The new Anglo-Catholics, however, were seeking to found episcopacy on deeper ground. Unlike most Episcopalians, they believed in a divine church, based on the Incarnation. A ministry could be divine only if it were the organ of a divine church with genuine sacraments. Only within this context could one properly approach the question of the form of the church and the ministry. Here the argument would be that the church as Christ's body must have unity and that this attribute is best represented in the external form of episcopacy.[35] Nevin did not say whether he found this argument conclusive. In a sense it must have seemed premature to him to press the question. First of all the belief in a divine church must become general before such questions could be properly approached or adjudicated. As the American church then stood, episcopal or otherwise, debates over forms of polity were futile. As Reinhold Niebuhr was to protest a century later to Archbishop Temple, "I told him that his conception of unity was irrelevant to the American ecumenical problem, where we would have to win the strong sectarian influence in the Churches

[33] *Ibid.*, pp. 448–49.
[34] Nevin, "The Anglican Crisis," *MR*, 1851, p. 377.
[35] Erb, *op. cit.*, p. 446.

over to some conception of Order rather than to any particular right order."[36]

Similar arguments from the nature of the church as the Body of Christ were used to support papacy, the fourth form of church government. With regard to the "idea" of the church, "two of her necessary attributes are unity and universality. She is an organization, but it belongs to the idea of an organization that it must have a visible centre. . . . Perhaps the ideal state of the Church would be [to have] such a visible centre, just as the best form of the state would be to have one. At least there is nothing objectionable in the idea of such a centre."[37] Attacks on the papal system as intrinsically anti-Christian rested on prejudice and ignorance.

This monarchical church structure was supported by the prerogatives of Peter, on whom in his faith Jesus Christ had promised to build his church. Like Schaff, Nevin accepted the ancient traditions that Peter suffered martyrdom at Rome and doubtless was a major influence in the church at Rome, but both men doubted that he had ever been bishop of Rome.

> This was assumed in order to prove the Papist claim. . . . The bishops of Rome always had the idea of supremacy before them and attempted to exercise it whenever they had an opportunity. . . . The Church in the beginning was organized after the pattern of the state, and Rome, being the centre of the state, naturally became the centre of the Church. Thus the Roman see soon stood at the head of the entire Western Church.

The system was eminently suited to the necessities of the church at that time; "it is not easy to see how the Church could have solved the problems, which she was called to solve over against the state, without such a visible centre, as she had in the Pope."[38]

While the papal system of church government was thus thoroughly respectable in principle and had been at times indispensable in practice, Nevin could not agree that it was neces-

[36] F. A. Iremonger, *William Temple* (London, New York, Toronto: Oxford University Press, 1948), p. 494.

[37] Erb, *op. cit.*, pp. 440–41.

[38] *Ibid.*, pp. 439–40.

sary to the existence of the church any more than episcopacy was. "As a republic may have a visible unity, so the Church may have a unity without an absolute head, as was the case in the first century, when the unity lay in the free councils and the free spirit of the Church." The church was able to exist without a papacy and had certainly done so. But "if the Church would be purely holy and catholic, it would perhaps be the best form of Church government. . . . So far as Papacy is wrong, it is so because in the present state of the world such a system cannot possibly be enforced without abuse." [39] Evidently Nevin's conception of the evangelical catholicism of the future involved some form of papacy, no doubt of the conciliarist type.

In his published essays, which were usually polemical, Nevin was less balanced and temperate than in his lectures to the students. In his essays on "Early Christianity" and "Cyprian" in particular we find him intellectually uncertain and emotionally disturbed, and it is a problem how far these essays are to be taken as representing his enduring judgments. In the "Dutch Crusade" of 1854 Nevin himself sought to separate these patristic studies from the Mercersburg platform in general and to have them viewed as private opinions. The German Reformed Church, he then contended, held that the rights and powers of the ministry were not derived from the people, but from Christ, and were thus more than earthly. And the church was not prepared to relinquish the idea of an apostolical succession in the ministry. "But," he concluded, "as this has not been made the subject of any particular controversy, it needs at present no farther notice." [40] There was no word here of several further conceptions which had been set forth in the patristic essays.

In "Cyprian" for example, Nevin presented in rather highly colored language a theory of hierarchy which was scarcely compatible with the views he and Schaff had previously expressed. The opinions, to be sure, are described as those of Cyprian, but the exposition is empathetic to the point of extra-

[39] *Ibid.*, p. 441.
[40] "The Dutch Crusade," *MR*, 1854, p. 93.

polation. For Cyprian "the only order here is downwards, not upwards. . . . The bishops hold from Christ, the presbyters and deacons from the bishops, and through this constitution all priestly, prophetical and kingly character, in any real form, descends to the people." Cyprian and his century would have been horrified at the "democratic" church polity of independency. This is "rank rationalism," to construct a church like a confraternity of free masons. The understanding of the ministry as representative of the universal priesthood of the church would not have been received much better.[41] Cyprian "was not a man to rest quietly in shadows or shams" or such "mournful pedantry" as a "mock episcopacy" deriving its authority from the people or even through the people. Thus even the old Presbyterian theory of a ministry by divine right would have been rejected out of hand in the ancient church.

Anglicanism was hierarchical but was irreconcilable with ancient Christianity on other counts. Episcopal authority in the third century presupposed the consensus and communion of all bishops, a communion which found its focus in the primacy of the bishop and church of Rome, "the root and mother of the Catholic church." A bishop or succession of bishops out of communion with Rome and the unity of the catholic episcopate was outside the Church. Nevin agreed with Newman and Wiseman that the modern Anglican position was that of Novatian in Cyprian's day, or the Donatists. "What charm can there be in an episcopate, that this rather than any other fragment of Peter's ship as it originally sailed towards heaven, should be taken to carry away with it now, *as a fragment*, the power of a true church life? No. Anglicanism is not Cyprianic Christianity. . . . The grand issue always, is that which lies between Protestantism and Romanism."[42]

Nevin could see no real reason to doubt the reliability of Irenaeus and Tertullian on the succession of bishops in apostolic sees, especially that of Rome. "It would be just as reasonable to

[41] Second article, MR, 1852, p. 362.
[42] *Ibid.*, p. 387.

question an appeal, at the present time, to the Gubernatorial succession of Pennsylvania, or Massachusetts, or New York, since the date of the American Revolution." "It is plain enough," he concluded, "that the government of the church, in the second century, was in this [episcopal] form; and we think it sufficiently clear also, that the See of Rome was regarded as possessing a central dignity in the system, a sort of actual *principality*, derived from the original primacy of St. Peter." [43] The primacy of Rome was as essential as hierarchy to the second- and third-century doctrine of the church.

Nevin made it clear, to be sure, that he did not necessarily accept Cyprian's views of polity by divine right. "It is quite possible," he wrote, "to conceive of an identity of life under great variations of outward form, while it may be wanting entirely where the outward show of variation is the least." [44] Episcopacy or liturgical forms as separate items prove no more for Anglicanism than the "pitiful and melancholy sham" [45] of baptismal regeneration among Campbellites does for that sect. "Mechanical similitude in this way is something widely different from organic communion." Nevin suggested even at this most Romanizing stage that the one true church might live with or without episcopacy or papal primacy provided it maintained community of life.

Herein lay the most distressing problem for Protestantism. The fathers saw the church as a divine society, as concrete as the Jewish theocracy, but mediating salvation in Christ. Faith involved submission to this social and historical reality. "Men must bow to its authority in this form, in order to be saved. To do so is faith; not to do so, involves at once the full condemnation of disobedience and unbelief." There was no room in this conception for even orthodox schism, nor for "the legitimate entrance of any such fact as the Reformation." Protestantism as a whole, with or without bishops, rested "upon a doctrine of

[43] Third article, *MR*, 1852, pp. 426, 428.
[44] *Ibid.*, p. 419.
[45] *Ibid.*, p. 449.

the church which is broadly at variance" with that of the second and third centuries.[46] How could it then be considered a continuation of the same "life"? Was not the modern church of Rome perhaps more clearly a continuation?

We are left somewhat uncertain as to precisely what doctrinal conclusions are to be drawn from Nevin's "Cyprian," but there is no such problem with his inaugural address for his successor, Professor Wolff. In this sermon of 1854 on "The Christian Ministry" Nevin did not declare for either hierarchy or papal primacy, but he insisted that institutional succession and administrative unity were both necessary for "validity." He made no reference whatever to the problem of reconciling these assertions with either the views or the fact of the Reformation. In no public deliverance did he ever depart further and more flatly from the teaching of the Reformation. Here a radical change in his views since his retirement was revealed. And he closed with an ominous adjuration to all ministers and laymen, as they valued their salvation, to inquire into the legitimacy of their ministry.

Nevin raised the question of priority between the ministry and the church, not temporally, for the two arose together, but in terms of rank.

> There is no room [he concluded] for the theory by which the Church . . . is taken to be the depository in the first instance, of all the grace and force which belong to the ministerial office. . . . The order of dependence here is not ascending but descending . . . from the few to the many, and not from the many to the few. [Contrariwise] . . . to say that there may be a Church without a bishop . . . a purely republican assembly of Christians in simply lay capacity, able to generate and produce from itself a full, valid ministration of the mystery of grace . . . without the intervention in any way, of the ministry constituted and commissioned for the purpose . . . to say, in other words, that the Church is before the Ministry, in the order of existence, and in no way dependent upon it, but complete without it . . . is a heresy.[47]

[46] *Ibid.*, pp. 439, 422, 419.
[47] *MR*, 1855, pp. 79, 80.

It is significant that Nevin uses political analogies almost exclusively. The role of the minister is put in terms of government, of supervision, of domination. The church is conceived as a kind of sacred *state*.

> In any government, the powers by which it exists and carries on its affairs, must form one single constitution. . . . Laws, titles, offices, functions, all have force only by virtue of their comprehension in the order which originates and sustains the whole. . . . To act officially in any polity, the single functionary must not only join himself with its general organization, but in doing so must bow also to the authority which already belongs to it as an actually existing constitution.[48]

The unity and the continuity described here seem purely institutional and legal. There is no word of unity of apostolic faith or love or service, or how variously they are related to administrative unity. There is no criterion of apostolicity save institutional continuity. It is easy to deride "tactual communication," Nevin says, and he had done so himself in younger days, but a valid succession must be kept in some way "to transmit the actual virtue of this first supernatural appointment from one generation still onward to another."[49] All seems to be a question of who is to sit on the right hand and the left hand in the Kingdom.

Both from its origin and its purpose, the ministry must be a single institution. "As there can be by the very conception of Christianity but one faith, one baptism and one Church, so can there be also but one Ministry."[50] The virtue of the ministry would fail if it were divided and its parts should try to function independently from each other. It would then belong to the realm of Antichrist. Just what implication Nevin meant to intend here is unclear. If one were to interpret this assertion in the light of Temple's comment "We are all in schism," it would seem to mean that there is *no* true ministry in existence. Nevin had agonized over this thought for years.[51] He evidently had also debated

[48] *Ibid.*, pp. 88–89.
[49] *Ibid.*, p. 82.
[50] *Ibid.*, p. 81.
[51] "The Anglican Crisis," *MR*, 1851, pp. 395–97.

for some time whether the safest solution was simply to affiliate with the largest remaining ecclesiastical fragment which claimed succession from the apostles.

Apparently Nevin never solved the doubt as to the validity of the ministrations of divided and independent successions in the ministry. Perhaps he felt he had discharged his responsibility to the best of his capacity when he laid the unanswerable problem formally before the church in his address. Thereafter he seems to have resumed full participation in the life of the German Reformed Church, as if convinced that its title to "legitimacy," however problematical, was as good as that of any other. The new liturgy, in its ordination service, was to lay claim to an unbroken succession of regular ordinations from the Apostles to the consecrations of the German Reformed Church, and to assert that the divine power of the office was thus transmitted irrevocably.

12/*The New Liturgy*

The theological tendency of Schaff and Nevin found its most specific practical expression in a new liturgy. Nearly every minister and congregation in the German Reformed Church was thereby forced to decide upon proposals for significant changes in the practice of worship. The resultant liturgical controversy was prosecuted with considerable bitterness for a generation and nearly tore the denomination apart. Many issues already canvassed were reopened in this debate—the nature of the Lord's Supper and baptism, for example, as defined in the forms for these sacraments and the meaning of the ministry as formulated in the ordination service. Certain more general issues were also involved in the decisions among alternative ways of worship, and these can be studied without attempting to enter on the later controversy.

The prevailing pattern of American Protestant worship in the nineteenth century was, of course, what was called "free" or "non-liturgical" worship. Such a pattern was almost unique in the Christian world, being virtually unknown on the European continent. There all the major churches used liturgies, not only the Roman Catholic and Lutheran, but also the Reformed churches of Switzerland, France, the Netherlands, Germany, and Hungary. Only in the English-speaking churches had there developed an antipathy to liturgies as such and systematic opposition to their use. Under the impact of the Puritan movement of the seventeenth century and the great English Civil War, the Protestantism of the English-speaking world had been permanently split on this issue. The royalist party sought to impose by police power the Anglican Book of Common Prayer; and the Presbyterians, Congregationalists, and Baptists reacted against all liturgies, including the Scots Presbyterians' own Reformation Book of Common Order. Not that Puritan worship was wholly extempore and formless; rather, the chief Puritan denominations conformed recognizably to a very definite pattern—that outlined in the Westminster *Directory for Worship*. This was the basis of the main American tradition, for in America the Anglicans constituted only a small minority in contrast to the heirs of the Puritans.

The original theological objection to reading prayers out of a book was that this was a poor substitute for the guidance of the Holy Spirit in the church. No drafting committee could foresee and adequately provide for the aspirations, fears, intercessory concerns of a given congregation, and the intrusion of an official manual of prayer could only stifle the devotion stirred by the present Spirit. This was still the prevailing American view of public prayer in the mid-nineteenth century. Yet it was recognized by many that such a conception of worship made religious demands which the average pastor could not always meet.

Hodge confessed that "as a general thing the public prayers in our churches do not meet the desires and exigencies of the people. We have felt this so often ourselves, we have heard the feeling expressed so often from all classes, that we presume the fact will not be denied." It was "lamentably true that the prayers are, in general, the least attractive and satisfactory part of our Church services." [1] Hodge and his Princeton colleagues were convinced that, at its best, free prayer was the most sensitive and flexible voice for the Holy Spirit. The more a church was marked by religious understanding and spirituality the less would be its inclination to forms. "Those who can walk are impatient of leading strings." Apparently, however, the mine run of ministers, and even many preachers of great distinction, had not yet learned to walk alone. The demand made of them was too high, and they were generally falling far short.

The patriarchal Dr. Miller, who had taught Nevin a quarter of a century before, published in 1849 his *Thoughts on Public Prayer*. Like Hodge he displayed considerable uneasiness at the prevailing quality of Presbyterian worship. He gave a depressing analysis of frequent faults of public "free" prayer, such as infelicities and solecisms of language, lack of organization and the omission of

[1] "Presbyterian Liturgies," *Biblical Repertory and Princeton Review* (hereafter cited as *BRPR*), 1855, pp. 461–62.

important elements, wearisome length, empty rhetoric, didacticism. It was understandable, he wrote, that many laymen were content to arrive just in time for sermons, and that the irreverent custom of remaining seated for prayer was spreading through the church. He was not ready to abandon the Puritan Covenanter position, but he followed Isaac Watts in recommending measures which considerably modified the original view. He urged that ministers should study great written prayers, as well as the Bible, to school themselves in appropriate ideas and phrases and should practice writing prayers. But they should not take these written prayers into the pulpit; the most he would concede to the formalists was the occasional use of the Lord's Prayer. He rehearsed all the stock Puritan arguments against the use of a prayer book. The American Presbyterians, Congregationalists, and Baptists as a whole stood pat on this position.

A further nuance had been introduced into this Puritan conception by the evangelical revival of the eighteenth and nineteenth centuries. The great overriding concern of the evangelical was to bring all men to the crisis of conversion, and in any given congregation the "unconverted" were likely to be in the majority. Sermons were consequently preached primarily to the impenitent, to convert them. Prayers were often appeals for them or to them; hymns were devised for their benefit and even addressed to them directly. In this way all these elements of Christian worship ceased to be primarily acts of homage to God and became devices to impress the irreligious. Direct and genuine worship of the old Puritan type was now largely transferred to the week-day prayer meeting or "lecture," where serious Christians met to seek communion with God more than to win over their neighbors.[2] Whether in the lecture room or on the Lord's Day, however, evangelical worship was extemporaneous, "free," and impatient of set forms.

One consequence of the use of elements of worship primarily for purposes of persuasion was to silence the congregation in sung praise, the sole remaining corporate liturgy of the Puritan

[2] J. W. Yeomans, "Forms of Worship," *BRPR*, 1846, p. 494.

tradition. At least there was widespread comment, about the middle of the century, on the prevailing disuse of congregational singing. The *Weekly Messenger* deplored the fact that congregational singing was becoming obsolete in some parts of the German Reformed Church.[3] Schaff contrasted American to German practice in this matter.[4] Hodge made similar observations about the widespread silencing of Presbyterian congregations.[5] He attributed the decline to the character of the hymns which had become current. These were often sermons in verse directed to the congregation rather than to God. Such hymns were used most naturally when sung by a choir *at* the congregation.

How were the immigrant Reformed churches from the Continent, with their liturgical traditions, to adapt themselves to the non-liturgical Puritan Evangelical pattern of the English-speaking Reformed churches? At first, the Continental churches sought to maintain their own liturgies in their own languages, but it soon became evident that the rising generations could not be retained by French or Dutch or Hungarian or German-speaking churches. All these Reformed groups lost large numbers to English-speaking denominations about them, and at last reluctantly accepted the necessity of changing over their worship into English. But how should they do it? Should they translate their European service books and align themselves with the Episcopalians in a small liturgical minority? Or should they give up the liturgical idea with their national languages and adopt the "free" worship of the main body of American Christians?

Of these Continental Reformed churches, only the Dutch had succeeded in retaining its liturgical character through the change of language. In Charleston, the old French Huguenot congregation had printed in 1836 a translation of its *Liturgy* (Osterwald's Neuchâtel order of 1737). One could not say, however, that the Huguenots had succeeded in maintaining their integrity as a de-

[3] September 8, 1847; August 16, 1848.
[4] "The New Liturgy," *Mercersburg Review* (hereafter cited as *MR*), 1858, p. 200.
[5] *BRPR*, 1858, pp. 725–26.

nomination through the loss of their language, for the bulk of the Huguenot congregations had passed into the Episcopalian, Dutch Reformed, and other denominations. The Hungarians were, of course, too few to survive. Only the Dutch survived, although with great losses. When English-language preaching was introduced in New York Dutch churches in 1764, an English-language liturgy was at hand—one that had been used in the Netherlands for refugee congregations. After the Revolution it was officially published as a service book for ministers and constituted the one functioning Reformed liturgy on the American scene beside the Anglican Book of Common Prayer.

The Anglicizing of the German Reformed came later than that of the Dutch, in the early nineteenth century, and was the occasion of much loss and controversy still in the days of Nevin and Schaff. For a time it had seemed problematical whether the denomination would survive or whether its materials might not, like those of the French Reformed in America, be parceled out among other churches. And for that portion seeking to reconstitute itself as an English-speaking body there was the question of how to worship in English. The Palatinate Liturgy had not been translated, and the one English-language liturgy which had come out of the committees assigned to the task, "Mayer's Liturgy" (1837), found little acceptance. The free prayer system had come to prevail almost without exception for regular services in the English-speaking congregations. For the sacraments and special occasions some pastors used the Dutch Reformed orders, others the Episcopalian, others Dr. Mayer's services, still others depended even here on their individual resources and the inspiration of the moment.

When Nevin took up the problem at the beginning of the 1840's, he promptly left behind him his anti-liturgical Presbyterian views. He set out to restore the genius of the German Reformed Church as expressed in its sixteenth-century formulations, and he must be given credit for reviving interest in the Palatinate Liturgy as well as in the Heidelberg Catechism. It was apparently some years before he saw a copy of the liturgy, but he knew that it was very similar to the liturgy of the Dutch Reformed Church.[6] He was chairman of the committee appointed by the joint convention of the Dutch and German churches in 1844, which proposed that the liturgy of the two denominations be conformed as closely as possible.[7] In the circumstances this probably meant that the German church should adopt substantially the English-language version of the Dutch liturgy.

Three years later Nevin evidently had still not seen the Palatinate Liturgy himself, for in his little sketch of the Heidelberg Catechism he used a description of it at second hand. The ancient pastor "Father" Pomp of Easton possessed a copy, reprinted in 1763 from the 1684 edition, which his father had brought to the colonies as a missionary; and Pomp's English-speaking colleague at Easton, John Bomberger, had sent Nevin an account of it. The work was evidently rare, for Nevin asked whether there were any other copies in the country, hoping to secure one for the seminary library.

In the Palatinate Liturgy, Nevin could now report to his readers, were set prayers for the regular Lord's Day service, for week-day morning and evening prayer, and festival prayers for Christmas, New Year's Day, Good Friday, Easter, Ascension, and Whitsuntide, as well as a schedule of Bible readings for the year. He called attention in particular to the service of preparation for the Lord's Supper, with its forms of confession and absolutions at the table, and to the baptismal service, with its high doctrine of baptismal grace and the use of the creed. The liturgy of the Reformed Dutch Church in America, while based on this order, included only a small part of it. The service of preparation for communion, for example, the burial service, and all the festival prayers were missing; and the creed was omitted from the form for baptism. The prayers for the Lord's Day service were somewhat changed. All this went to show, Nevin remarked, that the original and proper church life of the Heidelberg Catechism was

[6] *Weekly Messenger*, July 20, 1842.
[7] *Ibid.*, August 14, 1844.

something quite different from the spiritualistic baldness of modern "Puritanism." [8]

Most of this was doubtless news to the majority of the English-speaking pastors of the church. Probably Nevin's inquiries for copies of the liturgy among the German-speaking pastors stirred new interest in the subject. That spring (1847) East Pennsylvania Classis, in the old German area, discussed whether the Palatinate Liturgy should not be reprinted, and in the fall the synod received a request for either a reprinting of the Palatinate Liturgy or the drafting of another "in the spirit of our catechism." After much discussion the synod referred the matter to the several classes for their opinions.

The discussion throughout the bounds of the church achieved no clear resolution. Opinion was much divided. The Synod of 1848 referred the matter to a committee chaired by Bomberger, who—unable even to get his committee together—submitted to the Synod of Norristown in 1849 what amounted to a one-man report. He proposed that the synod seek to maintain its liturgical tradition by preparing a revised liturgy, based especially on that of the Palatinate. The synod debated the question two days. Many of the English-speaking pastors would have preferred that forms be provided only for the sacraments and such occasional services as funerals and weddings. Bomberger, however, wanted forms for the regular Lord's Day service, evidently preferring in general liturgical to "free" worship. He published a refutation of a Presbyterian attack on liturgies, noting that strictly applied its arguments would also rule out all psalmody and hymnody and even the minister's free prayer on behalf of a congregation of varied condition and experiences. The appeal to individual immediacy really left no room for corporate worship as such. The liturgical principle was the corporate principle. Bomberger's proposals were adopted with surprising unanimity, and the task of outlining a plan for such a liturgy was assigned to a large committee, of which Nevin was made chairman.

[8] *History and Genius of the Heidelberg Catechism* (Chambersburg, Pa., 1847), pp. 153–56.

Bomberger had also been translating Father Pomp's old copy of the Palatinate Liturgy, so that in 1850 and 1851 Nevin and the English-speaking section of the church were at last able to study their historical liturgy in English in the pages of the *Mercersburg Review*. This was the basis from which the liturgical committee was expected to work under the assignment of the Synod of Norristown.

The Palatinate Lord's Day service must have startled many with its full complement of set prayers. It began with a blessing and psalm, followed by the Bucer-Calvin prayer of confession, a prayer for saving apprehension of the Word, and the corporate Lord's Prayer. Then came the Scripture and sermon. A more specific confession of sin, to be recited by the congregation, followed. The absolution, which followed a declaration of grace, was full and explicit and accompanied by a declaration of condemnation against the impenitent. After it the Lord's Prayer was again recited in unison. An extended set of prayers of thanksgiving, supplication, and intercession, concluded by the Lord's Prayer for a third time, ended the prayers. (For this a long paraphrase of the Lord's Prayer might be substituted.) Then came the psalm and the Aaronic blessing. No place whatever was allowed for free prayer, but considerable corporate unison repetition was prescribed.

Set prayers were also provided for the week-day morning and evening services and for the Lord's Day afternoon sermons on the questions of the catechism. These services, like the preparatory service for communion, had, of course, fallen out of use in America generally. Probably even more surprising to the American congregations were the festival prayers, which were—on the days appointed—to head the chief prayer of thanksgiving, supplication, and intercession, for few American Christians had ever observed these festivals. Bomberger translated those for Christmas, Easter-day and Whitsuntide and gave in full the forms for baptism and Preparation for the Lord's Supper. The last, some no doubt observed, ended with a rubric instructing ministers to provide opportunity for private conference with those troubled in conscience. The book was completed by the orders for the

Lord's Supper, visitation of the sick, burial, and confirmation. Of these Bomberger left parts incomplete because of pages missing in Pomp's copy, and he omitted the long marriage service—already accurately translated in the Liturgy of the Reformed Dutch Church.[9]

A much wider range of sources had become conveniently accessible for readers of German in the first comprehensive collection from the various Continental Reformed liturgies, Professor Ebrard's *Reformiertes Kirchenbuch* (1846). Ebrard had sought to be of use at once to the scholar and to the practical churchman by altering archaisms of form and sense while retaining the original reading in footnotes. He had left each in its distinctive style—the "classical" French and Basel liturgies, the more dogmatical Dutch and Palatinate, the lively and psalmodic Neuchâtel, the childlike St. Gall with its deeply felt language. Parts of Ebrard's introduction were translated for the *Mercersburg Review* [10] by another member of the committee on the liturgy, B. C. Wolff of Baltimore. Ebrard's analysis here of the three types of Reformed worship (those of Zwingli, Calvin, and Melanchthon) although historically faulty, was at first sight a helpful approach. Ebrard also advocated the recognition, not merely of festival days in the worship of the church, but also of seasons, such as Advent and Epiphany. This carried the idea of the church year further than any historical Reformed liturgy except the Anglican had done.

The revival of historical liturgies, incidentally, was taking place in other Reformed churches in the 1840's and 1850's. Even in Scotland, where most Presbyterians doubtless supposed that the exclusive use of "free prayer" was the original custom of their church, a new current was perceptible. Dr. Cumming had republished "John Knox' Liturgy" in 1840, and in 1849 the Edinburgh edition of Calvin's works presented Calvin's *Form of Prayers* in English. In each case the editor had commended his

[9] J. H. A. Bomberger (trans. and ed.), "The Old Palatinate Liturgy of 1563," third article, *MR,* 1851, pp. 118, 123, 106.

[10] B. C. Wolff, "Public Worship," *MR,* 1850, pp. 296–307.

text as suggestive for modern practice. In 1852 an anonymous writer in the influential *Edinburgh Review* discussed the matter and estimated that some of the leading members of the Church of Scotland were ready to resume the Reformation tradition of a combination of set and extempore prayers. One hundred and eighty Scots ministers had contributed to a volume for *Family Worship* (1841), which constituted in itself a protest against the doctrinaire opposition to the use of forms in all circumstances. Although Scottish Presbyterianism was still "non-liturgical" in practice, the rationale behind the practice was being questioned.

The historical argument was presented to American Presbyterians in comprehensive fashion in 1855, when young Charles Baird drew on his experiences of the European reformed churches in producing his *Eutaxia, or the Presbyterian Liturgies: Historical Sketches*. Baird used Ebrard's studies, adding materials on the English, Scottish, and American Reformed churches which Ebrard had not included. Baird demonstrated unanswerably that the American practice of leaving everything to the "unaided individuality of the minister" was in conflict with the principle and practice of the Calvinistic reformation in every country. He argued that it was also inferior in practice. He urged Presbyterian ministers to resume the use of the Lord's Prayer, the Ten Commandments, and the Apostles' creed in regular Lord's Day services and to follow the Westminister Directory more faithfully, both in the pattern of their intercessions and in regular reading in public worship from both testaments. He looked to the day when Presbyterian congregations would again corporately join in the Lord's Prayer and Creed, as well as the Amen at the end of the minister's prayers. He wished that compilations of historical Reformed prayers would be sanctioned for the voluntary use of ministers in regular worship.

To further the last proposal, Baird published anonymously in 1857 *A Book of Public Prayer, compiled from the authorized Formularies of Worship of the Presbyterian Church, as prepared by the Reformers Calvin, Knox, Bucer and others. With sup-*

plementary Forms.[11] This work was a kind of English-language equivalent of Ebrard's *Kirchenbuch*, arranging its historical materials for practical use. Even these modest proposals for qualifying the puritanism of American Presbyterianism were to wait for half a century before realization in an official service book.

The Reformed Dutch in America, of course, had fewer inhibitions in liturgy than the Presbyterians. Their ministers were accustomed to a service book for the sacraments and special occasions, although the prayers for the Lord's Day service had largely fallen into disuse since the seventeenth century. Baird was satisfied with their offices for baptism, communion, and ordination but considered the order for ordinary services still defective, although "considerably in advance of the unmitigated baldness of our Scottish Presbyterian Service." A correspondent of the *Christian Intelligencer* complained [12] that many Dutch Reformed ministers habitually omitted the salutation and the Ten Commandments in the Lord's Day service. Others urged a revision of the service book and then more faithfulness to it. A committee was put to work contemporaneously with the liturgical committee of the German Reformed Church. Their proposed *Liturgy of the Reformed Protestant Dutch Church in North America*, which appeared in 1857, provides an interesting contrast to the new German Reformed liturgy of the same year.

The revised Dutch liturgy seemed in many ways a fulfilment of Bomberger's Norristown proposals for the German Reformed Church. In contrast to Presbyterian practice, it included an order for the Lord's Day. It began with an invocation and salutation, the Ten Commandments, the Scripture lesson, then *before* the sermon the long prayer of thanksgiving, confession, and intercession. After the sermon the service concluded with a short prayer and the benediction. The old prayers for week-day morning and evening services were provided, and those for the Sunday afternoon service based on catechetical preaching. This remained thus

[11] Enlarged edition (New York: Charles Scribner's Sons, 1858).
[12] March 10, 1853.

within the bounds of a revision of the Palatinate-Dathenus tradition. Unlike Bomberger and Ebrard, the Dutch revisers made no acknowledgment of the chief festivals of the church year, but they did supply a table of Scripture readings for every Lord's Day based on the principle of continuous reading through major books. A somewhat unexpected item was a litany, identified in a footnote as a literal translation from Bucer.

Some Scottish and American Presbyterians then, as well as the Dutch and German Reformed, seemed to have embarked in these years on the recovery of their liturgical heritage from the sixteenth century. One might have expected Schaff and Nevin to welcome this development. To a degree, they did. Yet none of these liturgical works satisfied them; their liturgical proposals were much more far-reaching.

Nevin began to declare his new views on the nature of worship shortly after he had published *The Mystical Presence.* The corporate and the objective emphases in religion, he now asserted, require the liturgical principle, "which may be said to consist mainly in this, that it sinks the individual and particular in the power of what is universal and constant." [13] Or again, "the power of Christian worship consists in this, that the worshippers be filled with the sense of a common church life, and present themselves in this consciousness as a living sacrifice to God. Its whole conception requires that it should move in the sphere of the objective, and not fall over to the sway of simply individual thought or feeling." [14]

This distinction of a corporate as against an individualistic understanding of worship usually, though not necessarily, coincided with the distinction between set forms and free worship. The important point was that the minister should be in public prayer the living organ of the whole congregation, submerging his individuality in his representative capacity and avoiding all singularities of sentiment or expression. It was possible to use a

[13] *The Church* (Chambersburg, Pa., 1847), p. 28.

[14] *Antichrist: or the Spirit of Sect and Schism* (New York, 1848), pp. 53-54.

good liturgical form in an unliturgical way, as a Methodist might, perhaps, with the Book of Common Prayer. Or, on the other hand, "free" worship might have liturgical character, although this rarely occurred. "Still we do at times," Nevin observed, "meet with men who pray by no book, and yet are like the sound of a divine liturgy throughout, in the midst of the great congregation, for which they are made soul as well as mouth." [15]

The prevailing taste in America, in contrast, made the individuality of the minister precisely the chief virtue in public prayer, and a man could be seriously complimented for "the most eloquent prayer addressed to a Boston audience." "Puritanism," as Nevin called the regnant evangelicalism, was universally unfavorable to a liturgical worship. "Under its influence," he wrote, "the creed itself is silenced in the pulpit, and even the Lord's Prayer is but seldom heard." [16] For him subjectivity in worship was one of the marks of the sect spirit, that Antichrist of American Protestantism. And he roundly announced that "sects as such . . . have no worship, in the only true sense of the term; and can hardly be said to know at all what worship, as a divine liturgical sacrifice, means." [17]

Rather than seeking novel forms of expression, Nevin held, public prayer should repeat itself to a great extent, for the spirit of devotion flows best in long consecrated channels. Herein lay the secret of the special satisfaction felt by thousands in the Book of Common Prayer. The great bulk of materials it contained were not Anglican but derived from remote antiquity. They were the common heritage of all Christians, and no liturgy informed by the ancient spirit of Christian worship would find it easy to dispense with them. If the movement for liturgy in the German Reformed Church was animated by "no sympathy whatever with the old catholic church service as it stood from earliest times," then the whole effort would have been vain.[18]

Before Nevin there seemed to hover some notion of a cosmic

[15] *WM*, February 9, 1848.
[16] *The Church*, p. 28.
[17] *Antichrist*, p. 53.
[18] *WM*, March 29, 1848.

liturgy, with which a worshiping congregation might be attuned. What was needed, he suggested, was sympathy with the divine liturgy of nature, the life of heaven still more, with "the music of the spheres, and with the song of the angels; the same mind that led the early Church into the universal use of liturgies." [19]

His whole conception of liturgical worship Nevin referred to frequently as "sacrifice," and associated with the idea of an "altar." He evidently felt that praise and adoration were too generally crowded out by pulpit rhetoric or moralizing. In heaven, he suggested, if there should be preaching at all, it would be greatly in the shade of the "altar." As against the "central pulpit" of the day, he contended that the pulpit must be ready to resign the whole "chancel," if need be, to the "altar." (Incidentally, Nevin gave no sign whatever of being aware of the classical Reformed view on this subject, and actually changed "table" to "altar" in reporting the rubrics of the Palatinate liturgy.) [20]

In setting forth these conceptions of worship, Nevin was clearly aware that he was not speaking for the German Reformed Church generally. He suspected that the majority of the Synod of 1847 had intended no more than a few forms for special occasions, assuming the basic pattern of free worship. For such "tinkering and splicing" he had little sympathy, and he prophesied as early as 1848 that the liturgical movement would "prove a miserable abortion." [21] Evidently he was pleasantly surprised with Bomberger's success at the Norristown Synod of 1849. But he never assembled the liturgical committee, and in 1850 he reported to the synod that the committee did not recommend the project of liturgical revision. If something must be done, a translation of the Palatinate Liturgy was probably the best recourse, although it might not be an enduring one. Thus even before Nevin began extricating himself from his ecclesiastical responsibilities, he had despaired of bringing the church in line with his conceptions of true liturgical worship.

[19] "The Liturgical Movement," *MR*, 1849, p. 612.
[20] *Heidelberg Catechism*, p. 155.
[21] *WM*, March 29, 1848.

It was in 1851 that the synod accepted Nevin's resignation as chairman of the committee for the liturgy and replaced him with Schaff, who was as sanguine of the possibilities as Nevin had been hopeless. His liturgical background, of course, was different from Nevin's, and he may not have realized so fully as Nevin the strength of the American anti-liturgical bias. He did charge American Protestantism with "a disproportionate esteem for the service of preaching, with a corresponding sacrifice in the case of the liturgy, the standing objective part of divine worship, in which the *whole congregation* is called to pour forth its religious life to God." [22] For a decade or so he had worshiped either in Lutheran churches or in the United Church of Prussia with its Lutheran type of liturgy as imposed by Frederick William III. He had not been in contact with any religious communion marked by a historical reaction against formalism. He repudiated iconoclasm and admired medieval religious art. In general, he preferred the Lutheran attitude toward traditional forms to that of the Reformed. He felt himself a part of the widespread contemporary movement in Germany to renew and enrich public worship "by thrusting aside all watery, rationalistic pretended improvements, and falling back in a proper way to the incomparable treasures of the old Church songs and liturgies." [23] In this movement modern historical scholarship had made accessible as never before "the wealth of all centuries." Under his leadership the German Reformed liturgical committee was to fall in with this trend toward liturgical renewal based on broad and ecumenical historical study.

Under Schaff's chairmanship the liturgical committee finally went seriously to work. Over the summer of 1852 the working nucleus (composed of those living in Mercersburg) met weekly, outlining "a general plan, also four forms for the regular service on the Lord's Day, two baptismal services, a form for the solemnization of matrimony, and a part of the Scripture lessons and collects for the ecclesiastical year." [24] Other members of the com-

[22] *Principle of Protestantism* (Chambersburg, Pa., 1845), thesis 64.
[23] *Ibid.*, pp. 84, 148.
[24] "The New Liturgy," *MR*, 1858, pp. 216–17.

mittee, like Bomberger, were assigned specific services to draft.

The general plan and principles which were set before the Synod of Baltimore in 1852 were significantly different from those contemplated by the Norristown Synod three years before or those embodied in the contemporary Presbyterian and Reformed Dutch liturgical revisions. The most striking change was the transfer of primary reference from the Reformed liturgies of the sixteenth century to the liturgies of the ancient catholic church. As the first principle of the report put it:

> The liturgical worship of the Primitive Church, as far as it can be ascertained from the Holy Scriptures, the oldest ecclesiastical writers, and the Liturgies of the Greek and Latin Churches of the third and fourth centuries, ought to be made, as much as possible, the *general base* of the proposed Liturgy; the more so, as they are in fact also the source from which the best portions of the various Liturgies of the 16th century were derived, such as the forms of confession and absolution, the litanies, the creeds, the Te Deum, the Gloria in Excelsis, the collects, the doxologies, etc. For the merit of the Reformation in the department of worship, if we except the hymnology, which has been very materially enriched, especially by the evangelical Churches of Germany, does not so much consist in producing new forms of devotions, as in transferring those handed down from former ages into the vernacular tongues, in purifying them from certain additions, in reducing them to greater simplicity, and in subordinating them to the preaching of the Gospel, as the principal part of Protestant worship.[25]

A liturgy so constructed in the nineteenth century would be "a bond of union both with the ancient Catholic Church and the Reformation."

Apart from the specific elements listed, in which the Reformation liturgies were dependent on those of the ancient church, Schaff's report found the language and style of the Reformed prayers often unsatisfactory. "The doctrinal tone, which predominates too much in most of the Calvinistic liturgies, ought to be used only within certain limits." [26] On these grounds, Schaff was to criticize Baird's *Book of Public Prayer*, Ebrard's *Kirchen-*

[25] *Ibid.*, pp. 218–19.
[26] *Ibid.*

buch, and other Presbyterian and Dutch proposals which confined themselves to Reformed formularies.[27]

A second striking principle of the general plan proposed by Schaff's committee was the insistence on a people's liturgy. Unlike the Norristown project, or the Dutch or Presbyterian proposals, the Schaff Report urged a book which—like the Bible, the catechism, and the hymn book—would be "the common property and manual of *every member of the Church.*" A service book which was merely for the optional use of ministers could not produce true congregational participation. "The laymen," argued the Report, "will take a far deeper interest in the devotional exercises, if they can follow the minister by their book, and respond at least with an audible *Amen* at the end of each prayer." [28] To promote such use, the committee proposed the inclusion of family prayers in the book.

Such a people's liturgy, of course, was the original pattern of Reformed worship, but few of the liturgical proposals of the mid-nineteenth century dared to make so frontal an attack on the freedom ministers had acquired to alter the order of service. So long as the service book was only in the hands of the minister, he might abridge, revise, supplement as he chose; but if the people were also to have the book in hand, the minister's discretion would be largely reduced to portions specifically allotted to free prayer. In the report no such provision for free prayer was contemplated in the regular Lord's Day service, although alternative forms were provided. It was proposed that room should be left for extemporaneous prayer "in connection with the Sunday afternoon and evening services, as well as in weekly Bible lectures, social prayer meeting, catechetical exercises, and on special occasions." [29] By 1857 Schaff was ready to accord free prayer some place in every major service of worship, but with it he wished to hear the congregational Lord's Prayer, Creed, Te Deum, and Gloria in Excelsis.[30]

27 *MR,* 1857, pp. 324–26.
28 Schaff, "The New Liturgy," *MR,* 1858, pp. 219–20.
29 *Ibid.,* p. 220.
30 *MR,* 1857, p. 325.

The third striking innovation of the Report of 1852 was its adoption of the ecclesiastical calendar. Schaff had been distressed that American churches generally ignored Easter, Pentecost, Christmas, and Good Friday; and his initiative had brought about the first recognition of such festivals at the Mercersburg Seminary. The general plan set before the Baltimore Synod proposed special prayers for the festivals and a complete set of Scripture readings and collects for all other Sundays. It abandoned altogether the old Reformed system of consecutive readings through major biblical books as maintained in the Dutch Reformed revision. The *Princeton Review* no doubt expressed the predominant Protestant viewpoint in America in rejecting the whole apparatus of lessons and collects, days and seasons; it "would require years of drill before the minister or people would know how to use such a book, or feel themselves at home with it." [31]

The "general plan" of 1852 thus embodied the characteristic theological views of Schaff and Nevin and for that reason differed significantly from most of the comparable proposals of the same period. The Mercersburg men conceived of a liturgy

> not simply in the light of convenience, decency and propriety, but as a sacred bond of union between the different ages of Christ's Church, as a guarantee against excesses of arbitrary freedom, as a conservative power in doctrine and discipline, as the organ for the exercise of the general priesthood, and as the artistic form which the very spirit of social worship instinctively assumes and which will characterize even the worship of the redeemed in heaven as a complete harmony of united thanksgiving and praise. . . . In one word, they desired a truly *scriptural, historical, evangelical catholic,* and *artistic* liturgy for the *people* as well as the ministry.[32]

The Synod of Baltimore accepted these principles with surprising celerity and authorized the preparation of a specimen liturgy. The Synod of Norristown, of course, had accepted Bomberger's proposals three years before with similar expedition. No doubt the majority had no very clear idea as to what was

[31] *BRPR*, 1858, p. 183.
[32] Schaff, "The New Liturgy," *MR*, 1858, pp. 208–9.

involved in these various proposals and waited to pass judgment on whatever should come from the committee.

The two years after the Baltimore Synod saw very little activity in the liturgical committee. In 1852–53 Schaff was burdened with the full responsibility of the seminary, and the other Mercersburg members of the committee were preoccupied with the removal of the college to Lancaster. Then came the closing of the seminary for 1853–54 and Schaff's trip to Europe. While he was abroad, however, the *Mercersburg Review* published several forms prepared by the committee, including those for baptism, marriage, the Lord's Day service (four alternatives), and Bomberger's communion and confirmation orders.

In this period the *Review* also published two articles by Henry Harbaugh, then serving as pastor of the First Reformed Church of Lancaster, on "Christian Cultus: Its Nature, History and Relations, with special reference to the German Reformed Church." [33] Harbaugh was secretary of the liturgy committee and, after Bomberger, the most active of the working pastors on the committee. His essays are historically inaccurate and theologically confused; he became hopelessly entangled in his attempt to interpret liturgical history in terms of the "sacrificial" and "sacramental" emphases. Some aspects of his presentation, however, are interesting. His general conception was evidently closer to Bomberger's proposals of 1849 than to Schaff's of 1852. He oriented himself entirely to Reformation precedents with no concern for the ancient catholic forms. He showed no interest in the church year beyond the great festivals and defended the rejection of the pericope system by the Reformed churches. He seems also to have been thinking of a minister's service book, not of a peoples' liturgy, since he expected and encouraged varying adaptations of the Lord's Day service he proposed. His conception of worship was primarily that of sacrifice, what we offer to God. He had a rather uncritical enthusiasm for "sacred" architecture and furnishings, steeples, stained glass, bells, organs, "the air of solemn mystery." He desired a high central pulpit with the

[33] *MR*, 1854, pp. 573–600; 1855, pp. 116–35.

"altar" at its base. All the prayers and Scripture readings should take place "in the altar." He took pride in the fact that the Reformation had restored the prophetic office of the ministry and although he declared that the pulpit points to the altar as John the Baptist to Christ, it was also a function of the "altar-service" to prepare for the reception of the Word.[34] Since Harbaugh was personally a strong supporter of the Mercersburg professors, it is striking that he shared so few of their leading ideas.

Schaff returned from Europe and revived the seminary for the academic year 1854–55. He reported for the liturgical committee at the synod in the fall of 1855, and the committee began again to work actively after its long pause. Schaff wrote Nevin that fall, apparently asking him to draft a communion service. Nevin was just in the process of moving from his retirement in Carlisle to Lancaster, where he would resume public activities, but he would not take on this assignment.

> I will try to furnish the family prayers you request for the Liturgy. But I must decline the task of the other services you mention. I have no helps here at hand, no access to the ancient Liturgies. . . . But what is worse I have no heart, no faith, no proper courage for any such work. A leitourgia (communion service) in the old sense demands a sort of faith in the real presence, which I am afraid goes beyond all that is possible to engraft on Protestantism, even in our G. R. version of it. And without this, I feel that it is for me at least a species of mockery to pretend to the use of the like words and forms. I cannot bear the sense of unreality which comes over me when I think of manufacturing on any such plan for public use a form of worship, into which our faith is not allowed to breathe the same mysterious soul.[35]

What Nevin declined, Schaff finally did himself. He had not been satisfied with Bomberger's communion service, based on the sixteenth-century models, and apparently he had hoped Nevin might do better. On his European trip he had gained a new

[34] *Ibid.*, pp. 124–25, 118, 128, 130, 134, 133.

[35] Letter to Schaff, December 3, 1835 (Library of the German Reformed Church, Franklin and Marshall College).

inspiration from the Catholic Apostolic Liturgy in Gordon Square in London. Although the chief American leader of the Irvingites, W. W. Andrews, had contributed four articles on the Eucharist to the *Weekly Messenger* in 1846 and both Schaff and Nevin had treated very seriously the *Lectures on Catholicism and Protestantism* of the Marburg convert, Professor Thiersch, the Catholic Apostolic Liturgy seems to have been unknown in Mercersburg before 1854. After spending a Sunday at Gordon Square, Schaff wrote his wife that this was "the most beautiful and perfect liturgical service I have yet attended," more so than that in the Roman Catholic cathedral of St. George's.[36] One can understand this enthusiasm, for the Catholic Apostolic Liturgy embodied the evangelical catholic principles of Schaff's liturgical report more fully than any other Reformed liturgy of the period. The Catholic Apostolic order then became through Schaff the stabilizing influence in the shaping of the Mercersburg communion service.

While in Germany in 1854 Schaff had also brought himself up to date on the current efforts to restore classical hymns for modern use.[37] A dozen or so important works on the history of hymnology had appeared, and numerous recent revisions, such as the hymnals of Elberfeld, Schaffhausen, Basel, Zurich, and Aargau, had profited from these researches. The Synod of 1855 commissioned Schaff and a committee to prepare a new hymn book for the German-speaking section of the church. Two years later the committee set before the synod the principles on which it proposed to work and had them accepted. Three to four hundred hymns were to be selected, including metrical psalms, from every period of the German Evangelical Church, especially the Reformed. Faults to be avoided were "subjective arbitrariness," didacticism, sentimentality, artificiality. Hymns selected were to be biblical and churchly; they should be organized on the order of the Apostles' Creed, with the church year assimilated to

[36] D. S. Schaff, *Life of Philip Schaff* (New York: Charles Scribner's Sons, 1897), p. 178.

[37] P. Schaff, "The Synod at Frederick," *MR*, 1859, p. 40.

it. So far as possible, original texts should be recovered, on the model of the *Deutsche Evangelische Kirchengesangbuch* issued by the Eisenach Kirchentag of 1856.[38]

The preceding year the synod had also instructed the liturgical committee to prepare and publish, with the English-language liturgy, a selection of about 150 psalms and hymns. These should include good translations of the best Latin and German hymns "which are so intimately interwoven with the history and piety of our mother Church in Europe, and which should be secured as far as possible for the devotional use of our English as well as our German congregations." [39] No better way of securing a people's liturgy could be found, of course, than by thus combining hymnal and liturgy.

The outcome did not in all respects correspond to the assignment. Difficulties of bulk no doubt caused the reduction by a third of the number originally planned to appear with the liturgy, and of translations from Latin and German there was a bare token. Over half the total were from Watts and Doddridge. Montgomery contributed seven and Charles Wesley but three. The criteria of selection and the arrangement were largely those specified by Schaff for the German collection.

In 1856 and 1857 the liturgical committee held five sessions of at least a week in length—the first four in Lancaster in the consistory room of Harbaugh's church, with Schaff coming up to Lancaster and staying with Harbaugh during the sessions. For much of 1856 Nevin and Harbaugh were meeting very often, laboring over the system of collects. Schaff had sent Nevin Strauss's work on the church year, which brought out the rationale of the appointed lessons in mystical exegesis. Nevin found that all the collects after Trinity and many before had to be original, "more full than the Episcopal and more true to the reigning idea of the lessons." [40]

[38] H. M. J. Klein, *History of the Eastern Synod of the Reformed Church in the United States* (Lancaster, Pa., 1943), pp. 234–35.

[39] *Ibid.*, p. 232.

[40] Nevin to Schaff, June 6, 1856 (Library of the German Reformed Church, Franklin and Marshall College).

No doubt as a gesture of deference, the committee asked Nevin to present their completed work to the synod in 1857. A volume of four hundred pages, he told the synod, was already in the printer's hands. Either it would quietly work its way into general use, or it would be allowed to fall into disuse. In this way a fair trial could be made, congregation by congregation, of "the possibility of incorporating the true conception of a Liturgy practically with the worship of the Reformed Church." Nevin himself was evidently still not sanguine of this possibility. If the *Liturgy, or Order of Christian Worship* could not win its way, he declared, "no other is ever likely to be formed that will be attended with any better effect." [41]

What was "the true conception of a Liturgy"? It was not merely a collection of prayers, even traditional ones. The interest being shown by some Unitarians, as at Harvard, in such forms of worship, was merely aesthetic, like their taste for Gothic architecture. The true idea of a liturgy, by contrast, presupposed the sacramental spirit, with its understanding of Christ and His new creation. In formal definition it was:

> A fixed scheme or system of worship, starting from the transaction of the Holy Eucharist, and everywhere resting on this as its original ground, in the use of which from week to week by ministers and people, it is made possible for them to offer themselves with joint action, their persons, praises and prayers, in the way of a living sacrifice to God, on the altar graciously consecrated for this purpose, through the death of his Son, in the bosom of the Christian Church.[42]

The distinctive element was not the fixity of form, which could conceivably be omitted, but the sense of worship as a sacramental sacrifice. Nevin's conception anticipated that of the twentieth-century Roman Catholic liturgical movement. As in early Christianity, he urged, liturgical worship must mean a real sacrificial oblation, Christ's passion presented to God by his people. The early church had no notion of any new sacrifice or repetition of the one Atonement on Golgotha. The Atonement had taken place

[41] Cited in Schaff, "The New Liturgy," *MR*, 1858, p. 225.
[42] Nevin, "The Idea of a Liturgy," *WM*, June 15, 1859.

once for all time and yet was a fact always present, a perennial reality before the throne of power, which was actually exhibited mystically in the Eucharist. With the offering to God of Christ's Passion were associated "the persons of his worshipping people themselves, with their prayers, praises, and their works of piety in general—the whole regarded in the light of a single sacrifice." [43] Such offerings of Christians, however, were only sacrificial when thus joined with that mystical oblation of Christ's body and blood, which the church continually brings before God. But in that priestly role of Christ the church and individual Christians were called to participate, just as in His prophetic and kingly functions.

The ancient fathers, Nevin observed, did not confine the conception of sacramental mystery to Baptism and the Eucharist. Their Platonism found the whole universe to be sacramental. All occasions in which the power of the new creation was seen actually at hand within the old were sacramental. The church itself was a sacrament. Even the natural creation as a medium of communication shared in something of this dignity. Thus, Nevin argued, commemorative festivals of the great events of the history of redemption had an intrinsic and necessary connection with the successive phases in the cosmic relations of earth, sun, and moon. Like the Jewish festivals of Passover, Pentecost, and Tabernacles, the Christian festivals of Good Friday, Easter, Ascension, and Pentecost had intrinsic connection with the changing relations of the powers of light and darkness, life and death through winter, the vernal equinox, the summer solstice, the autumn equinox.[44] The idea of religion in general as redemption from the powers of darkness and evil was represented in the parallel economies of created nature and supernatural grace—the one serving as a type and parable to the other. The festivals and seasons of the church year, consequently, were not merely appropriate, but even necessary for a firm hold on the facts of redemption. The church

[43] *Ibid.*

[44] Evidently it never occurred to Nevin that this mystical correspondence was realized only in certain latitudes of the Northern Hemisphere.

year was "a natural product from the Christian consciousness itself." Only the "Puritanic heresy" had set it aside. But without it

> there can be no right sense of the Church, no proper faith in the holy sacraments, no sound liturgical feeling, no active sympathy with the grand facts which are set forth in the Creed, no firm hold on the abiding power of these facts, as an order of grace moving onward in sublime correspondence with the order of nature to the end of time.[45]

Such were the primary historical meanings which, Nevin said, the liturgical committee had sought to adjust to the circumstances of the German Reformed Church. With the infrequent observance of the Eucharist customary in the church, it is hard to believe that Nevin thought that that service could really be the determinative one, the root and ground of all the others, even if the new *Order of Christian Worship* were scrupulously followed. The normal Lord's Day service there was a preaching service, and this surely would be the determinative service. His own conception would really have required something like the Catholic Apostolic Liturgy. And he obviously doubted that the German Reformed Church had enough sacramental spirit, sympathy with the church year, sense of the altar and the priestly element to find even the new *Order of Christian Worship* generally usable.

The liturgy, in fact, met with widespread interest but with rather limited adoption. Three printings were needed in the first year, a substantial portion of which was apparently sold outside the German Reformed Church. It seems unlikely, however, that in the decade of its experimental use the liturgy was really adopted regularly by more than a dozen congregations. Attempts to introduce it in the congregations related to the Mt. Washington Female College at Baltimore and to Franklin and Marshall College resulted in sharp controversies. Professor Porter, a member of the liturgical committee, used it at Easter of 1858 at Franklin and Marshall chapel for the first time without consulting anyone. "It was well received," he reported, "and no one seemed taken by surprise." [46]

[45] Nevin, "The Christian Year," *MR,* 1856, p. 478.

[46] Porter to Steiner, April 6, 1858 (Library of the German Reformed Church, Franklin and Marshall College).

Harbaugh followed suit that evening at First Church in Lancaster.

> The whole service of the liturgy was used, and spontaneously without any previous direction or concert, *responses* were given by a goodly number in the congregation, Dr. Nevin leading with his full deep tone. The ice is broken and the day is not far distant when the Regular service for the Lord's Day will take its proper place.[47]

Porter, however, was too optimistic; Harbaugh's use of the book was indignantly protested by members of his consistory and a disgraceful row ensued, which eventually resulted in his leaving the congregation.

Although the liturgy was in this sense a failure, it was at least a qualified success as a minister's service book, a "pulpit liturgy."

> It was wonderful to see [Nevin wrote] how it worked notwithstanding as a silent influence among us, in favor of sound ideas on the subject of Christian worship. It wrought a change, far and wide, in the spirit and form of our sanctuary services. It served to deepen among us the power of the liturgical movement, which had given it birth. . . . The Church might not be prepared at all for this new order of worship; but it was just as clear, that she could not now be satisfied with any such book of forms as was thought of in the beginning.[48]

A year after the *Liturgy* Schaff's *Deutsche Gesangbuch: Eine Auswahl geistlicher Lieder aus allen Zeiten der Christlichen Kirche*[49] was published and adopted. The collection included about five hundred classical hymns, including metrical psalms, the best Greek and Latin hymns of the ancient church, and Reformation and modern Protestant hymns, especially those of German Reformed writers such as Neander, Lampe, Tersteegen, Lavater, the Krummachers, Lange, and Schaff's friend Meta Heusser. Great effort had been expended to restore and date the original texts. The arrangement, as with the English hymns in the liturgy, combined the order of the Apostles' Creed with that of the church year. Under each topical division and subdivision the hymns were arranged in historical order. That they represented a

[47] *Ibid.*
[48] *Vindication of the Revised Liturgy* (Philadelphia, 1867), p. 26.
[49] Philadelphia and Berlin, 1859.

contrast to the views of popular rationalism is indicated by the comment of a Cincinnati reviewer: "These are the same old orthodox embers reheated." [50]

This collection probably accomplished more in the "evangelical catholic" direction than either the opponents or advocates of liturgical reform realized, but its influence was doomed, of course, by the diminishing use of the German language in America. A more enduring influence, on the other hand, was exerted by the *Order of Worship* and its revisions—the cause of the great liturgical controversy which destroyed the peace of the church for half a generation.

[50] D. S. Schaff, *op. cit.*, p. 208.

Epilogue

In 1862 and 1863 Confederate troops raided and then invaded the region about Mercersburg. The seminary was suspended in the summer of 1863, and the buildings used as a hospital for wounded Southerners after the battle of Gettysburg. Schaff taught at Andover as a visiting professor in 1862–63 and left Mercersburg finally in 1863, taking up residence in New York City.

The creative period of the Mercersburg movement thus came to an end. It remained a very live subject within the German Reformed Church. In fact, the most bitter controversy over the liturgy dates from 1861, when Bomberger broke out of the Mercersburg camp to lead the opposition. But little if anything new in principle emerged in that dispute. What had been a theological challenge in American religious thought generally subsided into a denominational controversy from the time of the Civil War.

In part the change was owing to the departure of Schaff and the relative inactivity of Nevin. The power and interest of the movement were almost completely dependent on these two gifted theologians. They had been called into the service of the German Reformed Church from elsewhere at the beginning of the 1840's. In each case the call came as a complete surprise. Coming from old-school Presbyterianism and from the United Church of Prussia, respectively, they found an astonishing convergence of theological and religious interests. No doubt the cultural transplantation helped in each case to break the hold of intellectual conventions and to provide a fresh perspective. These two men, so happily matched, were then given virtual control of the educational institutions of a denomination still in its formative period. From that base they were enabled to assess and call to account the whole character and tendency of American religious thought—that of Lutherans and Roman Catholics, as well as of the mainstream of British Protestant background.

The Civil War, however, turned men's minds from the theological concerns of the Mercersburg men. In Europe the parallel catholicizing movements lost the center of the stage in the last third of the century. After the Civil War Nevin was drafted into the presidency of Franklin and Marshall College to meet the critical situation there. Under his leadership the institution did recover and prosper. He retired for a second time in 1876 at seventy-three. He had recently embarked in a new direction theologically which diverged sharply from that of his Mercersburg period. Schaff, likewise, had a second career. In 1870, he transferred to the Presbyterian Church and joined the faculty of Union Theological Seminary. He became the country's leading organizer of ecumenical activities and the study of church history. In several important respects, however, his views changed materially from those of his Mercersburg days.

The Mercersburg heritage was conserved theologically for a time by E. V. Gerhart and T. Appel in the institutions of the German Reformed Church. But the post–Civil War generation had new interests. Darwinism, biblical criticism, the social problems of urbanization and industrialism, psychology of religion, and the religious education movement crowded aside Christology, the church, and sacraments. By the early twentieth century the Mercersburg theology had ceased to exist as an aggressive thological force, although the Mercersburg liturgy was still a living tradition in many congregations—and is to this day.

Outside the German Reformed Church, Nevin and Schaff had made themselves felt. Their contribution to the defeat of the "American Lutheranism" of B. Kurtz and S. S. Schmucker and the triumph of a more traditional Lutheranism has been variously assessed, but probably was significant. In the Episcopal Church W. Muhlenberg's *Evangelical Catholic* derived its name and much of its conception from this source, and the ablest Episcopal theologian of the century, W. P. DuBose, was set on his way by the *Mercersburg Review*. A considerable diffused influence in Presbyterian circles may be surmised, although documented only with difficulty. As Archibald Alexander Hodge said at Nevin's memorial service, his father, Charles Hodge, had always regarded Nevin, in spite of their profound disagreements, as his greatest student.

The influence of Mercersburg is hard to assess in part because it converged with so many other tendencies at the end of the century. In several respects Nevin and Schaff led the German Reformed Church in the 1840's and 1850's through a transition which the major American Reformed bodies, the Presbyterians and Congregationalists, experienced only in the 1880's and 1890's. The New England theology and that of the Presbyterian old school then finally collapsed in favor of German modes of thought. The old two-level universe of nature and supernature, the propositional conception of revelation, philosophical predestinarianism—all were replaced by modes of thought comparable to those used by Schaff and Nevin and deriving ultimately from Schleiermacher and his contemporaries. Similarly static orthodoxy—or static rationalism—was replaced by the new consciousness of historical development. Even the dominance of evangelical individualism with its hostility to liturgy in worship and its indifference to the sacraments perceptibly weakened at the end of the century. In all these matters the Mercersburg movement was a kind of paradigm before the Civil War of what would happen to the American Reformed churches generally by the end of the century.

It is only the generation since the mid-1930's, however, which has come once again to place in the foreground the specific issues which were the distinctive emphasis of Nevin and Schaff. Since that time the social gospel and the evolution controversy have ceased to attract interest. The agenda of the twentieth-century ecumenical movement, on the other hand (at least on its "faith and order" side) read like the heads of the Mercersburg controversy. Christ and the church, tradition and traditions, ministry and sacraments, ways of worship, the nature of church unity—on all these contemporary themes of ecumenical study, Nevin and Schaff speak with startling actuality. They seem, for example, to foreshadow that fruitful interplay of Reformed and Lutheran theology which has emerged in recent ecumenical conversation. Their particular solutions will not commend themselves universally, but they are often instructive.

Appendix

Philadelphia Classis at its meeting on September 16, 1845, passed the following resolutions:[1]

1. Resolved, That we regard the doctrine, that the Scriptures are the only rule of faith and practice, as fundamental and essential to the existence of Christianity, and that we utterly deny the propriety of asserting that Scripture may under any circumstances be undervalued in favor of human addition or tradition. (Rev. 22:18, 19.)

2. Resolved, That we regard faith in Christ as the life-giving principle of Christianity, (Gal. 2:20.) and that under no circumstances may the efficacy of the sacraments be represented as superior to that of faith.

3. Resolved, That we deem the sentiment, that the sacraments depend not for their efficacy upon the spiritual state of the receiver, as contravening the great truth that the sacraments without faith are unavailing. (Remember Judas.)

4. Resolved, That we hold as a fundamental doctrine that we derive our religious life from Christ by the truth, through the quickening influence of the Spirit, and that whilst the ordinances of the Church are channels through which spiritual blessings are conveyed, they cannot confer religious life.

5. Resolved, That we hold that Christ is not bodily present with his people in the celebration of the Lord's Supper, in any other way than symbolically, but is spiritually present with them to the end of time, and that this institution is intended to remind us of his death, till he come the second time in his glorified body; that we cannot admit that the presence of Christ in the Lord's Supper is corporeal as it was in the days of his flesh, because his presence with his Church on earth is no longer human, but divine and spiritual, and that in all cases in which the flesh and blood of Christ are said to be received in the Sacrament of the Supper, the language is to be understood symbolically and not literally.

6. Inasmuch, as it is believed by many that sentiments contrary to the above essential doctrines of God's Word are inculcated in a work entitled the "Principle of Protestantism" (pp. 122–124), therefore,

Resolved, That the attention of Synod be called to the work in question.

[1] H. M. J. Klein, *History of the Eastern Synod of the Reformed Church in the United States* (Lancaster, Pa., 1943), pp. 204–5.

Bibliographical Note

The theological world of such German universities as Tübingen, Halle, and Berlin about 1840 is a large subject, on which it is scarcely feasible to enter here. To a lesser degree this is also true of American theology in the first half of the nineteenth century. The following references will be confined to the Mercersburg movement proper.

In the first half-decade of the Mercersburg movement there appeared seven or eight significant tracts: *The Anxious Bench* (2d ed.; Chambersburg, Pa., 1844); *The Principle of Protestantism*, with Nevin's "Catholic Unity" as an Appendix (Chambersburg, 1845); *What Is Church History?* (Philadelphia, 1846); *The Mystical Presence* (Philadelphia, 1846); *History and Genius of the Heidelberg Catechism* (Chambersburg, 1847); *The Church* (Chambersburg, 1847); and *Antichrist, or the Spirit of Sect and Schism* (New York, 1848). Of these the second and third were by Schaf, the rest by Nevin.

In these same years a very large amount of material by, for, and against the Mercersburg professors was being published in the *Weekly Messenger* of the German Reformed Church (Chambersburg). A very useful Index to the *Messenger*, compiled by Guy P. Bready, is available at the library of the Historical Society of the Evangelical and Reformed Church, Franklin and Marshall College. The Index is not, however, complete; there are, for example, probably twice as many contributions by Nevin in the *Messenger* in this period as are indicated in the Index.

The Reformed Dutch *Christian Intelligencer* (New York) for the same period is probably, among the weeklies, the repository of the largest amount of anti-Mercersburg material, followed by the *Lutheran Observer* (Baltimore). Unfortunately, few if any libraries contain all three or even two of these periodicals, so that it is difficult for the historian to follow the debate week by week.

The 1848 volume of the *American* (or "Whig") *Review* contains several articles by Nevin and Schaff. That same year Schaff began publication of *Der Deutsche Kirchenfreund*, and in 1849 a committee of Marshall alumni launched the *Mercersburg Review*, with Nevin as chief contributor. These journals, especially the last, contain the chief publications of the Mercersburg men up to Nevin's retirement from the *Mercersburg Review* at the end of 1852 and Schaff's from *Der Deutsche Kirchenfreund* at the end of 1853. The one major exception is Schaff's *History of the Apostolic Church*, which appeared first in German (Mercersburg, 1851) and then in E. D. Yeoman's English translation (New York: Charles Scribner, 1853). Important articles by Nevin and Schaff were published after 1852 in the *Mercersburg Review*, but much less frequently than in the first four volumes.

C. H. Ranck compiled a very useful list of articles and notices bearing on Mercersburg theology from some twenty-four contemporary periodicals, entitled, "As Others See Us in the Magazines, 1840–1860," *Reformed Church Review*, July, 1913. Two quarterlies which should be added to his list are the *Protestant Quarterly Review* and the *New Brunswick Quarterly Review*. Ranck also prepared the Index for the *Mercersburg Review* (later *Reformed Church Review*), 1849–1926.

Three sets of student notes on Nevin's lectures in systematic theology were collated by W. H. Erb and published as *Dr. Nevin's Theology, Based on Manuscript Class-room Lectures* (Reading, Pa., 1913). They provide a valuable correction to the impression given by the more polemical articles.

The chief *Lives* of the two principals, that of Schaff by his son David S. Schaff (New York: Charles Scribner's Sons, 1897), and that of Nevin by T. Appel (Philadelphia: Reformed Church Publication House, 1889) were written while the wounds of the controversy still smarted. They minimize or omit the Romanizing phase at Mercersburg and are generally inadequate for setting Mercersburg views in the context of the history of theology. The most important historical work from the opposing viewpoint, J. I. Good's *History of the Reformed Church in the United States in the Nineteenth Century* (New York: Board of Publication of the Reformed Church in America, 1911) is the most circumstantial of all and an excellent guide to the literature of the controversy. It is so unsympathetic to Nevin and Schaff, on the other hand, as to be of little value in the understanding of their thought.

There are biographies also of several related figures: H. H. Ranck's *Life of the Rev. Benjamin Bausman* (Philadelphia, 1912), Linn Harbaugh's *Life of Henry Harbaugh* (Philadephia, 1900) and Elizabeth Clarke Kieffer's Life of the same (*Proceedings of the Pennsylvania German Society*, Vol. LI [Norristown, 1945]), and the Ursinus College symposium *John H. A. Bomberger* (Philadelphia, 1917). Charles E. Schaeffer treated B. C. Wolff in *A Repairer of the Breach* (Lancaster, Pa., 1949). Autobiographies include George B. Russell, *Four Score and More* (Philadelphia, 1908) and T. Appel's *Recollections of College Life at Marshall College* (Reading, 1886).

The *Bulletin of the Theological Seminary of the Evangelical and Reformed Church* has published excerpts from the diaries of E. V. Gerhart (July, 1932), William Rupp (October, 1930), U. H. Heilman (January, 1932), and J. Spangler Kieffer (July, 1930).

There are substantial histories of the educational institutions involved: J. H. Dubbs's *History of Franklin and Marshall College* (Lancaster, 1903), H. M. J. Klein's *Century of Education at Mercersburg, 1836–1936* (Lancaster, 1936), and G. W. Richards' *History of the Theological Seminary of the Reformed Church in the United States, 1825–1934, Evangelical and Reformed Church, 1934–1952* (Lancaster, 1952). Each of these has a bibliography.

The minutes of most of the ecclesiastical bodies concerned with the movement were published at the time in the *Weekly Messenger*. The official *acta* of the synod are conveniently accessible in H. M. J. Klein's *History of the Eastern Synod of the Reformed Church in the United States* (Lancaster, 1943).

A number of articles and theses are devoted to Mercersburg themes. The chief concentration of recent articles is in the *Bulletin of the Theological Seminary of the Evangelical and Reformed Church.* Among the theses might be mentioned two dealing with the liturgy: W. W. Moyer (B.D., Mt. Airy Lutheran Seminary, 1936) and Bard Thompson (B.D., Union Theological Seminary, New York, 1949); also, K. Plummer "Theology of John Williamson Nevin to 1852" (Ph.D., Divinity School, University of Chicago, 1958), W. W. Wetzel, "Debates and Discussions in the Society of Inquiry" (B.D., Lancaster Seminary, 1954), and H. J. B. Ziegler's published Columbia University thesis, *Friedrich Augustus Rauch* (Lancaster, 1953). A recent thesis, not available at time of writing, is Klaus Penzel's study of Schaff's ecumenical activities (Ph.D., Union Theological Seminary, New York).

The library of the Historical Society of the Evangelical and Reformed Church, housed in the Fackenthal Library of Franklin and Marshall College, possesses by far the largest collection of pertinent manuscript materials. Here are the records of the synod and the classes, and of the liturgical commission; Schaff's notes and studies from his student days and the manuscript lectures for his Mercersburg courses; student notes on Nevin's courses in systematic theology, pastoral theology, ethics, and aesthetics; and correspondence of both Nevin and Schaff, as well as of related figures such as Gerhart, Bomberger, Bausman, Harbaugh. Here are diaries of Harbaugh, Gerhart, T. Appel, G. B. Russell. More student notes on Nevin's lectures are in the Franklin and Marshall library, and the manuscript Heyser diary and another collection of Schaff correspondence in the theological seminary across the street. The Good Collection at Eden Theological Seminary, St. Louis, the chief archive of the anti-Mercersburg party in the denomination, has some manuscript notes of Nevin's lectures as well as most of the relevant published material, including a good collection of Reformed liturgical materials. Here and at Lancaster are some German periodicals of the time not easily accessible elsewhere in this country. The most important single Schaff collection of letters, his correspondence with W. J. Mann, is at Mt. Airy Lutheran Seminary in Germantown; and some Schaff diaries and notes are at Union Theological Seminary in New York. The letters in Nevin's exchange with Brownson and McMaster are at the University of Notre Dame, South Bend, Indiana.

Index

www.ingramcontent.com/pod-product-compliance
Lightning Source LLC
LaVergne TN
LVHW020529100826
845148LV00010B/1403